赤本メディカルシリーズ
Akahon Medical Series

私立医大の
英語〔長文読解編〕

3訂版

西村真澄 編著

K 教学社

02

はしがき

If you don't know the content, you cannot understand these kinds of articles.
「内容を知らなかったら，この種の文を理解できないだろう」

　これは，元ケンブリッジ大学講師の David Chart 氏に，私大医学部の入試問題についての分析と感想を伺ったときの，最初の一言でした。私大医学部入試の英語長文は，医学雑誌を出典とするなど，**最新医療の時事問題**や，脳の神経伝達，癌の発達など，医学・生物学の専門的な内容の出題頻度が高く，難度も高い傾向がみられます。冒頭の David 氏の言葉のように，あらかじめそのテーマの内容を知っていないと，とうてい太刀打ちできなくなっています。

　医系テーマに読み慣れるために，本書では，私大医学部および，同レベル・同傾向の私大薬学部や国公立大医学部の**過去問を徹底的に分析**し，その中から，背景知識の有無や医系単語への慣れにより，大きく点差をつけることができる，**最も重要な頻出長文16題を厳選**しています。さらに，それらの長文を，生殖器系・神経系・呼吸器系など，部位別に9分類しました。この**部位別習得法**は，米国の医学部の病理のテキストでも効果的習得法として多く適用されており，**将来の実践で役立つ，医学英語の基盤**となります。

　本書では，各 Chapter の初めの，「テーマ理解」に「知っておきたい医系用語」のリストを掲載し，たくさんの**イラスト**を用いて重要な背景知識の概念をわかりやすく解説しています。イラストは，医師として臨床医学に携わりながら，主に医学書で漫画家・イラストレーターとしても活躍されている茨木保先生に描いていただきました。イラストがあることで視覚的に記憶に残りやすく，生物を選択していない受験生や再受験生，さらに高校2年生でも，**将来に直結する専門的な内容を，短期間で楽しみながら習得できます。**また，「長文読解」「速読訓練」「プラス α」に分けて，入試問題や医学英語の記事を収載し，医系入試問題の読解力の確実な向上を目指しています。

　本書で取り上げたテーマは，**医学において大切な普遍性のあるもの**です。医学部で必要となる内容ばかりで，本書の勉強は決して無駄にはなりません。私大医学部に限らず，国公立大医学部の英語や，小論文対策としても活用していただけますし，将来，医師になってから必須となる医学論文の読解にもきっと役立つことと思います。

　一人でも多くの受験生が楽しみながら本書を活用し，合格を勝ち取られることを心より祈ります。

編著者しるす

CONTENTS

| ☆★ | やや易 | ☆★★ | 標準 |
| ☆★★★ | やや難 | ☆★★★★ | 超難問 |

本書の構成

本書は以下の4つの要素で構成されています。

テーマ理解
イラストで楽しみながら医系用語を学ぼう！

問題演習を進める前に，医学英単語を身につけましょう。イラストを用いて，背景知識をわかりやすく解説しています。

長文読解
厳選された入試問題を解いてみよう！

別冊問題編で厳選された問題を解き，本冊で答えあわせ，解説を読むことでさらに理解が深まります。解説中の **攻略ポイント** も確認しましょう。

速読訓練
目標解答時間に解けるようになろう！

私大医学部の入試問題で出題された問題の中から，*Science* や *Nature* など医学論文レベルの英文を扱っています。解説では **速読攻略** も示してありますので，学習の一助としてください。

［解答編のみ］
プラスα
幅広く医系テーマに読み慣れよう！

知っている背景知識や医系テーマが多ければ多いほど，本番で類似のテーマが出題されても，問題に落ち着いて取り組めます。英文を読む目標時間を設定していますので，その時間を目安に英文を読めるように練習しておきましょう。

本書の利用法

1 医系テーマを把握する

　まず，**テーマ理解** で「知っておきたい医系用語」の重要な用語をおさえ，イラストつきの解説で背景知識を頭に入れてから，別冊問題編を使って，16 題分の **長文読解** **速読訓練** の問題を解いてみましょう。目標解答時間を設定していますので，解答時間内で解けるように意識しながら，解いてみましょう。

　幅広く医系テーマに読み慣れるために，**プラスα** では入試問題で出題された医系テーマの英文や医学英語の記事を 13 題収載しています。2019 年以降，最新の治療・手術・薬剤，また定義の変更などに関する医学論文レベルの記事が，入試問題で取り上げられる傾向にあります。その対策として，**プラスα** を用いて色々な医系テーマに読み慣れ，医学論文レベルの速読読解力の強化を図りましょう。

　本書では，医学英語の重要なテーマの「知っておきたい医系用語」および巻末付録として「医学論文読解のための必須単語」をまとめています。これらの医学英単語はすべて読める程度にはなじんでおきましょう。また，本書は重要な医系テーマをおさえるだけでなく，医学論文読解力の速読強化を図れるよう構成されており，将来医師となってからも，必須となる医学論文読解への確実な基礎固めとなります。

2 速読のための全訳の読み方

　本書では左ページに英文，右ページに全訳を掲載しており，**赤字**で示されている語は重要な医系表現です。**赤字**の数語をかたまりとしてとらえることで，正確な速読力が身につくようになっています。下線箇所はイディオムや文法上のポイントです。繰り返し読んで覚えていきましょう。正確な速読ができるようになれば，文の内容が容易に理解できるだけでなく，解答に多くの時間を割くことができるので，高得点を狙えます。

3 速解のための解説の読み方

　実際の入試では，時間配分が大切になります。特に私大医学部は，試験時間に比して問題量が多い傾向にあります。そこで本書では，実戦に即した読み方・解き方で解説しています。また，大問ごとの解説ページに，**攻略ポイント** や **速読攻略** などをちりばめています。**medi** は関連して覚えておくとよい医系表現です。あわせて確認しておきましょう。

　本書で紹介している解き方はあくまで一例ではありますが，参考にできるところを吸収し，自分に合った方法を見つけてください。

速読対策

2019 年以降，最新の治療・手術・薬剤，また定義の変更などに関する *Science* または *Nature* の論文記事が，一部の私大医学部や国公立大医学部の入試で取り上げられる傾向にあります。設問数は以前と同じですが，読解英文自体の難易度が上がっているため，最新医療記事の速読が必要です。日頃から 1 ～ 3 年前のオンライン最新記事に目を通しておくとよいでしょう。

　私大医学部は，試験時間に比して問題量が多い傾向にあり，90 分で 65 ～ 70 の設問が出題されている大学もあります。つまり，解答時間は設問を読む時間を含め 1 問 1 ～ 2 分以内が目安となり，かなりのスピードが必要になると考えられます。時間内に解けるまで繰り返し，解答スピードを身につけて試験に臨みましょう。

　段落順に設問のある大学，全体を読まないと解答が探せない問題が設問にある大学などがあります。大学の出題形式にあらかじめ慣れておき，全体を読まないと解けない問題を最後に回すなど，解答する時間配分を想定しておきましょう。

✅ 速読・速解法の一例

1 先に 3 ～ 4 問分の設問を読み，選択肢の相違点や key words を頭に入れます。同じフレーズは，縦読みして重複箇所を読み飛ばしましょう。

> ▶縦読み例　重複箇所②～④（彼女たち）は読み飛ばす。
> ①彼女たちが　食べたいのならピーナッツを食べることができる
> ②彼女たちは　木の実を食べることができる
> ③彼女たちは　ピーナッツを食べることはできない
> ④彼女たちは　たくさんピーナッツを食べ過ぎてはならない

2 解答を探しながら本文を読み進め，該当する段落を特定しましょう。

• 必須フレーズやパターンセンテンスは，一語として読みましょう。

> ▶例 1 「～の患者」
> ☐ case of hypertension「高血圧患者」
> ☐ a patient with diabetes mellitus「糖尿病患者」
>
> ▶例 2 「病気・症状が発現する，現れる」
> ☐（病気・症状）develops／occurs／appears
> ☐ A patient develops（病気・症状）(× A patient appears／occurs（病気・症状）)
> ☐ A patient has／suffers from（病気・症状）「（病気・症状）がある」

• 場所，氏名，所属など固有名詞はある程度読み飛ばし，内容理解に焦点を当てましょう。

3 設問を再確認し（選択問題の場合は選択肢間の相違を確認），解答の根拠となる文を特定して確実に正解しましょう。

速読・速解のコツ

　試験時間に比して問題量が多く，速読・速解力が求められる私大医学部の英語対策として，ここでは，英文の構造や論理展開の仕方に注目して，内容をすばやく的確につかむコツを紹介します。

✎ コツ1 英語論文の構造を知る

　英語の論文の多くは，次のような形になっています。この構造を頭に入れておけば，内容に関する設問の解答の根拠を，すばやく見つけることができます。

> ▶第1段落
> 広い話題から入り，段落の最後で文全体のキーセンテンスを述べる。
> ▶第2段落〜
> 最初に段落ごとのキーセンテンスを述べ，続いて，具体的な理由や例をあげ，キーセンテンスをサポートする。
> ▶最終段落
> 段落ごとの要点を繰り返しながらまとめ，結論を述べる。

✎ コツ2 医系英文でよく用いられる比較の展開

　私大医学部の長文は350〜700語程度で「ある1つのテーマについての結論」を導いている場合がほとんどです。したがって，結論が"positive"「よい」か"negative"「悪い」か，あるいは賛否両方か，早い段階で判断できると内容を把握しやすくなります。賛否どちらの結論が導かれる場合でも，テーマの中で比較・対照が行われることが多いので，比較表現に注目して賛否を推測することができます。

> ▶比較の展開パターン
> ①テーマの導入
> ②結論をサポートするための比較群（control group）の提示
> ●比較群を導入する熟語・接続詞
> ☐ compared with〜「〜と比較して」（＝comparing〜）
> ☐ in contrast to〜「〜と対照的に」　　☐ by contrast「対照的に」
> ☐ while〜「〜なのに対し」　　☐ whereas〜「〜であるのに対し」
> ③結果の相違から結論を推測する
> ☐ positive／negative「肯定的／否定的」　　☐ proponent／opponent「賛成者／反対者」
> ④テーマの結論
> ●結論を導く語
> ☐ therefore「したがって」　　☐ thereby「それによって」
> ☐ in conclusion「要するに，結論として」

● 本書で用いている主な記号・略号

- S　　　　　主語
- V　　　　　動詞
- O　　　　　目的語
- C　　　　　補語
- *A, B, C*　任意の語句が含まれていて，そのすべてが名詞のときに使用。
　　　　　　　例：take *A* to *B*「*A* を *B* に連れて行く」
- ～, …　　　任意の語句が含まれていて，上記の定義に該当しないときに使用。
　　　　　　　例：the＋比較級～，the＋比較級…
　　　　　　　「～すればするほど，ますます…」
- …　　　　　中略
- (　)　　　　省略可能
- 〔　〕　　　言い換え可能
- ［　］　　　同じ例文中で使用可能な別表現
- to *do*　　　to 不定詞
- *doing*　　　動名詞や現在分詞
- *do*　　　　原形動詞
- *done*　　　動詞の過去分詞
- be　　　　　be 動詞
- *one's*　　　人称代名詞の所有格（his, their など）の代表形
- *oneself*　　再帰代名詞（himself, herself など）の代表形

《全訳》において
　　赤字：重要な医系表現を示しています。
　　下線：イディオムや文法上のポイントを示しています。
　　(※　)：補注や，構文読解のヒントを示しています。

《解説》において
　　l.：本冊解説編での英文の行数を示しています。
　　medi：関連して覚えておくとよい医系表現であることを示しています。
　　🔵攻略ポイント：英文の読み進め方，設問を解く上でのヒントです。
　　☑速読攻略：英文の読み進め方，速読のためのヒントです。

医系長文読解

医系長文読解の本冊では，計 16 題の 長文読解 速読訓練 の入試問題と，読解の素材として計 13 題の プラスα の入試問題や医学英語の記事を収載しています。重要な医系テーマに読み慣れ，問題演習を重ねることは，医学論文読解への確実な基礎固めとなります。また，問題演習を進めるうえでは，医学英単語を身につけておく必要があります。「知っておきたい医系用語」で，重要な用語をおさえ，イラストつきの解説で背景知識を深めておきましょう。

Chapter 1 ≫ 医 療
Medicine

知っておきたい医系用語

● 医　療

☐ **preventive medicine**「予防医学」
　発症後に行う従来の「治療医学」に対し，発症前の予防を目的とする医学。

☐ **evidence-based medicine**「科学的根拠に基づく医療（EBM）」
　医療行為の有効性を批判的な立場で見直し，科学的根拠を明らかにした医療。

☐ **hospice care**「ホスピス・ケア」ホスピスとは，癌などの末期患者が生を全うするために，延命治療ではなく肉体的・精神的苦痛を除く緩和ケアを行う施設。
　◆ reimbursement hospice care「ホスピスの医療費の払い戻し」

☐ **terminal care ／ end-of-life care**「末期治療」

● 患　者

☐ **outpatient**「外来患者」

☐ **inpatient**「入院患者」

☐ **healthy people**「健常成人」

☐ **the contacts**「患者の接触者」

☐ **carrier**「保菌者」

● 診　察

☐ **clinical practice**「臨床診察」

☐ **early diagnosis**「早期診断」

☐ **early detection**「早期発見」

☐ **medical chart**「カルテ」

● 態　度

☐ **doctor-patient relations**「医師と患者の関係」
　◆ epitomize good doctor-patient relations
　　「医師と患者のよい関係を典型的に示す」

☐ **be proactive**「主体的である」［prouǽktiv］

インフォームド・コンセント（Informed Consent）

patient（患者）は，**medical personnel**（医療従事者）から検査・治療・手術について十分に説明を受け，検査・治療・手術を受けることに同意する。その第一歩は，患者と医療従事者とのコミュニケーションである。

　Truth-telling can be very challenging in the clinic, especially when the truth is bad news. Over time, Japan has developed ethical codes and formal, legal rules that require **information disclosure** and **informed consent**. In addition, patients are taking a more active role in the **decision-making process** about their **diagnosis and treatment**.

　臨床において真実を告げることは，特にその（告げようとする）真実が悪いニュースの場合〔病気が深刻な場合〕は大変難しい。日本において，倫理コードおよび，情報開示やインフォームド・コンセントを必要とする正式な法律規定が整備されてきている。加えて，患者は診断と治療の意思決定（の過程）にますます積極的な役割を果たしている〔医師が患者の診断と治療をする際に，これまでと比較し，患者は，ますます積極的に関与してきている〕。

長文読解 ☆★★☆☆

1 医師と患者のコミュニケーション

自治医科大学（医学部）   438 語

[1] The communication skills of health care professionals can make their interactions with patients easier and bring about a better treatment result. Medical professionals need to be good at both verbal and nonverbal communication. Nonverbal behavior, such as facial expressions, voice tone, eye contact, hand movements and other gestures, often modifies what is spoken, expressing more about a person's thoughts and feelings. Besides controlling their own nonverbal behavior, observing and interpreting the patient's nonverbal messages are essential skills for health care providers.

[2] Attentive listening can help **caregivers** recognize the patient's needs. This requires **empathy**. Patients are often unable to identify their feelings and have difficulty talking about them. So, while listening, health care providers need to put themselves in the patient's situation.

[3] Various verbal skills are also (5)critical for **therapeutically effective** communication. They include such (6)techniques as clarifying what is meant by a patient's statement and asking **open-ended questions**. Clarifying a patient's statement is to make a guess and restate the basic message if necessary. The following example shows how to clarify what is implied.

Patient : There is no point in asking for a pain pill.

Nurse : Are you saying that no one gives you a pill when you have pain?
        Or, are you saying that the pills are not helping your pain?

[4] Open-ended questions and statements, such as "How did you feel in that situation?," "I'd like to hear more about that," and "Tell me about that," can invite patients to (7)discover and explain their feelings.

[5] Just as it is important to learn ways of fostering **therapeutic** exchanges, it is also helpful to recognize responses that interfere with effective communication. Below are some examples of such nontherapeutic forms of expression.

[6] Feelings expressed by patients such as anger or worry often make caregivers uncomfortable. Common responses to those situations are: "Don't worry about it, everything will be fine." or "Please don't cry." Such responses inhibit the expression of feelings. It is best to encourage the patient to voice his/her feelings and examine them objectively.

🎓同様のテーマが出題されたことのある大学

順天堂大(医)・産業医科大(医)・日本医科大・藤田医科大(医)・久留米大(医〈医〉)

1 医療専門家のコミュニケーション技術は，患者との相互関係をよりよくし，より
よい治療成果をもたらすことができる。医療専門家たちは，言語によるコミュニケー
ションおよび非言語コミュニケーションの両方に優れている必要がある。顔の表情や
声の調子，アイコンタクト，手の動き，その他の身振りなどの非言語行動によって，
人の考えや感情についてさらに多くのことを表現し，話す内容を修正することが多い。
自身の非言語行動を調整することに加え，患者の非言語メッセージを観察し，解釈す
ることは，医療提供者にとって必要不可欠な技術である。

2 注意深く聞くことは，介護者が患者の必要とすることを認識するのに役立つ場合
がある。これには感情移入をすることが必要である。患者は自分の感情がはっきりわ
からない場合が多く，また自分の感情について話すことは困難である。したがって，
医療提供者は聞いている間，その患者の身になることが必要である。

3 さまざまな話術もまた，治療上有効なコミュニケーションにとってきわめて重要
である。話術は，患者の発言が何を意味するかを明確にする，自由回答式質問をする，
などの技術を含む。患者の発言を明確にすることとは，推測し，必要に応じて基本的
なメッセージを言い換えるということである。次の例は，患者がほのめかしているこ
とをいかにして明確にするかを示す。

　　　患　者：鎮痛剤をお願いしてもだめでしょうね。

　　　看護師：痛みがあるときに，誰も鎮静剤をくれないという意味ですか，それとも，
　　　　　　　鎮静剤が痛みに効かないとおっしゃっているのですか。

4 「その場合にどんなふうに思いましたか」「そのことについてもっと聞きたいので
すが」そして「それについてもっと話してください」などの自由回答式質問または，
叙述により，患者は自分の感情を発見し，説明することができるようになる。

5 治療目的の会話を強化する方法を学ぶのが重要であるように，効果的なコミュニ
ケーションを妨げるような返答を認識することも役に立つ（※ここでの response は「反
応」〈医系の意味〉ではなく，「返事・返答」）。以下は，治療上好ましくない表現の例である。

6 患者によって表現される怒りや心配などの感情は，介護者を不快にさせることが
多い。そのような状況でよくある返事は，「そのことは心配しないでください。すべ
てうまくいきますよ」または，「どうぞ泣かないでください」である。このような返
事は，感情の表現を抑制する。患者が感情を言葉で表現し，患者自身の感情を客観的
に深く考えるように仕向けることが一番である（※ examine「～を深く考える」）。

6

7 Judgmental statements that indicate how patients should feel deny a patient's true feelings and suggest that they are inappropriate. An example of such statements is: "You shouldn't complain about the pain, many others have gone through this same experience without complaint."

8 In addition to these communication strategies, health care providers need to be aware that a person's style of communication is often affected by factors such as his/her health condition, stress level, **fatigue**, education, and culture. Good therapeutic communication skills are at the heart of all the medical professions. These skills can lead to accurate assessment and improvement of a patient's health status and well-being.

≫ 解説

長文を読み始める前に，設問（**1〜4**）に目を通して頭に入れ，該当段落を探しながら長文を読み始める。**1〜4**の設問の要点は，
1. 「nonverbal communication とは…」
2. 「health care providers（医療提供者）が必要なことは…」
3. 「caregivers（介護者）が必要なことは…」
4. 「good communication skills（よいコミュニケーション技術）ができることは…」

1.「nonverbal communication（非言語コミュニケーション）は（言語によるメッセージと比較して）…」1 *ll.* 3-8 を参照して，
Ⓐ「**医療提供者の感情をより表していることが多い**」➡ *ll.* 4-6 と一致。
Ⓑ「医療提供者のメッセージを患者に伝えるときに，同程度に重要である」➡ *l.* 3 に「両方に優れている必要がある」とあるが重要性について言及していない。
Ⓒ「患者の必要とするものを理解するとき，より有用である」➡有用性についての比較には言及していない。
Ⓓ「介護者は，患者の言語によるコミュニケーションと同様に，患者の非言語コミュニケーションをコントロールする必要がある」➡ *ll.* 6-8 と不一致。

2.「医療提供者が患者の必要なことを認識するために必要なことは…」1・2 を参照して，
Ⓐ「患者の行動を注意深く観察する」➡ 1 *ll.* 7-8「患者の非言語メッセージを観察し，解釈する」と不一致。
Ⓑ「患者の訴えを聞く」➡ 2 *l.* 1「注意深く聞くことが介護者が患者の必要とすることを認識するのに役立つ」と不一致。
Ⓒ「患者に同情（sympathy）する」➡ 2 *l.* 2「感情移入（empathy）」と不一致。
➡Ⓐ・Ⓑ・Ⓒはそれぞれ正確に言い換えている文がない。

7 患者がいかに感じるべきかを示唆するような，自分の意見が一番という発言は，患者の真の感情を否定し，それらが不適切であると示唆する。そのような発言の一例としてあげれば，「あなたは痛みを訴えるべきではない。他の多くの人は痛みを訴えずに同じ経験をしてきたんです」である。

8 これらのコミュニケーション戦略に加え，医療提供者は，人のコミュニケーションスタイルというのは，健康状態，ストレスの程度，疲労，教育，文化などの要因によってしばしば影響されることを認識する必要がある。治療目的の十分なコミュニケーション技術は，すべての医療専門家にとって核心部分である（※ medical professions「医療専門家」）。これらの技術によって，患者の健康状態と幸福の正確な判定と改善をもたらすことができる。

   Ⓓ「患者の立場になる」➡ 2 *l*. 4 と一致。
    ◆put *oneself* in a person's shoes「～の立場になって考える」≒ put *oneself* in a person's situation

3.「caregivers（介護者）が，効果的なコミュニケーションを抑制（＝inhibit the expression）しないために必要なことは…」6 を参照して，
   Ⓐ「患者に体調について心配しないように促す」➡不一致。
   Ⓑ**「断定的にならず（non-judgmental），患者に話させるように仕向ける」**➡最終文と一致。
   Ⓒ「客観的でいて，患者の意見を，感情的に深く考える」➡不一致。
   Ⓓ「自分たちの感情と患者の訴えを抑える」➡不一致。

4.「よいコミュニケーション技術ができることは…」この内容は 8 *l*. 4 以降（Good therapeutic communication skills are …）にあるので，設問 **5 ～ 7** を先に解いてもよい。
   Ⓐ「介護者の地位を上げるのに役に立つ」➡不記載。
   Ⓑ**「患者が適切に取り扱われるのに不可欠である」**➡ 8 最終文「患者の健康状態と幸福の正確な判定（accurate assessment）と改善をもたらす」と一致。
   Ⓒ「社会福祉および医療を促進させる」➡不記載。
   Ⓓ「介護者が患者を助けるために役立つ」➡介護者に関しては明確に言及していない。

5. critical の意味は
   ①重大な（➡ここではこの意味なのでⒸ **essential** がもっとも近い）
   ②批判的な
   ③危機的な ◆ critical condition「危篤状態」 critical state「重体」 critical

care unit「集中治療室（CCU）」

④臨界の　◆critical accident「臨界事故」

> 「重要な」を表す essential, vital, crucial などの訳語を問う問題は比較的多いので，まとめて覚えておこう。

6． techniques〔tekníːks〕

Ⓐ professional〔prəféʃənl〕　　　Ⓑ **treatment**〔tríːtmənt〕

Ⓒ caregiver〔kéərgìvər〕　　　Ⓓ interpret〔intə́ːrprit〕

7． 空所の文は「自由回答式質問により，患者が自分の感情を（　　　）し，説明するように誘導する」。➡Ⓓ **discover**「～を発見する」が適切。

8． 表題について，

Ⓐ「介護者にとっての言語によらないコミュニケーションの重要性」➡言語によるコミュニケーション技術も述べているので不適切。

Ⓑ「病院でのコミュニケーション技術の改善法」➡技術の「改善法」ではなく，「患者の健康状態の改善」（improvement of a patient's health status）〔⑧最終文〕であるので，不適切。

Ⓒ「コミュニケーションが，患者と医師との関係にいかに影響するか」➡影響は患者と医師の関係にとどまらないので不適切。

Ⓓ **「医療専門家にとってのコミュニケーション技術の有用性」** ➡ therapeutically effective communication「治療上有効なコミュニケーション」〔③ *ll.* 1-2〕など，全体を通して述べられており，正解。

ANSWER

1 —Ⓐ　　2 —Ⓓ　　3 —Ⓑ　　4 —Ⓑ

5 —Ⓒ　　6 —Ⓑ　　7 —Ⓓ　　8 —Ⓓ

1

💡攻略ポイント

自治医科大学の，論旨に合う文を選択する問題は，不正解の選択肢の文が，一見，本文と類似しているものが多い。したがって，本文の内容を正確に言い換えている文を特定できるように注意しよう。

速読・速解法！

「カタマリで読む方法」

数語のまとまりでよく出てくる表現は，一語のように読み慣れると，正確さとスピードを上げることができる。

例）

☐ be more likely to develop「発現しやすい」

☐ a patient who is suffering from diabetes「糖尿病患者」

☐ an incidence rate of the kidney failure「腎不全の罹患率」

「選択肢を縦に読む方法」

同じ箇所（love is）は省いて，is より後ろの相違を読む。

例）

Ⓐ　love is like a pain in the neck

Ⓑ　love is │ expressed by sincere actions

Ⓒ　love is │ visible, like cars and food

Ⓓ　love is ↓ to have many good friends

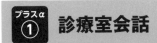 診療室会話

診察室でよく使われる表現

- ☐ 「初診」first visit
- ☐ 「再診」return visit
- ☐ 「カルテ」medical chart
- ☐ 「健康保険証」medical insurance card
- ☐ 「処方箋」a prescription
- ☐ 「処方薬」prescription drugs〔medicine〕
- ☐ 「予防」prevention
- ☐ 「診察室」the consultation room
- ☐ 「健康診断」medical check-up
- ☐ 「診察する」examine
- ☐ 「診断する」diagnose / make a diagnosis
- ☐ 「治療をする」give treatment
- ☐ 「乳児検診」baby health check-up
- ☐ 「注射をする」give a shot〔an injection〕
- ☐ 「点滴をする」give an IV drip
- ☐ 「予防注射をする」give a vaccination

会話例

1. 「今日はどうしましたか？」
   What is bothering you today? / What seems to be the trouble today? / What is the problem today? / How can I help you today?

2. 「症状［現病歴／既往歴／家族歴］はありますか？」
   Do you have symptoms [a disease / a past history of disease / a family history of disease]?

3. 「大きく息を吸って止めて，吐いてください」
   Breathe in deeply and hold it, then breathe out.

4. 「それでは，お腹［背中］を診ましょう」
   Let's have a look at〔examine〕 your stomach [your back].

5. 「胸の音を聴きますから大きく息を吸って，吐いて，吸って」
   Please breathe in deeply while I listen to your chest … breathe out … and breathe in.

6. 「では，背中を診ますから，後ろを向いてください」
   Right, I'll have a look at your back. Please turn around.

7. 「診察台に仰向けに寝てください」
   Please lie down on your back on the examination table. / Please lie face up.

8. 「 病気 があるかを調べるために，血液検査［尿検査／ CT スキャン／ MRI ／レ
ントゲン］が必要です」
You need a blood test［a urine test / a CT scan / an MRI / an X-ray］to see if
you have 病気 .

9. 「 病気 の可能性を否定するために，MRI をとる必要があります」
You need to have an MRI to rule out 病気 .

10. 「検査の結果は陽性［陰性］でした」
Your test result was positive［negative］.

11. 「あなたの症状や検査の結果から，あなたは 病気 でしょう」←診断の表現
Considering your symptoms and your test results, you may have 病気 . /
Your test results show that you may have 病気 .

12. 「 病気 と診断された」
I was diagnosed with 病気 .

13. 「しばらく様子をみてみましょう」
We will see how things go for a while.

14. 「経過観察が必要です」
You need to make a follow-up appointment.

15. 「あなたの症状に効く薬を出しましょう」
I will give you some medicine for your symptoms.

16. 「この分野の専門家に紹介状を書きましょう」
I will write a referral letter for you to a specialist in this field.

17. 「もし，具合が悪くなったら，すぐにいらしてください」
If you feel that something is wrong, please come back immediately.

18. 「お大事に」
Take care of yourself.

テーマ理解

Chapter 2 》 生殖器系／遺伝子
The Reproductive System

知っておきたい医系用語

● 生　殖
☐ **reproductive system**「生殖器系」
☐ **embryo**「胎児（妊娠2カ月まで）」［émbriòu］
☐ **fetus**「胎児（妊娠3カ月から生まれるまで）」
☐ **in vitro fertilization**「体外受精」
☐ **ovary**「卵巣」
☐ **mutate**「突然変異する」
☐ **mutation**「突然変異」

● 生殖補助医療／再生医療
☐ **surrogate mother**「代理母」［sə́ːrəgèit mʌ́ðər］
☐ **remove egg ／ withdraw egg**「卵子を取り除く」
☐ **differentiate**「分化する」
☐ **proliferate**「増殖する」
☐ **cultured cell**「培養した細胞」
☐ **culture dish**「培養皿」
☐ **regenerative medicine ／ tissue engineering**「再生医療」
☐ **embryonic stem cell**「胚性幹細胞」［èmbriánik stém sél］
☐ **therapeutic cloning**「治療目的クローニング」［θèrəpjúːtik klóuniŋ］

● 遺伝子操作
☐ **genetic screening**「遺伝子走査」
☐ **gene test**「遺伝子検査」
☐ **gene therapy**「遺伝子治療」
☐ **decode**「～を解読する」
☐ **encode**「～をコード化する」
☐ **gene manipulation**「遺伝子操作」［dʒíːn mənipjuléiʃən］
☐ **genetically engineered animal**「遺伝子組換え動物」

□ **genetically engineered plant**「遺伝子組換え植物」

2

● 遺伝子検査の影響
□ **violation of privacy**「プライバシーの侵害」
□ **discrimination**「差別」
□ **health insurance system**「医療保険制度」
□ **social security**「社会保障」

● 差　別
□ **a person with handicaps［disabilities］／ the disabled**「障害者」
□ **Hansen's disease ／ leprosy**「ハンセン病」癩菌の感染によって起こる慢性伝染病。

● 生態系
□ **ecosystem**「生態系」
□ **food chain**「食物連鎖」
□ **organism**「有機体，生物」

● 健　康
□ **diet and exercise**「食事（療法）と運動」
□ **healthy diet**「健康食」
□ **succumb to the attraction of fast food**「ファストフードの魅力に屈する」
□ **regimen**「養生法」［rédʒimèn］
□ **mortality rate**「死亡率」
　　◆ The mortality rates have been declining.「死亡率が減少してきている」
□ **aging**「老化，加齢」

細胞（Cell）

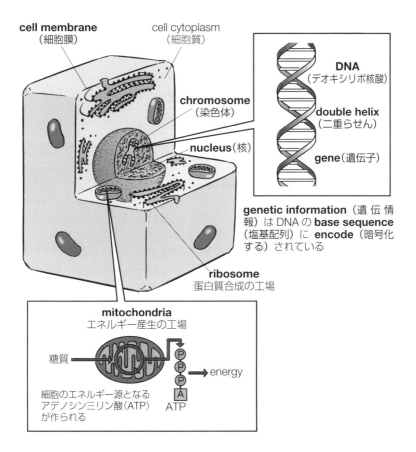

cell membrane
（細胞膜）

cell cytoplasm
（細胞質）

DNA
（デオキシリボ核酸）

chromosome
（染色体）

double helix
（二重らせん）

nucleus（核）

gene（遺伝子）

genetic information（遺 伝 情 報）は DNA の **base sequence**（塩基配列）に **encode**（暗号化する）されている

ribosome
蛋白質合成の工場

mitochondria
エネルギー産生の工場

糖質

energy

細胞のエネルギー源となるアデノシン三リン酸（ATP）が作られる

ATP

イラスト 茨木保

蛋白質の合成（Protein Synthesis）

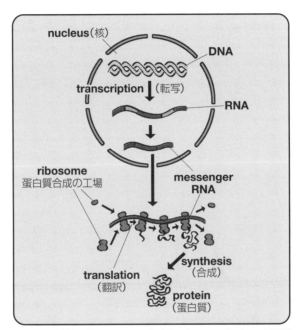

DNA の遺伝情報が RNA に写し取られ〈**transcription**（転写）〉，
RNA の情報を元に蛋白質が作られる〈**translation**（翻訳）〉

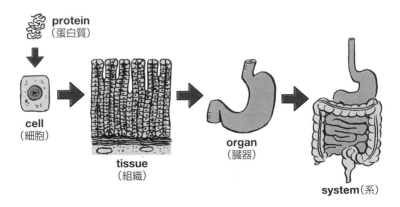

体外受精・胚移植(IVF-ET：In Vitro Fertilization and Embryo Transfer)

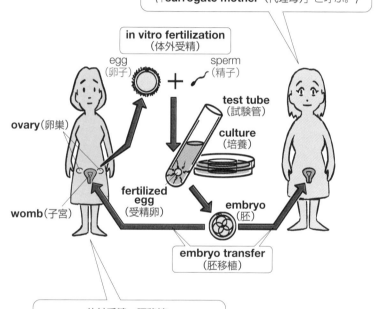

借り腹（**host mother**）
夫婦の胚を妻以外の女性の子宮に **transplant**
（移植する）して懐胎させること。
夫の精子を妻以外の女性の子宮に **inject**
（注入する）して懐胎させた場合は
「**surrogate mother**（代理母）」と呼ぶ。

in vitro fertilization
（体外受精）

egg
（卵子）

sperm
（精子）

test tube
（試験管）

culture
（培養）

ovary（卵巣）

**fertilized
egg**
（受精卵）

embryo
（胚）

womb（子宮）

embryo transfer
（胚移植）

体外受精・胚移植
卵巣から取り出した卵子と精子を体外
で **fertilize**（受精させる）させ，胚を
子宮内に戻す方法。

ES 細胞（Embryonic Stem Cell）

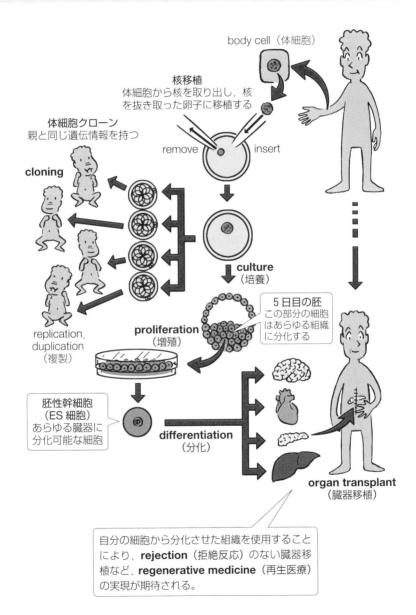

body cell（体細胞）

核移植
体細胞から核を取り出し，核
を抜き取った卵子に移植する

remove　insert

体細胞クローン
親と同じ遺伝情報を持つ

cloning

**replication,
duplication**
（複製）

proliferation
（増殖）

culture
（培養）

5 日目の胚
この部分の細胞
はあらゆる組織
に分化する

胚性幹細胞
（ES 細胞）
あらゆる臓器に
分化可能な細胞

differentiation
（分化）

organ transplant
（臓器移植）

自分の細胞から分化させた組織を使用すること
により，**rejection**（拒絶反応）のない臓器移
植など，**regenerative medicine**（再生医療）
の実現が期待される。

イラスト 茨木保

再生医療（Regenerative Medicine）

iPS cells（iPS 細胞）

Induced pluripotent stem cells, or iPS cells are generated directly from human somatic cells. iPS cells are created by introducing certain genes into human somatic cells. The process was discovered by a team lead by Professor Yamanaka at Kyoto University.

人工多能性幹細胞すなわち iPS 細胞は，人の体細胞から直接創作される。iPS 細胞は，体細胞に特定の遺伝子を導入することによって作られる。この過程は，京都大学の山中教授が率いるチームによって発見された。

Researchers hope that iPS will be applied not only to the development of regenerative medicine, but also to the study of the development process of currently incurable disease, or their causes and to drug development.

iPS は再生医療だけでなく，難病の発生過程およびその原因の研究，また，創薬開発への応用が期待されている。

Genes created during visionary stem cell research are sensitive to the whole visible spectrum. Therapy has successfully restored sight to blind rats.

幹細胞による視覚再生研究において創出された遺伝子は，可視光全域に感受性をもっている。これまでに，その遺伝子を用いた治療で，失明したラットの視覚を回復させることに成功している。

Therapy using these genes has drawn global attention as a possible way to restore vision to the blind.

同遺伝子を用いた治療は，失明者の視覚を回復できる治療法として，世界的にも注目を浴びている。

2

これからの研究

近い将来，**cell sheet**（細胞シート）などを作製し，再生医療が利用される研究が進んでいる疾患例：

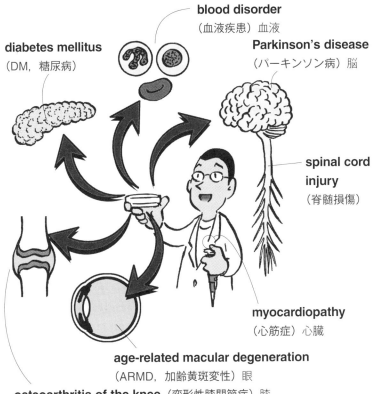

blood disorder
（血液疾患）血液

diabetes mellitus
（DM，糖尿病）

Parkinson's disease
（パーキンソン病）脳

spinal cord injury
（脊髄損傷）

myocardiopathy
（心筋症）心臓

age-related macular degeneration
（ARMD，加齢黄斑変性）眼
osteoarthritis of the knee（変形性膝関節症）膝
　関連用語 **the cartilage**（軟骨）

その他
amyotrophic lateral sclerosis（ALS，筋委縮性側索硬化症）
atopic dermatitis（アトピー性皮膚炎）皮膚
periodontal disease（歯周病）歯

ゲノム分析の利点と懸念点

| genetic diagnosis（遺伝子診断） | gene therapy（遺伝子治療） |

genetic testing
（遺伝子検査）

疾患の原因遺伝子を見つけ，欠陥を修復したり正常遺伝子を導入したりすることで，**treatment**（治療）・**prevention**（予防）を行う。

new drug development（新薬開発）

遺伝子を解析することで，個々人の体質に合った，効果が高く，**side effect**（副作用）の少ない新薬を作ることができる。

2

invasion of privacy（プライバシー侵害）と**genetic discrimination**（遺伝子差別）

あなたの遺伝子プロファイルによると
40歳で糖尿病になりますから，
入社は無理ですね。

保険会社の保険加入，
会社採用などの際に
遺伝子情報が用いられると…

面接官

受精卵の遺伝子操作・着床前診断

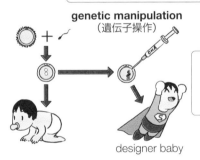

genetic manipulation
（遺伝子操作）

ethics issue（倫理問題）
human rights violation（人権侵害）
能力・外見・性格・性別を親が選択する
難病や障害をもつ子供を排除する

designer baby

2 遺伝子検査

順天堂大学（医学部）　　　　　　　　　　　　　　　　　　553 語

[1]　I've just had my **genome scanned**, and unfortunately **the test results** show that I have some common **mutations** that give me a slightly increased **genetic risk** for **diabetes** and **heart disease**. More worrisome is the news that I have three times the average risk for getting **Alzheimer's disease**.

[2]　On the other hand, the test also shows that I don't have lots of other dangerous mutations, like those associated with various forms of cancer. All in all, the **analysis** of 130 of my **genetic markers** suggests that my overall **health expectancy** is better than that of the average person. This should be comforting news. But it also makes me wonder about the future.

[3]　This kind of **genetic screening** may be the Next Big Thing in medicine. It offers a glimpse of how **genetics** will transform human life in this century. "We'd like to do away with much of **the health care system**," said Charles Cantor, the chief scientific officer of Sequenom, the genetic discovery company that tested my DNA. "We'd like to keep people very healthy, until they die suddenly and painlessly of old age. I think genetic screening will give doctors and patients much better disease **prevention** tools."

[4]　What is scary is not the technology itself. Rather, it is that we are slipping toward "our post-human future," as Francis Fukuyama put it, without public understanding or debate, and without adequate laws to prevent **genetic discrimination**.

[5]　The kind of broad genetic scan that I underwent may be commonly available to the general public within ten years. Such screening could give the benefits of alerting people to their medical weaknesses so that they could get **early treatment** for diseases, possibly saving their lives.

[6]　But genetic screening also will raise many difficult personal and ethical questions we need to wrestle with now, rather than simply allowing them to go unanswered. Among the problems — getting the results of a genetic screening can be emotionally troubling to the patient. "People need to be really sure they want to do this," emphasized Dr. Harry Osterer, the genetic specialist who advised me. For example, do people really want to know that they are at risk for Alzheimer's? Such information can change the way people see

🎓**同様のテーマが出題されたことのある大学**

川崎医科大・東海大〈医〈医〉〉

2

⬛1　私は今，ゲノム走査を受けたところである。残念なことに検査の結果は，私にはいくつかのよくある変異があり，糖尿病や心臓病の遺伝子リスクを少し高めていることを示した。さらに心配なことは，アルツハイマー病のリスクが平均の3倍高いという情報である。

⬛2　一方，検査は，多様な形態の癌に関係するような，ほかの危険な変異が多くないことも示した。全体的には，遺伝マーカー〔遺伝形質〕130個の分析は，私の総合的な健康寿命が平均的な人よりも良好であることを示した。これはほっとする知らせである。しかしそれは，私に将来について考えさせることにもなる（※wonder「あれこれ考える」）。

⬛3　この種の遺伝学的スクリーニングは，医学における「未来に注目されること」であるかもしれない（※スクリーニング：症状がない段階で病気を発見するための検査）。それは今世紀，遺伝学が人間の生活をいかに変えるかを垣間見せてくれる。「私たちは，現在の健康保険制度の多くを廃止したいと思うのです」と，私のDNAを検査した遺伝子検査会社，シーケノムの科学部門の部長であるチャールズ=キャンターは言った。「私たちは，人々が老衰でぽっくり苦痛を伴わずに死ぬまで，彼らの健康を維持したいと思っています。遺伝学的スクリーニングは，医師と患者にこれまでよりもずっとすぐれた病気の予防法を提供するだろうと思います」

⬛4　恐ろしいことは技術そのものではない。むしろ，一般人の理解を得ず，また公開討論をせず，そして遺伝子差別を防ぐための適切な法律をつくらずに，フランシス=フクヤマが言うような「新人類の未来」に向かってなし崩し的に進もうとしていることが恐ろしいのである。

⬛5　私が受けた種類の広域遺伝子走査は，10年以内に一般利用が可能になるだろう。そのようなスクリーニングは，病気を早期治療し，ことによると救命できるように，人々の医学的弱点に警鐘を鳴らすという恩恵を与えることができるだろう。

⬛6　しかし，遺伝学的スクリーニングはまた，多くの難しい個人的・倫理学的問題を生むだろう。その問題は単に未解決のままにするのではなく，今こそ取り組む必要がある。その問題の1つに，遺伝学的スクリーニングの結果を得ることが，患者にとって感情的な困難になりうるということがある。「この種の検査をしたいのかどうかについて，人々は本当に確信をもつ必要がある」とハリー=オステレル博士は強調する。彼は私に助言をした遺伝子の専門家である。たとえば，人々はアルツハイマー病になるリスクがあるということを本当に知りたいだろうか。そのような情報は，自分自身

themselves.

7 And then, <u>what about</u> issues of privacy and discrimination? For example, should voters be allowed to see **the genetic records** of candidates for political offices? What if the genetic records of a presidential candidate showed that he or she had a high risk for some disease? Would this affect the way people voted? <u>What if</u> genetic records were stolen, or made up falsely by opponents?

8 And then, what about the effects on **the medical insurance system**? Would people whose gene-scans showed low risk of disease stop paying for insurance, believing it an unnecessary use of money? This could make insurance companies go bankrupt. And on the other hand, insurance companies might be tempted to engage in genetic discrimination. They might, for example, try to reject people whose gene-scans showed higher risk for dangerous diseases.

9 So now, while this technology is still in its infancy, is the time to debate this issue and to enact suitable laws to prevent genetic discrimination. **Genetic technology** is a grand technology we are quickly moving toward, but we need to shape it, rather than allow it to shape us.

>>> 解 説

設問 **1**～**4** の要点は,
1．「この文章で筆者が一番懸念していることは何か」 ⇨大意のようなので，最後にまわす。
2．「チャールズ=キャンターが遺伝学的スクリーニングの可能性について考えていることは何か」
3．「遺伝子走査検査の結果を得たのち，筆者への最大の影響は何だったか」
4．「『新人類の未来』という句が示唆している主要な問題は何か」

1.「この文章で筆者が一番懸念していることは何か」大意なので最後に解く（大意・表題などの問題が最初にくる場合がある）。結論である**最終段**（ 9 ）を参照して,
　① 「アルツハイマー病になることへの恐怖」
　② 「遺伝子走査の保険制度への影響」
　③ **「遺伝子差別の可能性」** ➡ *ll*. 1-2 と一致。
　④ 「遺伝子走査による感情的な苦痛」
　⑤ 「遺伝子走査による政治への影響」
2.「チャールズ=キャンターが遺伝学的スクリーニングの可能性について考えていることは何か」 3 を参照して，選択肢の相違を確認する。
　① 「新人類の未来を懸念」　　　　② 「老衰で死ぬ人々を懸念」

に対する見方を変える場合がある。

[7]　それから，プライバシーと差別の問題<u>はどうであろうか</u>。たとえば，行政官庁を志望する人の**遺伝子記録**を，有権者が閲覧することが許されるのだろうか。大統領候補の遺伝子記録が，ある病気に対して高いリスクを示したらどうだろうか。これが，人々の投票行動に影響するだろうか。遺伝子記録が盗まれたら，または対立候補によって<u>でっちあげられたらどうなるだろうか</u>。

[8]　さらに，医療保険制度への影響はどうなるだろうか。遺伝子走査で病気のリスクが低いことがわかった人々は，不必要な出費であると考えて，保険料の支払いをやめないだろうか。これによって保険会社が破産するかもしれない。一方，保険会社が遺伝子差別をしようとするかもしれない。たとえば，遺伝子走査で危険な病気のリスクが高いことがわかった人々を拒否しようとするかもしれない。

[9]　したがって，この技術がまだ未熟期にある今こそ，この問題を議論し，遺伝子差別を防止する適切な法律を制定する時である。**遺伝子技術は偉大な技術であり，我々は急速にそこへ向かっている。しかし，この技術が我々を形成するのではなく，我々がこの技術を形成する必要がある。**

③「健康保険制度廃止への意欲」
④「**多くの病気の予防に役立つと予言**」➡最終文と一致。
⑤「経費を懸念」

3.「遺伝子走査検査の結果を得たのち，筆者への最大の影響は何だったか」[1]・[2]（the test results show that …）を参照し，①〜⑤の相違を確認する。
①「アルツハイマー病になることを知った」
②「癌になることを知った」
③「**寿命が平均より長いとわかった**」➡[2] *ll.* 2-4 と一致。
④「遺伝子走査は用いられるべきでないと確信」
⑤「遺伝子走査の経費を心配」

4.「『新人類の未来』（our post-human future）という句が示唆している主要な問題は何か」[4]を参照して，選択肢の相違（何の問題か）を確認する。
①「感情」
②「**倫理**」➡ *ll.* 1-4 の後半で遺伝子差別を防ぐ法律の必要性にふれている。
③「経済」
④「身体」
⑤「歴史」

設問 **5** ～ **7** の要点は,

5.「遺伝学的スクリーニングでもっともももたらされそうな恩恵とは何か」

6.「遺伝子走査技術によってもたらされうる結果として示唆されていないものはどれか」

7.「筆者が示唆しているもっとも重要なことは何か」

5.「遺伝学的スクリーニングでもっともももたらされそうな恩恵とは何か」 ⑤ *ll.* 2-4
   (Such screening could give the benefits …) を参照して,
   ① **「遺伝子に関係している病気の早期診断と早期治療」** ➡一致。
   ② 「医療の経費削減」
   ③ 「医療倫理問題の解決」
   ④ 「医師と患者間の信頼の高まり」
   ⑤ 「医療におけるプライバシー拡大の促進」

6.「遺伝子走査技術によってもたらされうる結果として示唆されていないものはどれか」 ⑨ (this technology is …) を参照して,
   ① 「ヒトの生活を変えうる」
   ② 「投票行動に影響を及ぼしうる」
   ③ 「命を救いうる」
   ④ 「社会的・経済的問題が起こる」
   ⑤ **「技術を未熟期にとどめる（進歩しない）」** ➡不一致。

7.「筆者が示唆しているもっとも重要なことは何か」 ⑨ (So now, … is the time ….
   … we need to …) を参照して, 選択肢の相違を確認する。
   ① 「遺伝学的スクリーニングの禁止」 ➡不記載。
   ② 「遺伝子技術の禁止」 ➡不記載。
   ③ 「医療保険制度の改善」 ➡不記載。
   ④ **「遺伝子差別の予防のための法律の議会通過」** ➡ ⑨ *ll.* 1-2 と一致。
   ⑤ 「遺伝子走査技術における医師の訓練」 ➡不記載。

💡攻略ポイント

順天堂大学の出題を見ると, 選択肢の相違は比較的明確で解きやすい反面, 設問数が多い。選択肢の相違の確認には,「**選択肢を縦に読む方法**」(➪ p. 9) を活用するなど, 速読・速解の訓練をしておこう。

ANSWER
1 —③   2 —④   3 —③   4 —②
5 —①   6 —⑤   7 —④

2

速読・速解法！

論理展開に重要な頻出熟語

英語には，「～〈原因〉が…〈結果〉をもたらした」という因果関係を示す熟語が数多くある。言うまでもなく，「物事の原因が何か」をはっきりさせることは，文章の内容を把握する上で極めて重要である。因果関係を示す熟語に注目して，「原因」と「結果」を正確につかむようにしよう。

「A〈原因〉⇨ B〈結果〉」を表す熟語

☐ A result in B「A〈原因〉が B〈結果〉をもたらす」
　≒ A lead to B
　≒ A cause B

☐ A contribute to B「A が B の一因となる」

☐ A be responsible for B「A は B の原因である」

「B〈結果〉⇨ A〈原因〉」を表す熟語

☐ B result from A「B〈結果〉は A〈原因〉に起因する」
　≒ B arise from A
　≒ B stem from A
　≒ B come from A

☐ B is caused by A「B〈結果〉は A〈原因〉によって引き起こされる」
　≒ B is due to A
　≒ B is triggered by A

理由・結果を導く接続表現

☐ therefore「それゆえ」　　　　☐ and thus「したがって」

☐ and then「それから」　　　　☐ thereby「それによって」

文頭において理由・結果を導く表現

☐ As a result,「～の結果として」　☐ Due to A,「A のため」

☐ Ultimately,「結局のところ」

☐ As ～「～ので，～して」
　≒ Since ～

3 遺伝子治療

北里大学（医学部）　　　　　　　　　　　　　　935 語

1 Scientists have long known that **specific genes** <u>are associated with</u> a **number of serious diseases** and **birth defects**. Scientists have used this knowledge to develop tests to **identify defective genes**, which are the result of **mutation**: a natural process that **alters genetic material**. Researchers **have identified a large number of genes** that <u>are responsible for</u> **life-threatening conditions**, such as cystic fibrosis and Huntington's disease. (1)Once these genes are identified, **genetic tests** for many such diseases become available. These tests can indicate if a person has a specific defective gene. By 2011, researchers had developed more than 2,000 genetic tests, which allow doctors to inform patients if they have inherited these genes and if they risk <u>passing them on to</u> their children.

2 This testing is a significant milestone in genetic research, because these tests provide **people who have genetic defects** (2)with important information. However, the tests also introduce complex ethical issues. If patients find out that they have a dangerous genetic defect, they may not know <u>what to do</u>. Their decision will depend on several factors. First, **in some cases**, identification of the gene only suggests the likelihood that the patient will **develop the disease** <u>associated with</u> that gene. For example, women who have inherited the harmful BRCA gene mutation <u>have a much higher chance of</u> developing breast cancer than other women do. (3)Thus, it is likely that women with **the genetic mutation** will develop cancer, but it is not certain. A second important **factor in the decision** is whether there is a treatment, and if so, what kind of treatment. **In the case of BRCA gene mutation**, a frequent treatment is **major surgery** before **the cancer develops**. Women who **test positive for the mutation** must decide between this treatment and the possibility of dying of cancer.

3 Unfortunately, for some genetic diseases, **there is no treatment**, which (6)<u>gives rise to</u> even more complex ethical issues. Would patients want to know that they are going to **die young** or become very sick if there is no treatment? Some may want to know so that they can prepare themselves. If there is a chance they could <u>pass the disease</u> to their future children, they may decide not to have children. For others, however, the news could ruin their lives. They might prefer not to know about their **condition** and enjoy their lives **while they**

🎓 同様のテーマが出題されたことのある大学

岩手医科大（医）・埼玉医科大（医）・久留米大（医〈医〉）

2

1　特定の遺伝子が多くの重篤な疾患や先天性欠損症に関連していることは，以前より科学者たちに知られている。科学者たちは，この知識を用いて，欠陥遺伝子を同定する検査を開発した。欠陥遺伝子は，突然変異の結果であり，突然変異は遺伝物質を変化させる自然の過程である。研究者らは囊胞性線維症やハンチントン病のような生命を脅かす病態の原因となる，多数の遺伝子を同定している。いったんこれらの遺伝子が同定されると，多くの遺伝子疾患の遺伝子検査が可能になる。これらの検査により，ある個人が特定の欠陥遺伝子をもっているかどうかを示すことができる。2011年までに，研究者らは 2,000 を超える遺伝子検査を開発してきたが，こうした検査によって，医師は，患者に，これらの欠陥遺伝子を受け継いでいるかどうか，また，欠損遺伝子を子供に伝えるリスクがあるかどうかを知らせることができる。

2　このような検査は遺伝子研究において画期的な出来事である。なぜなら，これらの検査は，遺伝的欠陥をもつ人に重要な情報を提供するからである。しかし，これらの検査はまた，複雑な倫理問題をもたらす。たとえ患者が自分に危険な遺伝的欠損があることを知ったとしても，どうしたらよいのかわからないかもしれない。彼らの決断はいくつかの要素次第である。第1に，ある症例では，遺伝子の同定は，患者がその遺伝子に関係する疾患を発現する可能性を示唆するにすぎない。例えば，有害なBRCA 遺伝子（※乳癌感受性遺伝子）変異を受け継いでいる女性は，受け継いでいない女性と比較し，乳癌を発現する可能性が極めて高い。したがって，遺伝子変異を伴う女性は癌を発現するだろうが，確実というわけではない。決断する際の第2の重要な要素は，治療法が存在するかどうかということである。そして，もし治療法があるなら，どのような種類の治療があるか，ということである。BRCA 遺伝子変異の症例で，頻繁に行われる治療は，癌の発現前に，大手術をすることである。検査で遺伝子変異陽性例の場合，女性はこの治療を受けるか，または癌で死ぬ可能性をとるかを決断しなければならない。

3　残念ながら，遺伝病によっては，治療法がない場合もあり，このことにより，さらに複雑な倫理問題が生じる。治療法がない場合，患者は，自分は若死にするだろうとか，重病になるだろう，ということを知りたいだろうか。自ら備えるために知りたいと思う人もいるかもしれない。将来の子供に病気が遺伝する可能性があるなら，子供をもたないという決断をするかもしれない。しかし，そうした情報が人生を台無しにしてしまう人もいる。そのような人は自らの病状について知らない方がいいと思い，健康な間に人生を楽しむだろう。それゆえ，彼らは遺伝子検査を全く受けないという

are healthy. So, they may decide not to get genetic tests at all.

4 Most researchers expect that the next step will be gene therapy that **repairs or replaces the defective gene**. This would mean, for example, that BRCA patients could receive a treatment that actually changes their genetic material. If that came true, most people would probably decide to take genetic tests.

5 At the end of the 20th century, researchers began to develop treatments for a variety of **life-threatening** genetic diseases. The early results seemed very ₍7₎encouraging, and, consequently, **people with genetic diseases** became hopeful that they would soon see a cure. In 2000, for example, French doctors treated **babies with a** rare **genetic disorder**, commonly ₍8₎referred to as "bubble boy disease," that **affected their immune systems**. They injected the babies with a **healthy replacement gene**. Ten months later, the children's immune systems appeared completely normal.

6 To these early achievements, however, considerable problems and limitations were attached. Results were ₍4₎mixed; success occurred in only a small number of **patients with rare conditions**. Sometimes the therapy caused more problems than it solved. For example, **in the French case**, several of the children **developed leukemia**, one of whom died. In addition, enthusiastic researchers sometimes ₍9₎underestimated the time it would take for discoveries in the laboratory to become practical therapies, a difficulty that persists today, often leading to disappointment and a lack of confidence in the field of **gene therapy**.

7 In spite of these ₍5₎setbacks, many scientists pursued their research in gene therapy. They believed this form of treatment still held great potential. However, three basic technical challenges ₍10₎stood in the way of their progress. First, gene therapy is not like other kinds of treatments in which a patient can **take a pill** that sends **medicine** throughout the body. It must be introduced into specific genes. Second, scientists need **a way to deliver the therapy** directly into a cell. In many cases, they have used a virus to do this, but they have to be sure that the virus will not harm the patient. Finally, they have to be sure that the new or **repaired gene** will not "turn off" after it is introduced into the cell.

8 After years of research and trials, scientists had made considerable progress in solving these problems. In the first years of the 21st century, positive results began to emerge, arousing renewed interest in the field. In **a small clinical trial** in 2007, **patients with Parkinson's disease** received genes

決断をするかもしれない。

4　研究者の多くは，次の段階は欠陥遺伝子を修復または交換する遺伝子治療であることを期待している。このことは，たとえば，BRCA をもつ患者は，自分の遺伝物質を実際に改変する治療を受けることが可能になることを意味する。それが実現すれば，多くの人は遺伝子検査を受ける決断をするだろう。

2

5　20 世紀末に，研究者らは，命を脅かすさまざまな遺伝病の治療の開発を始めた。初期の結果は極めて有望に思えた。その結果，遺伝病のある人は，まもなく治療が現れるだろうと期待した。たとえば，2000 年に，フランスの医師が，免疫系に影響する「バブルボーイ症候群」と一般的に呼ばれる，希少な遺伝性疾患の乳児らを治療した。医師らは乳児らに正常な遺伝子に置き換えた遺伝子を注射した（※ inject A with B「A を B に注射する」）。10 カ月後，この小児らの免疫系は完全に正常になったように思われた。

6　しかし，これらの初期の成果には重大な問題と限界が伴っていた（※ A be attached to B「A が B に伴う」）。結果にはさまざまなものが入り混じっていた。成功したのは，希少難病患者のうちのほんの少数だけであった。この療法は，それが解決する以上の問題を引き起こした場合もあった。たとえば，フランスの症例では，小児数人が白血病を発現し，そのうち 1 人が死亡した。加えて，熱心な研究者らは，実験室での発見が実用的な療法になるまでにかかる時間を過小評価したことも時にはあり，そうした難点が今日でも根強く存続し，しばしば，遺伝子治療の分野での失望と自信の欠如につながっている。

7　これらのつまずきにもかかわらず，科学者の多くが遺伝子治療の研究を追究した。彼らはこの種の治療が依然として大きな潜在的可能性をもつと信じていた。しかし，3 つの基本的な技術上の難題が，その進歩に立ちはだかった。第 1 に，遺伝子治療は，患者が体中に薬を送る錠剤を服用できるような他の種類の治療とは異なっている。遺伝子治療は特定の遺伝子に対して導入されなければならない。第 2 に，科学者らにとって，細胞に直接治療を施す方法が必要である。多くの症例では，遺伝子治療を行うためにウイルスを用いてきたが，そのウイルスが患者に害を及ぼさないことを確認しなければならない。最後に，新しい遺伝子や修復された遺伝子を細胞に導入した後に「スイッチが切れる」ことがないことを確認しなければならない。

8　長年の研究と治験後，科学者らはこれらの問題を解決する上でかなり大きな進歩を遂げてきた。21 世紀の最初の数年間で，有望な結果が出始め，この分野への新たな関心を呼び起こした。2007 年の小規模臨床試験において，パーキンソン病の患者が，欠損している重要な蛋白質を産出する遺伝子を投与された。患者 12 名すべては，

for **production** of an important protein that they lacked. All 12 patients experienced an improvement in their condition **with no negative effects**. In 2011, researchers successfully treated **patients with hemophilia**, a disease that impairs the body's ability **to clot blood**, by injecting them with **the healthy form of a defective gene**. These were major achievements, but they are particularly exciting because the treatments are for **major diseases** that affect large numbers of people.

⑨ All of these positive results have revived the public's interest in gene therapy. Many researchers and scientists have renewed their belief in the prospect of its enormous **potential** to treat **killer diseases** like **cancer**, **diabetes**, cystic fibrosis, etc. However, they are now more careful to caution patients and society that many effective genetic therapies may still be years, or decades, in the future.

≫ 解 説

1. (1)接続詞の問題。「研究者らは…多数の遺伝子を同定した。（　　　）これらの遺伝子が同定されると，多くの遺伝子疾患の遺伝子検査が可能になる」➡この構造をとれるのは，③ **Once**「いったん」。

(2) provide *A* with *B* で，正解は⑤ **with**。前置詞選択問題は，熟語をチェックする。

(3)接続詞の問題。前の文には，BRCA 遺伝子変異を受け継いでいる女性は乳癌リスクが高くなる，とある。「（　　　），遺伝子変異をもつ女性は癌を発現するだろう」は順接の関係なので，正解は，⑤ **Thus**「このようにして」。Thus は論文などに用いられることが多い。

(4)治療はプラスの結果とマイナスの結果を引き起こしたので，② **mixed** が正解。
①費用対効果　③時間的な正確さ　④反映的　⑤嫌々➡これらはいずれも不適切。

(5)「これらの（　　　）にもかかわらず，研究者らは追究した」➡④ **setbacks**「逆行」が正解。

2. (6) give rise to ～「～を引き起こす」＝ bring about ～

(7) seemed encouraging「有望に思えた」 promising「有望な」

(8) referred to as ～「～と呼ばれる」＝ called

(9) underestimate「～を少なく見積もる」➡②以外は高くなり，反対の意味になる。よって②の「～を不正確に判断する」が正解。

(10) stand in the way of ～「～の邪魔をする」＝ block「～を阻害する」

病状が改善され，悪影響はなかった。2011 年に，研究者らは，欠陥遺伝子を正常化したものを注射することによって，血液を凝固させる身体の能力を損なう血友病の患者の治療に成功した。これらは大きな成果であった一方，今でも，その治療は，多くの人々に影響を与える重篤な疾患を対象とし，特に興味深い。

2

⑨　これらの有益なすべての成果により，一般人の遺伝子治療への関心を再び集めた。多くの研究者や科学者は，遺伝子治療が，癌，糖尿病，嚢胞性線維症などの致命的な病を治療する潜在的可能性が極めて高くなる，と新たに信念をもった。しかし，彼らは，遺伝子治療の多くは有効になるのがまだ数年あるいは数十年先である，と患者や社会に対して以前より慎重に注意を促している（※ many effective genetic therapies「多くの効果的な遺伝子治療」は，effective「効果的な」という形容詞を動詞「効果的になる」で訳すと，意味がとりやすくなる。このように，名詞や形容詞を動詞の形で訳す方法がある）。

🔍 攻略ポイント

設問 3 の⑾と⒀は，斜め読み速読で選択肢に目を通そう。「選択肢を縦に読む方法」（⇨ p.9）

3 . ⑾「遺伝子治療開発の最終的な目的は何か」

　　①欠損遺伝子の永久の修復と置換➡ 7 *ll.* 8-9「遺伝子を細胞に導入した後にスイッチが切れないようにする」とあるので，これが正解。

　　②欠損遺伝子の同定➡遺伝子検査の目的なので，不正解。

　　③欠損遺伝子のある人を同定するための遺伝子検査の開発➡遺伝子検査の目的なので，不正解。

　　④ウイルスが用いられていないシステムの開発➡不記載。

　　⑤体中に薬剤を送るための錠剤の開発➡不記載。

　⑿「遺伝子検査はどのように役立つか，の例はどれか」

　　①免疫系の増強によって➡不記載。

　　②正常遺伝子の保護によって➡不記載。

　　③複雑な倫理問題を引き起こすことによって➡役立つ例ではない。

　　④遺伝病があるかどうかを知らせないことによって➡役立つ例ではない。

　　⑤子供をもつかどうかを情報に基づいて決定することによって➡ 3 *ll.* 4-6 より，これが正解。

(13) ⑦ に３つ述べられている。
  (A)見つけなければいけない　　治療を細胞に誘導する➡⑦ $ll.$ 6-7 に一致。
  (B)確実にしなければいけない　新しい遺伝子や修復された遺伝子が活性したまま
      である➡⑦ $ll.$ 8-9 に一致。
  (C)確実にしなければいけない　血液がけがのあと固まるか➡不記載。
  (D)確信しなければいけない　　治療に用いられるウイルスが害がない➡⑦ $ll.$ 7-8
      に一致。
  (E)説得しなければいけない　　さらに多くの医師が治療に参加する➡不記載。
(14)内容真偽の問題。
  ④「**実用的な遺伝子治療の開発にかかる時間の問題は完全には解決していない**」
   が正解。➡⑨ $ll.$ 4-6「遺伝子治療が有効になるのは，まだ先である」と一致。
(15)今日の遺伝子治療の現状を要約する問題。可能であれば，重要箇所を斜め読みし，
  正解を選択する。
  ①「いかなる遺伝子治療も世界中で使用可能になる」➡不記載。
  ②「これからも希少遺伝病の患者のみが，遺伝子研究の恩恵を受けるだろう」➡
   ⑧ 最終文に不一致。
  ③「**遺伝子治療が将来的により使用可能になると期待されている**」➡⑨ $ll.$ 2-4
   に一致するので，これが正解。
  ④「遺伝子治療の総括的な価値について懐疑的になるほどの失敗があった」➡本
   文は遺伝子治療について否定的でないので，不一致。
  ⑤「BRCA 患者が，大手術をするか，または癌で死亡する可能性を選ぶか，と
   いう選択を迫られる時代はすでに終わっている」➡② 最終文に不一致。

ANSWER

1. (1)—③　(2)—⑤　(3)—⑤　(4)—②　(5)—④
2. (6)—①　(7)—④　(8)—①　(9)—②　(10)—⑤
3. (11)—①　(12)—⑤　(13)—②　(14)—④　(15)—③

2

誤訳しやすい，ちょっと気になる単語

　医系の英文では，やさしい単語でも，一般の英文で用いられる場合の意味と，全く異なる意味で用いられる場合があります。

☐ general「一般の」⇨「全身の」
　◆ general anesthesia「全身麻酔薬」
☐ constitutional「憲法の」⇨「全身の」
　◆ constitutional symptoms「全身症状」
☐ manifestation「明示・表明」⇨「症状，徴候」
☐ case「場合」⇨「症例」
　◆ first case of bird flu「トリインフルエンザの初めての症例」
☐ subject「主題」⇨「被験者，被験体」
　◆ trial subject「被験者」
☐ preparation「準備」⇨「薬の調合，製剤」
　◆ medicinal preparation「医薬製剤」
☐ agent「代理人」⇨「①菌（株）」，「②薬剤」
　◆ infectious agent「感染菌」
　◆ therapeutic agent「治療剤」

☐ follow-up「追跡調査」
　follow-up は「追跡調査」と訳しますが，患者さんの経過を観察していくことを意味します。しかし，The patient is followed. や，The doctor followed the patient. のように up を省くと，「患者は追いかけられる」「医師は患者のあとを追った」となってしまいます。

☐ germ「病原体」病気をもたらす bacteria「細菌」，virus「ウイルス」，fungus「カビ」など，微生物の総称を意味します。

日本大学（医学部）　857 語

HUMAN-PIG 'CHIMERAS' MAY PROVIDE VITAL **TRANSPLANT ORGANS**, BUT THEY RAISE ETHICAL DILEMMAS

1　**Transplantation** is one of modern medicine's success stories, but it is hampered by a scarcity of donor organs. Figures for the UK published by the NHS Blood and Transport Service show that 429 patients died in 2014–2015 while awaiting an organ. What's more, many of the 807 removed from the waiting list will have been removed because they became too ill to receive an organ and are likely to have died as a result.

2　So while there is a strong ethical imperative to increase the supply of **donor organs**, many of the methods(S) tried or proposed —— **presumed consent**, allowing organs to be bought and sold, and using lower-grade organs such as those from donors with HIV —— are(V) themselves controversial. And even if we accept these approaches it's unlikely they will be sufficient to meet the demand.

3　Gene editing techniques such as CRISPR could provide the answer. These techniques allow us to make precise changes in the DNA of living organisms with exciting prospects for treating disease —— for example by modifying human DNA to remove genes that cause disease or insert genes associated with **natural immunity to** conditions such as HIV/AIDS. However, gene editing the DNA of animals could prove equally important for the medical treatment of humans.

4　Scientists are now working on a technique that would allow human organs to be grown inside pigs. The DNA within a **pig embryo** that enables it to grow a **pancreas** is deleted, and **human stem cells** are **injected into** the embryo. These **stem cells** have the ability to develop into any type of cell within the

2

ヒトとブタの「キメラ」が重要な移植用臓器を提供する可能性はあるが
それらは倫理的問題を孕む

1　移植は現代医療の成功事例の１つであるが，臓器ドナー不足によって阻まれてい
る〔臓器ドナー不足が障壁となっている〕。NHS 献血臓器移植機構によって公表され
たイギリスに関する数値によると，2014 年から 2015 年に臓器を待つ間の死亡は 429
例となった。さらに，待機リストから除外された 807 例のうちの多くは，容態が悪く
なり臓器を受け取ることができなくなったために待機リストから削除されるだろうし，
結果的に死亡する傾向にある。

2　したがって，ドナー臓器の供給を増やすのに強い倫理的な義務があるのだが，試
験された，あるいは提案された多くの方法は(S)，つまり，推定同意，臓器売買を許容
すること，そして HIV ドナーから提供された臓器のような質の低い臓器を用いるよ
うな方法は，それら自体が議論の的である(V)（※構文説明：主節の主語は many of the
methods で，動詞は are である。presumed consent, allowing organs to be bought and sold,
using lower-grade organs such as those from donors with HIV は，the methods tried or
proposed の例）。そしてたとえこれらの方法を受け入れたとしても，（移植の）需要を
満たすのに十分（な数）ではないだろう。

3　CRISPR といった遺伝子編集技術が答えを提供しうるだろう（※ CRISPR: DNA 二
本鎖を切断してゲノム配列の任意の場所を削除，置換，挿入することができる新しい遺伝子改変技術）。
これらの技術のおかげで，私たちは病気を治療するのに十分な期待をもって，生きた
臓器の DNA を正確に変化させることができる。例えば，病気を引き起こす DNA を
取り除くために，あるいは HIV/AIDS といった病態への自然免疫に関連する遺伝子
を注入するために，ヒト DNA を改変することによって（変化させる）（※構文説明：
allow 人 to do「人が〜できるようにする」 make changes in 〜「〜の変化をする」 by modifying
「改変することによって」は，make … changes「変化する」にかかる。remove「取り除くため」と，
insert「注入するため」は，modifying human DNA「ヒト DNA を改変する」にかかる）。しかし，
動物の DNA を編集している遺伝子は，ヒトを治療することにとって同じくらい重要
であるとわかっている。

4　科学者らは現在，ブタの体内でヒトの臓器を育てることを可能にする技術に取り
組んでいる。膵臓を育てることを可能にするブタの胚内の DNA を取り除き，ヒト幹
細胞をその胚に注入する（※受動態を能動態で訳す）。これらの幹細胞は体内のいかなる
細胞にも成長する能力をもっている。そしてラットやマウスを用いた先行実験は，そ

body, and previous experiments using rats and mice suggest that they will automatically fill the gap created by the missing pancreas genes and form a pancreas that consists of **predominantly genetically human cells**.

⑤ The idea of **transplanting organs** from pigs into humans is not new. **Transplants between different species**, or **xenotransplantation**, was considered **promising** in the 1990s but fell from favour due to (A)the challenges of preventing the human immune system from rejecting pig organs, and (B)concerns about the possible transmission of infectious diseases from pigs to humans. Modern gene editing techniques may help alleviate both concerns: rejection is less likely since the organ will be more closely resemble a human one, while other scientists have demonstrated that CRISPR can also be used to delete retroviruses from the pig genome.

⑥ However, some will undoubtedly protest that the risks are still too high. Often these objections appeal to the so-called **precautionary principle**, which states that action should be taken to avert risks even if their existence and magnitude is uncertain. Attractive though this idea is, the precautionary principle is only defensible if it is evidence based, and balances the risks of innovation against the known harms of not using the technology.

PRACTICAL MEDICINE MEETS PRACTICAL ETHICS

⑦ Others will argue that it is inherently wrong to create **human-animal hybrids**, so-called **chimeras**; that it(S) is(V1) contrary to human dignity, or **constitutes**(V2) "playing God". It's hard to understand the rationale for such claims given that **humans' biological nature** is neither fixed nor categorically separated from that of other organisms. Even without **technological interventions** we(S) share(V1) much of our DNA with other species, host(V2) millions of non-human cells within our bodies, and may have absorbed(V3)some of their DNA by horizontal transfer.

⑧ Even if creating human-animal chimeras is not intrinsically wrong, is there an ethical problem in **harvesting organs** from a creature that is part-human? It has been suggested that human stem cells might become incorporated into the pig's brain, making the pig "more human". But even if stem cells enhanced the

れらが失った膵臓の遺伝子によってできた<u>ギャップ</u>を<u>自動的に埋め</u>，<u>遺伝的に主にヒ</u><u>ト細胞からなる</u>膵臓を形成するということを示唆する。

2

⑤　ブタからヒトへ臓器を移植するという概念は新しいものではない。異種間移植，つまり異種移植は，1990 年代に有望であると考えられていたが，ヒトの免疫システムが，ブタの臓器を拒絶する<u>ことを防ぐ</u>〔免疫系によって拒絶反応が出ることを防ぐ〕という課題（challenges）と，ブタからヒトへ感染症が伝播する可能性についての懸念から，<u>支持されなくなった</u>（※構文説明：fell from favour due to ₍A₎the challenges …and（due to）₍B₎concerns about …　(A)「～の課題」と　(B)「～の懸念」は，due to にかかる）。現代の遺伝子編集技術は<u>両方の懸念を軽減する</u>手助けとなるだろう。つまり，臓器は，さらにヒトの臓器に近づいているので，拒絶反応は，<u>さらに起こりにくくなり</u>，他の科学者らは，CRISPR をブタのゲノムから<u>レトロウイルスを削除するのに</u>用いることもできると実証している。

⑥　しかし，リスクはまだ高すぎると明らかに反論する者もいる。これらの反対意見はいわゆる予防原則に訴えていることが多い。予防原則は，たとえリスクの存在や程度が不確かであっても，リスクを回避するために<u>対応をするべきである</u>と述べている。魅力的ではあるが，それが，エビデンスに基づいていて，その技術を用いないことの被害と，新たな技術の導入のリスクとのバランスを取るなら，予防原則は単に防御でしかない。

実地医療が実践の倫理に即す

⑦　ヒトと動物の交配種，いわゆるキメラを作成することは本質的に間違っていると主張する人たちもいる。つまりそれは₍S'₎人間の尊厳に<u>相反する</u>₍V'1₎こと，または「神のようにふるまう」という性質のものである₍V'2₎（※ constitute「～の性質である」 cf.constitution「体質」）。ヒトの生物学的性質が定まっていないし，他の生体の生物学的性質と分類上分離されていないということを<u>鑑みると</u>，そのような主張の根拠を理解することは難しい（※構文説明：given that S V「～であることを鑑みれば」）。たとえ技術的介入がなくても，ヒトは₍S₎DNA の多くを他の種と共有しており₍V1₎，ヒトの体内に何百万もの非ヒト細胞を宿しており₍V2₎，そして個体間における水平伝播によってそれらの DNA を吸収している可能性がある₍V3₎（※ share A with ～「～を A と共有する」）。

⑧　たとえヒトと動物のキメラを作成することが本質的に間違っていないとしても，部分的にヒトである生き物から臓器を得ることにおいて倫理的な問題があるのだろうか。ヒト幹細胞がブタの脳に<u>取り込まれ</u>，ブタを「よりヒトらしく」するかもしれないと示唆されてきている。しかしたとえ幹細胞がブタの脳の機能を向上させたとして

pig's brain function, it seems implausible that the pig would acquire anything like the **cognitive sophistication** that would put it morally <u>on a par with</u> humans.

⑨ We might question whether the use of pigs as a source of organs for humans is permissible, even <u>leaving aside</u> any suggestion that their moral status is somehow enhanced by the presence of human cells. Jeremy Bentham, the father of utilitarianism, famously wrote: "The question is <u>not</u>, can they reason? Nor, can they talk? <u>But</u>, can they suffer?"

⑩ <u>If this is the case</u>, pigs undoubtedly qualify for moral consideration. It is often argued that since pigs and other livestock animals are routinely sacrificed for our culinary pleasure, it would be odd to prohibit their use in **life-saving medical research and treatment**. But meat-eating itself is under increased ethical scrutiny today which, even while it is unlikely to be banned anytime soon, makes for a weak foundation on which to justify <u>extending</u> animal exploitation <u>to</u> a new arena.

⑪ Other approaches(S) such as laboratory-grown organs, or organs grown in "zombie" animals genetically engineered to lack sentience, could in the future **offer**(V) **the benefits** of the chimera technique without the **animal welfare problems**. Until then, we shouldn't try to duck difficult judgements about <u>weighing up</u> human and animal welfare. If the risks can be sufficiently controlled, then it's hard to **envisage** society choosing to **forego the life-saving opportunities** of this technology. But we must also recognise that the choices we face now are influenced by earlier decisions about research priorities, and that these too require careful ethical consideration.

も，道徳的にヒトと<u>同等の</u>高度の認知（能力）のようなものをブタが獲得するとは到底信じがたい（※ on a par with ~「~と同等の」）。

9　ヒト細胞の存在によって倫理的地位がいくぶん高められるという<u>提案</u>はさておき，私たちはヒト用の臓器源としてブタを用いることが許されるかどうかを疑問に思うかもしれない（※ question　ここでは動詞）。功利主義の父である，ジェレミー＝ベンサムが，「問題は，理性を用いることができるか，会話をすることができるか<u>ではなく</u>，苦痛を感じられるかということである」と記載した（※構文説明：not *A* but *B*「*A* ではなく，*B* である」）。

10　もしこれがそのケースに当てはまるなら，ブタは疑いなく倫理的考慮をする資格がある。ブタや他の家畜は日常的に我々の食の楽しみのために犠牲になっているので，ブタを，生命救助の医学研究や治療に用いることを禁止するのは，奇妙だろうとよく議論される。しかし肉食自体が，すぐに禁止されることはなさそうではあるものの，今や，倫理的に精査されることが増えていることから，動物搾取を新たな分野に<u>広げ</u>ることを正当化する根拠を弱いものにしている（※ make for ~「~を促進する」　extend *A* to ~「~に *A* を広げる」）。

11　実験室で育てた臓器や，感覚をもたないために遺伝子操作された「ゾンビ」動物で育てた臓器，といった他の手段は(S)，将来，動物福祉の問題なく，キメラ技術の恩恵を提供するだろう(V)。それまでは，ヒトと動物の福祉を<u>重視する</u>ことについての難しい判断を避けようとするべきではない。この（ヒトと動物の福祉の）リスクを十分に抑えれば，この技術による人命救助の機会を捨てるという選択を社会がすると考えるのは困難である〔社会は，人命救助の機会に，この技術を用いることを容易に選択する〕。しかし，我々が今直面している選択は，研究の優先についての早期の決心によって影響される〔研究の優先について，早期に決心することが，今直面している選択に影響する〕ことと，また，これら（の選択）は，注意深い倫理的配慮が必要であることも認識しなければならない（※構文説明：we recognise that S V, and (we recognise) that S' V' the choices we face「我々が直面している選択」）。

>>> 解 説

1.「①の内容について，以下のうち間違って（NOT）いるのは」

選択肢を頭に入れ，解答を探しながら①を読もう。

① 「移植は素晴らしい医療革新ではあるが，利用可能な臓器に（数の）問題がある」➡ ① *l.* 2 a scarcity of donor organs と一致。

② 「多くの人が臓器移植手術を待つ間に亡くなった」

③ **「待機リストから省かれた 809 例のうち，429 例が臓器を待っている間に亡くなった」** ➡ ① *ll.* 4-6「807 例中の…する傾向にある」と不一致なので，正解。

④ 「病状が悪化しすぎたために，臓器移植手術を待つ何人かの患者は待機リストから外された」

2.「④で，以下のうちどれが embryo の意味に近いか」

① 「ブタの細胞」

② 「ブタの血」

③ **「生まれていない発育中のブタ」** ➡正解。

④ 「生まれて間もないブタ」

　medi embryo「胚」　fetus「胎児」　neonatal infant「新生児」

3.「④の内容を最もよくまとめているのは」

選択肢を頭に入れて，解答を探しながら④を読もう。

① 「ヒトの臓器は主に遺伝的にヒト細胞で構成されている」

② 「将来，ブタと他の動物は進化し，自動的にヒトの臓器を育てるかもしれない」

③ **「科学者たちは動物の体の中でヒトの臓器を育てる方法を開発している」** ➡ ④ *l.* 1 Scientists are now … と一致しているので，正解。

④ 「幹細胞は科学者が興味をもつ新しい刺激的な能力を発達させた」

4.「⑤で，異種移植（xenotransplantation）の初期の発展を最もよく表現しているのは」

選択肢を頭に入れて，解答を探しながら⑤を読もう。⑤ *l.* 2 Transplants between different species, or xenotransplantation の～ , or …は「～,すなわち…」 xenotransplantation は「異種移植」の意。

2

①「スタートはよかったが，その後問題になった」 ⇒ 5 *ll.* 3-4 considered promising … but fell from favour due to the challenges of … とあるので,正解。

②「遺伝子編集が病気の伝播につながる」 遺伝子編集とは，遺伝子情報の特定の塩基配列を変化させる技術のことをいう。

③「1990 年代には，実践できないほど費用が高かった」

④「臓器を移植することはヒトからブタにのみ可能であった」

5.「 6 で，予防原則（precautionary principle）の意味を最もよく反映しているのは」

予防原則（precautionary principle）とは，安全性などについて，環境や人への悪影響の因果関係がエビデンスに基づいて（evidence based）いなくても，予防のための決定をすることをいう。

☑️速読攻略
選択肢を頭に入れて，解答を探しながら 6 を読もう。

①「革新は本来的にリスクがある」

②「リスクは科学的エビデンスによって引き起こされる」 ⇒非論理的。

③「**リスクは想定され，避けられるべきである**」 ⇒ 6 *l.* 3 action should be taken to avert risks … と一致しているので，正解。

④「リスクは利益のため無視されるべきである」

6.「 7 の内容を最もよく反映しているのは」

☑️速読攻略
選択肢を頭に入れて，解答を探しながら 7 を読もう。選択肢の内容から②と予想できれば，確認のために 7 を読もう。

①「動物はヒトの恩恵のために存在する」 ⇒非論理的。

②「**ヒトは他の動物とそれほど相違がない**」 ⇒ 7 *ll.* 4-5 humans' biological … と一致しているので，正解。

③「ヒトと動物の交配種を作成することは危険である」 ⇒不記載。

④「神だけが DNA を改変することを許される」 ⇒不記載。

44

7.「⑧で，ヒトの幹細胞をブタの胚に注入すると，どのような結果になり得るか」

☑速読攻略

ブタの胚に注入すると，変化が起きるのは，ヒト（① or ②）かブタ（③ or ④）のどちらであるかを予測しながら⑧を読み進めよう。

① 「より高い機能性の脳をもったヒト」
② 「ブタの DNA をもったヒトの交配種」
③ 「倫理的な決定ができるブタ」➡ ⑧ *ll.* 5-7 it seems implausible that … と不一致。脳の機能を高めたとしても，ヒトと同じような倫理観をもつような複雑な認識は得られないだろう。
④ **「より能力の高い脳をもつブタ」**➡ ⑧ *ll.* 4-5 making the pig "more human". But even if stem cells enhanced … と一致しているので，正解。

☑速読攻略

設問 8 および 9 の選択肢を頭に入れて，解答を探しながら ⑨⑩を読もう。

8.「⑨と⑩で，"If this" とは」

If this の直前の記述を参照する。The question is not, can they reason? … But, can they suffer?（reason = do rational thought） 問題は理性的でないとか，話せないということではなく，苦痛を感じられるということである。
① **「もしブタが痛みと恐怖を経験することができるなら」**➡ ⑨ *ll.* 4-5 "The question is not, … can they suffer?" と一致しているので，正解。
② 「もしブタが理性的な思考ができないなら」
③ 「もしブタが倫理的にヒトと等しくないのなら」
④ 「もしブタがヒトの細胞をもつなら」

9.「⑩で，なぜ肉食の議論は弱い根拠（weak foundation）をもつと表現しているか」

☑速読攻略

⑩ *l.* 6 makes for a weak foundation の直前の文を注意深く読み，解答を探そう。

① 「なぜならば肉を食べることは危険ではないから」➡不記載。
② 「なぜならば肉を食べることは自然で健康的だから」➡不記載。
③ **「なぜならば多くの人が肉を食べることは倫理的ではないと考えるから」**➡ ⑩ *ll.* 4-5 But meat-eating itself … 「倫理的に精査されることが増えていること」と一致しているので，正解。

④「なぜならば多くの人は，遺伝子組み換えは倫理的ではないと考えるから」

10.「11で，将来，どのようにして，動物福祉問題（animal welfare problems）を克服すると示唆しているか」

①「ヒトの DNA を変えることによって」

②**「苦痛を感じることができない動物を作り出すことによって」** ➡ 11 *ll.* 1-2 organs grown in "zombie" animals … to lack sentience（lack sentience「感覚がない」→「苦痛を感じない」の言い換え）と一致しているので，正解。

③「肉の消費のために動物を殺すことをやめることによって」

④「リスクを十分に制御することによって」➡キメラの恩恵を受けるまではリスクを十分に制御すると本文にある。将来のキメラ技術の提供をする際の設問なので，④は本文に記載はあるが，設問内容に対する答えではない。

💡攻略ポイント

英文では各パラグラフの最初の一文に，要点（key sentence）をもってくることが多い。したがって，各パラグラフの最初の一文は，十分に注意して英文を読もう。

ANSWER

1—③	2—③	3—③	4—①	5—③
6—②	7—④	8—①	9—③	10—②

テーマ理解

Chapter 3 ≫ 神経系／脳
The Nervous System

知っておきたい医系用語

●神　経
- □ **nervous system**「神経系」
- □ **central nervous system**「中枢神経系」
- □ **neuron**「ニューロン（神経単位）」
- □ **nerve signal**「神経信号」
- □ **neurotransmitter**「神経伝達物質」[n(j)ùəroʊtrǽnsmítər]
- □ **acetylcholine**「アセチルコリン」
- □ **serotonin**「セロトニン」
- □ **sensory**「感覚の」

●記　憶
- □ **hippocampus**「海馬」大脳辺縁系の一部で記憶の形成にかかわる。
- □ **long-term memory**「長期記憶」
- □ **short-term memory**「短期記憶」
- □ **declarative memory**「陳述記憶」長期記憶のうち，言葉で表現できる記憶。
- □ **nondeclarative memory**「非陳述記憶」長期記憶のうち，自転車の乗り方のように，言葉で表現できない記憶。

●記憶の三段階
- □ **recognition ／ cognition ／ acquisition**「認識」
- □ **register**「登録」
- □ **recall**「想起」

●睡　眠
- □ **REM sleep**「レム睡眠」（**REM：rapid eye movement**「急速眼球運動」）全身の筋肉は弛緩しているが，脳は覚醒している状態。眼球がすばやく動いており，夢を見ていることが多い。
- □ **insomnia ／ vigilance**「不眠症」

● アルコール
☐ **alcohol abuse**「アルコール乱用」
☐ **alcoholism**「アルコール中毒」

● 症　状
☐ **anxiety**「不安」
☐ **depression**「鬱」
☐ **chronic**「慢性の」
☐ **acute**「急性の」
☐ **progressive**「進行性の」

● 部　位
☐ **lesion**「病巣」［líːʒən］
☐ **diseased area**「患部」
☐ **site**「部位」
☐ **region**「領域」

● 病　気
☐ **etiology**「病因論」［ìːtiálədʒi］病気の原因を追究する学問のこと。
☐ **susceptibility**「感染しやすさ」［səsèptəbíləti］
　（≒ **vulnerability**「傷つきやすさ」）
☐ **ward off** 〜／ **fend off** 〜／ **fight off** 〜「〜を撃退する」

● 薬
☐ **painkiller**「痛み止め」
☐ **anesthetic**「麻酔薬」［æ̀nisθétik］
☐ **concentration**「濃度」

● 微生物
☐ **microorganism**「微生物」
☐ **bacteria**「細菌」
☐ **germ**「病原菌」
☐ **virus**「ウイルス」［váiərəs］
☐ **pathogen**「病原体」［pǽθədʒən］
☐ **fungus**「カビ」［fʌ́ŋgəs］

3

中枢神経系（CNS：Central Nervous System）

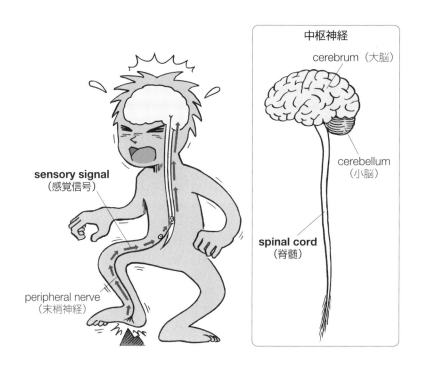

中枢神経

cerebrum（大脳）

cerebellum（小脳）

spinal cord（脊髄）

sensory signal（感覚信号）

peripheral nerve（末梢神経）

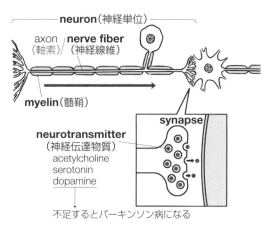

neuron（神経単位）

axon（軸索）/ **nerve fiber**（神経線維）

myelin（髄鞘）

synapse

neurotransmitter（神経伝達物質）
acetylcholine
serotonin
dopamine

不足するとパーキンソン病になる

脳（Brain）

3

cerebral cortex（大脳皮質）

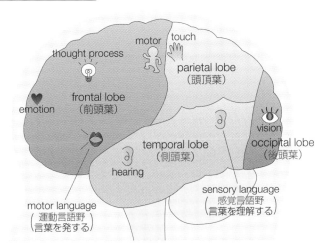

brain-stem（脳幹）
生命維持に重要な機能を司る
脳幹死は日本の脳死の基準

diencephalon（間脳）
視床・視床下部などからなり，
自律神経系・内分泌系を制御

midbrain（中脳）
姿勢保持，眼球の運動

pons（橋）
大脳・脊髄，右脳・左脳の連絡

medulla oblongata（延髄）
respiratory center（呼吸中枢）
cardiac center（心臓中枢）
muscle contraction（筋収縮）
muscle dilation（筋拡張）

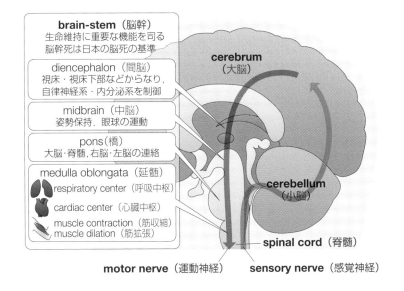

長文読解

★★☆☆☆

5 AI を活用した脳腫瘍診断法

久留米大学（医学部医学科）   389 語

[1] A new **machine learning approach** classifies a common type of **brain tumor** into **low or high grades** with almost 98% accuracy, researchers report in the journal IEEE Access. Scientists in India and Japan, including from Kyoto University's Institute for Integrated Cell-Material Sciences (iCeMS), (1)developed the method to help clinicians choose the most effective treatment strategy for individual patients.

[2] **Gliomas** are a common type of brain tumor affecting **glial cells,** which provide support and **insulation for neurons. Patient treatment** varies depending on **the tumor's aggressiveness,** so it's important to **get the** (2)**diagnosis** right for each individual. **Radiologists** obtain a very large amount of data from **MRI scans** to reconstruct a 3D image of the scanned tissue. Much of the data available in MRI scans **cannot be detected** by the naked eye, such as details related to the tumor shape, texture, or the image's intensity.

[3] **Artificial intelligence (AI) algorithms** help **extract** this data. **Medical oncologists** have been using this approach, called radiomics, to improve patient diagnoses, but accuracy still needs to be (3)enhanced. iCeMS bioengineer Ganesh Pandian Namasivayam collaborated with Indian data scientist Balasubramanian Raman from Roorkee to develop a machine learning approach that can (4)classify gliomas into low or high grade with 97.54% accuracy.

[4] Low grade gliomas include grade I **pilocytic astrocytoma** and grade II low-grade glioma. These are **the less aggressive and less malignant** of the glioma tumors. High grade gliomas include grade III malignant glioma and grade IV **glioblastoma multiforme,** which are much more aggressive and more malignant with a (5)relatively **short post-diagnosis survival time.**

[5] The choice of patient treatment largely depends on being able to determine the glioma's grading. The team, including Rahul Kumar, Ankur Gupta and Harkirat Singh Arora, used a dataset from MRI scans belonging to 210 people with high grade gliomas and another 75 with low grade gliomas. They developed an approach called CGHF, which stands for computational decision support system for grouping gliomas using hybrid radiomics and stationary wavelet-based **features.**

3

1　新しい機械学習の方法が，一般的なタイプの脳腫瘍を低悪性度と高悪性度に，ほぼ98％の精度で分類したと，研究者らは，IEEE Access ジャーナルで報告している。インドと日本の科学者らは，京都大学物質−細胞統合システム拠点（iCeMS）の科学者も含むが，臨床医が個々の患者に対する，最も有効な治療戦略の選択を手助けする方法を開発した。

2　グリオーマは，ニューロンを支持または分離するグリア細胞に由来する一般的なタイプの脳腫瘍である。患者の治療は，腫瘍の侵襲性によって異なり，そのため個々の患者にとって正しい診断を得ることが重要である。放射線科医は，スキャンされた組織の3D画像を再構築するために，MRI スキャンから非常に多くのデータを得る。MRI スキャンで得られるデータの多くは，腫瘍の形状，テクスチャ，あるいは画像の強度に関連する詳細等であり，裸眼では検出できない。

3　人工知能（AI）アルゴリズム（※アルゴリズムとはコンピュータにおける計算方法のこと）は，このデータを抽出するのを手助けする。腫瘍内科医は，患者の診断を改善するためにラジオミクス（radiomics）と呼ばれるこの方法を用いているが，さらに精度を向上させる必要がある。iCeMS の生体工学者 Ganesh Pandian Namasivayam はルールキー出身のインド人データ科学者 Balasubramanian Raman と協力し，97.54％の精度でグリオーマを低悪性度と高悪性度に分類することができる機械学習の方法を開発した。

4　低悪性度のグリオーマには悪性度 I の毛様細胞性星細胞腫と悪性度 II の低悪性度グリオーマがある（※ include「～がある」）。これらは侵襲性が低く，悪性度が低いグリオーマ腫瘍である。高悪性度グリオーマには悪性度 III の悪性グリオーマと悪性度 IV の多形性膠芽腫があり，それらはより侵襲性が強く，悪性度が高く，診断後の生存期間が比較的短い。

5　患者の治療選択は，グリオーマの悪性度の決定ができるかどうかに大きく左右される。Rahul Kumar, Ankur Gupta そして Harkirat Singh Arora らのチームは，高悪性度グリオーマ210例と，低悪性度グリオーマ75例の，MRI スキャンで得られたデータセットを用いた。彼らは CGHF と呼ばれる手法を開発したが，これはハイブリッドラジオミクスと定常ウェーブレットに基づく特徴を用いた，グリオーマの分類のためのコンピュータによる判定サポートシステムの略語である。

6 They chose specific algorithms for extracting features from some of the MRI scans and then (6)trained another **predictive algorithm** to process this data and categorize the gliomas. They then **tested** their model on the rest of the MRI scans to **assess its accuracy**. "Our method outperformed other state-of-the-art approaches for predicting glioma grades from brain MRI scans," says Balasubramanian. "This is quite considerable."

>>> 解 説

1.

(1)「科学者らは，the method を （　　）」
   (a)「～を育てた」　　　　　(b)「～を捨てた」
   (c)**「～を開発した」**➡正解。
   (d)「～を非難した」
(2)「患者の治療は腫瘍の侵襲性によって異なるので，個々の患者にとって正しい（　　）を得ることが重要である」
   (a)**「診断」**➡正解。
   (b)「法令」　　　　　(c)「忘却」　　　　　(d)「合理性」
(3)「さらに精度は（　　）必要がある」
   (a)「想定される」　　　(b)「鼓舞される」　　　(c)「減らされる」
   (d)**「高められる」**➡正解。
(4)「グリオーマを低悪性度と高悪性度に 97.54％ の精度で（　　）ことができる機械学習の方法を開発した」
   (a)**「～を分類する」**➡正解。1 l. 1 A new machine learning approach classifies …が同じ意味の文であり，ヒントとなる。
   (b)「～を混同させる」　(c)「～を拒絶する」　(d)「～を悪化させる」
(5)「…は，生存期間が（　　）短く，より侵襲性が強く，悪性度が高い」
   (a)「長引いて」
   (b)**「比較的」**➡正解。
   (c)「ほとんど～ない」　(d)「広く」
(6)「MRI スキャンから特徴を抽出する特定のアルゴリズムを選び，このデータを処理するために別の予測アルゴリズムを（　　）」
   (a)「～を治療した」　　(b)「～を強要した」
   (c)**「～を訓練した」**➡正解。
   (d)「～を破壊した」

⑥ 彼らは MRI スキャンから特徴を抽出するために，特定のアルゴリズムを選んだ。そして，このデータを処理してグリオーマを分類するために，別の予測アルゴリズムを訓練した。それから，その精度を評価するために，残りの MRI スキャンで彼らのモデルを検査した。「我々の方法は，脳の MRI スキャンからグリオーマの悪性度を予測するための他の最先端の手法よりも優れていました」と Balasubramanian は述べる。「これは，極めて重要なことです」

3

2.

(a) 「グリオーマは，脳腫瘍を引き起こす一般的なタイプの細胞である」➡ ②*l.* 1 より，グリオーマは細胞ではなく腫瘍なので不一致。

(b) 「**放射線科医は，組織の 3 次元画像を再構築するために MRI スキャンからデータを入手する**」➡ ②*ll.* 4-5 に述べられているので，正解。

(c) 「**低悪性度のグリオーマは，高悪性度のグリオーマより危険性は低い**」➡ ④*ll.* 2-5 に述べられているので，正解。

(d) 「新しいタイプの機械は，脳腫瘍へアプローチする方法を高い精度で学んでいる」➡ ①*l.* 1「新しい機械学習の方法は脳腫瘍を分類した」に不一致。

(e) 「AI アルゴリズムは，患者が自分の診断について調べるのに役立つ」➡ ③*l.* 1 「AI アルゴリズムは，データの抽出を行うのを手助けする」に不一致。

(f) 「議論されているグリオーマの種類は，患者の治療法には関係しない」➡ ⑤*ll.* 1-2 より悪性度によって，治療法が異なるので不一致。

(g) 「腫瘍の形状やテクスチャ等の詳細は，MRI スキャンを見れば簡単にわかる」➡ ②*ll.* 5-6「MRI スキャンで得られるデータの多くは，裸眼では検出できない」に不一致。

(h) 「**インドの科学者によると，彼らの方法は，脳の MRI スキャンを用いてグリオーマのタイプを推定するのに，はるかに優れていた**」➡ ⑥*ll.* 4-6 "Our method outperformed …と一致するので，正解。

ANSWER

1. (1)—(c) (2)—(a) (3)—(d) (4)—(a) (5)—(b) (6)—(c)

2—(b)・(c)・(h)

☆★★☆☆

6 アルツハイマー

帝京大学（医学部）　　　　　　　　　　　　　　　　691 語

1 ①Exercise may help to keep the brain robust in people who have an increased **risk of developing Alzheimer's disease**, according to an inspiring new study. **The findings** suggest that even moderate amounts of physical activity may help to slow the progression of one of the most **dreaded diseases** of aging. For the new study, which was published in May in *Frontiers in Aging Neuroscience*, researchers at the Cleveland Clinic in Ohio recruited almost 100 older men and women, aged 65 to 89, many of whom had **a family history of Alzheimer's disease**. Alzheimer's disease, characterized by a ②gradual and then quickening **loss of memory and** ③cognitive functioning, can strike anyone. But scientists have discovered in recent years that people who harbor **a specific variant** of a ₍A₎gene, known as the APOE epsilon4 allele or the e4 gene for short, **have a substantially increased risk** of developing the disease. ④Genetic testing among the volunteers in the new study determined that about half of the group **carried** the e4 gene, although, at the start of the study, none showed **signs of memory loss** beyond what would be normal ⑤for their age.

2 But then some studies began to suggest that exercise might affect **the disease's progression**. A 2011 **brain scan study**, for instance, conducted by some of the same researchers from the Cleveland Clinic, found that elderly **people with** the e4 **gene** who exercised regularly **had significantly more brain activity** during **cognitive tests** than people with the e4 gene who did not exercise, suggesting that the exercisers' brains were functioning better. But that study looked at the function, not the structure of the brain. ⑥Could exercise also be affecting the physical shape of the brain, the researchers wondered, particularly in people with the e4 gene? To find out, they asked the volunteers in their new ₍B₎experiment how often and intensely they exercised. About half, as it turned out, didn't move much at all. But the other half walked, jogged or otherwise **exercised moderately** a few times every week.

3 In the end, the scientists divided their volunteers into four groups, based on their e4 status and **exercise habits**. One group included those people with the e4 gene who did not exercise; another consisted of those with the e4 gene who did exercise; and the other two groups were composed of those without the gene who did or did not regularly exercise. The scientists then **scanned**

🥢 同様のテーマが出題されたことのある大学

順天堂大(医)・東京女子医科大(医)・東邦大(医)・愛知医科大(医)・金沢医科大(医)・兵庫医科大(医)

3

[1]　素晴らしい新研究によれば，運動をすることが，アルツハイマー病の発現リスクが高い人の脳を健常な脳に保つのに一助となるかもしれない。その所見は，適度の身体活動でさえ，老化のもっとも重篤な一疾患の進行を遅らせるのに役立つかもしれないと示唆している。5 月に『老化神経科学の最前線』で発表されたその新研究に関して，オハイオ州クリーブランド・クリニックの研究者たちは，アルツハイマー病の家族歴のある 65 歳から 89 歳までの高齢の男女約 100 名を募集した。徐々に，その後速まっていく記憶および認知機能の喪失が特徴であるアルツハイマー病は，誰にでもかかる可能性がある。しかし，最近，APOE epsilon4 対立遺伝子（※表現型：アポ e4），あるいは，略して e4 遺伝子として知られる遺伝子の特定のバリアント〔変異体〕を有する人は，事実上，アルツハイマー病の発現リスクが高いことを科学者らは発見した。研究当初は，年齢に対して正常でない範囲に入る記憶喪失の兆候を誰一人示さなかったものの，その新しい研究によって，被験者間の遺伝子検査から，その群の約半数が e4 遺伝子を保有していると決定づけた。

[2]　しかし，それから，いくつかの研究は，運動すればその病気の進行に影響を与えるかもしれないことを示唆し始めた。たとえば，クリーブランド・クリニックの同じ研究者らの一部によって行われた 2011 年の脳スキャン検査から，定期的に運動している，e4 遺伝子保有の高齢者は，運動をしない e4 遺伝子保有者よりも，認知力テスト中，脳活動が有意に高いことがわかり，運動している人の脳のほうがよりよく機能していることを示唆した。しかし，その研究が見ていたのは機能であって，脳の構造ではなかった。運動が，特に e4 遺伝子保有者において，脳の物理的形態にも影響を及ぼすだろうかと，研究者らは疑いの念を抱いた。それを知るために，彼らは，新しい実験の被験者らに運動の頻度と強度（※名詞節）について尋ねた。約半数の人が，ほとんど動いていなかったことが判明した。だが，残り半数は，ウォーキングやジョギング，あるいは別の方法で，毎週 2，3 回中等度の運動をしていた。

[3]　最後に科学者たちは，e4 遺伝子状態と運動習慣に基づいて，被験者を 4 群に分けた。1 群は，運動をしない e4 遺伝子保有者である。別の 1 群は，e4 遺伝子を保有し運動をしている群である。そして，残り 2 群は，e4 遺伝子非保有者で，運動を規則的にしている群と運動をしていない群である。その後，科学者らは，特に海馬に重点を置いて，被験者の脳スキャンをした。18 カ月後，彼らはもう一度スキャンを行

their volunteers' brains, with particular emphasis on their hippocampi. Eighteen months later, they repeated the scans. In that brief interval, the members of the group carrying the e4 gene who did not exercise had **undergone significant atrophy** of their hippocampus. It had **shrunk** (7)by about 3 percent, on average. Those volunteers who carried the e4 gene but who regularly exercised, however, showed almost no **shrinkage of their hippocampus**. Likewise, both groups of volunteers who did not carry the e4 gene showed little change to their hippocampus. In effect, the brains of (8)physically active volunteers **at high risk for Alzheimer's disease** looked just like the brains of people at much lower risk for the disease, said Stephen M. Rao, a professor at the Schey Center for Cognitive Neuroimaging at the Cleveland Clinic, who oversaw the study. Exercise appeared to have been (9)**protective**.

4 Meanwhile, the brains of sedentary people **at high risk** appeared to be slipping, structurally, toward **dysfunction**. "This occurred in a very compressed time frame," said Dr. Rao, who described the differences in brain structure as "quite significant." How exercise was guarding people's hippocampi remains unclear, he said, although the e4 gene is known to alter **fat metabolism** within the brain, he said, as does exercise, which could be counteracting some of the undesirable effects of the e4 gene. More research needs to be done to better understand the interplay of exercise and Alzheimer's disease risk. But even so, Dr. Rao said, "there's good reason to tell people to exercise" to protect their memories. Many of us do not carry the e4 gene, but everyone has some chance of developing Alzheimer's disease. And if exercise **reduces that risk** in any way, Dr. Rao said, "then why not (10)get up and move?"

>>> 解 説

1. gene と neat の発音がともに [iː] なので,正解は②。

2. experiment と expensive の発音がともに [e] なので,正解は④。

3. (ウ)は「アルツハイマー病を発現する(リスク)」(risk of) developing Alzheimer's disease とするのが正しい。risk of Alzheimer's disease to be developed は,誤り。disease is developed「病気は発現される」ではなく,develop disease「病気を発現する」となる。

った。その短い間隔でも，運動をしない e4 遺伝子保有群が，有意に海馬が萎縮をしていた。海馬は，<u>平均約 3 パーセント萎縮していた</u>。しかし，e4 遺伝子を保有し，規則的に運動している被験者らは，<u>海馬の萎縮をほとんど示さなかった</u>。同様に，e4 遺伝子を保有していない被験者両群は，海馬への変化をほとんど示さなかった。実際に，<u>アルツハイマー病罹患リスクが高い身体的に活発な〔運動をしている〕被験者の脳は，アルツハイマー病罹患リスクがかなり低い人の脳とまさに似ていた</u>〔ほぼ同様であった〕と，研究を監督した，クリーブランド・クリニックのシャイ認知神経画像検査センター教授スティーブン゠M.ラオは述べた。運動は予防的であったようだ。

3

④　その一方で，（罹患）リスクが高い座っている時間の長い人の脳は，構造的に，<u>機能不全へ向かって悪化している</u>ようであった。「これは非常に圧縮された時間枠〔短時間〕で起きました」とラオ博士は言い，脳の構造の違いを<u>「極めて有意」と述べている</u>（※ describe *A* as *B*「*A* を *B* と描写する」）。ラオ博士は，「どのように，運動が人の海馬を保護しているかは明確ではない」と言い，「e4 遺伝子は脳内で脂質代謝を変えることが知られているが」と続け，「運動も同様で，e4 遺伝子の望ましくないある影響〔悪影響〕を<u>防御している可能性がある</u>」と述べた。運動とアルツハイマー病のリスクとの相互作用をさらによく理解するために，さらなる研究を行う必要がある（※ more research needs to be done は，よく用いられるフレーズ）。しかし，たとえそうであっても，記憶力を守るために「人々に運動しなさいと<u>警告するだけの理由があります</u>」とラオ博士は続けた。私たちの多くは，e4 遺伝子を保有していないが，アルツハイマー病を発現する可能性は皆にある。運動によって，何らかのアルツハイマー病のリスクが減少するならば，「起き上がって，動いたらどうでしょうか」とラオ博士は述べた。

4 ．⑦「徐々に」　④「同時期に」　⑦「突然の」　⑤「圧倒的な」➡アルツハイマー発症のプロセスは「最初はゆっくりと，そしてそれから速まる」ので，正解は⑦。

5 ．cognitive は「認知の」の意。➡⑦「**あることを知り，理解し，学ぶ過程に関連した**」が正解。　④「思い出される価値がある」　⑦「健全な判断力をもつ」　⑤「高度に発達した知性をもっている」

6 ．e4 遺伝子をもっているかどうかが明らかにされた testing「検査」なので，遺伝

58

子 gene の形容詞形である⑨ **Genetic** を入れれば文脈に合う。

medi a genetic code「遺伝情報」 a genetic disorder「遺伝病」

7 . for their age「彼らの歳にしては」 熟語。➡︎⑦が正解。「7月にしては」

8 .「〜と研究者らは疑念を抱いた」の〜にあたる文を選ぶ。

　⑦「運動は，脳の物理的な形にも影響すべきだったか」

　⑦「運動は，脳の物理的な形にも影響されるだろうか」

　⑨「運動は，脳の物理的な形にも影響するだろうか」➡︎正解。

　⑤「運動は，脳の物理的な形にも影響したであろうか」

9 . 正解は，⑤ **by**（about 3 percent）。「約3パーセント縮小した」 差を表す by。

cf. reduced <u>by</u> 〜 percent「〜パーセント減少した」

10.「運動をしている」を意味するので，反対は「運動をしない，動かない」。➡︎

　4 *l.* 1 にある **sedentary**「いつも座っている」が正解。

11.「運動することが，アルツハイマーになることを防ぐ」という流れ。➡︎⑤

　protective「予防的な」が正解。ここでは，protective は「守る」ではなく「予

　防的な」の意味。

12. ⑦**「起き上がって動きなさい」**が正解。 ⑦「家で静かにしていなさい」 ⑨「記

　憶喪失を回復しなさい」 ⑤「昇って，輝きなさい」

13. ⑤が正解。運動することが予防的に働くが，どの程度，運動がアルツハイマー病

　のリスクを低減するかは，依然として研究中であるという主旨をとらえられるかが

　ポイント。 3 最終文の Exercise appeared to have been protective. や 4 *ll.* 7-8

　の More research needs to be done …. などが一致。

特定遺伝子と病気の関係を扱った記事である。また，アルツハイマー，老化，記憶など
は，入試で扱われる頻度の高いテーマの1つである。

ANSWER

1 —⑦	2 —⑦	3 —⑨	4 —⑦
5 —⑦	6 —⑨	7 —⑦	8 —⑨
9 —⑤	10. sedentary	11—⑤	12—⑦
13—⑤			

記憶（Memory）

記憶の三段階

recognition（認識）　　**register**（登録）　　**recall**（想起）

記憶の分類

short-term memory（短期記憶）
短期間保持され，時間経過とともに
忘却される。

long-term memory（長期記憶）
長期間保持され，忘却しないかぎり
死ぬまで保持される。

長期記憶の種類

declarative memory（陳述記憶）
言葉で表現できる記憶。

nondeclarative memory（非陳述記憶）
言葉で表現できない記憶。

イラスト　茨木保

長文読解　　　　　　　　　　　　　　　　　　☆☆★★☆

7 睡眠と記憶

聖マリアンナ医科大学　　　　　　　　　　　　　　　387 語

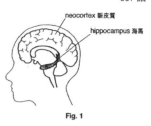

Fig. 1

1　It is widely believed that memories of events and spaces **are stored** briefly in **the hippocampus** before they are combined and strengthened in **the neocortex** for permanent storage (Fig. 1). (a)Experts have long suspected that part of the process of turning temporary **short-term memories** into lasting **long-term memories** occurs during sleep. Now, Professor Susumu Tonegawa and his team have shown that mice prevented from "replaying" their activities from **waking hours while asleep** do not remember them.

2　At research facilities around the world, mice learn to run through complex mazes, find chocolate-flavored rewards, and after an interval, run the mazes again very efficiently, quickly collecting all the rewards. However, Professor Tonegawa and his team created **mutant mice** in which a change of diet **blocked** a specific part of the mouse hippocampus, **the area of the brain responsible for learning and memory**. Consequently, these mutant mice (b)could not perform these tasks.

3　In the experiment with these mutant mice, the researchers **implanted electrodes** in their brains and **monitored the activities of their brain cells** as the mice ran a maze and then slept (Fig. 2 & 3). Researchers examined a **circuit** within the hippocampus known as the **synaptic pathway**. While the mice were still awake and running, they formed within their brains **a pattern of neurons that was activated** to recognize the maze the mice had learned to find their way through. During their post-run sleep, particularly during a deep

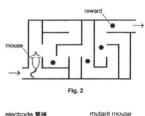

Fig. 2

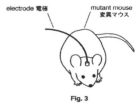

Fig. 3

sleep phase called **slow-wave**, the specific **sequence** of brain cells that had been activated during the run was "replayed" in a similar sequence. However, with these mutant mice, this replay process during the slow-wave sleep **was harmed**. Generally, the animals were able to form long-term memories of the maze only

🎓 同様のテーマが出題されたことのある大学

帝京大(医)・順天堂大(医)・慶應義塾大(医)・東海大(医〈医〉)・日本医科大

1　事象と空間の記憶は，長期記憶をするために新皮質で結合され強化される前に，海馬で短期的に蓄積される〔海馬で短期的に蓄積され，その後，新皮質で結合され強化されて長期記憶になる〕，と広く考えられている（図1）。一時的な短期記憶が永続的な長期記憶に変換される過程の一部は，睡眠中に起こるのではと，専門家は長い間疑念を抱いてきた。さて，利根川進教授と彼のチームは，睡眠中に覚醒時間の活動を「再現すること」を妨げられたマウスは，その活動を覚えていないことを示唆している。

2　世界中の研究施設で，マウスは複雑な迷路を走り抜けられるようになり，チョコレート味の褒美を見つけ，その後しばらく経ってから，迷路を再び効率よく走り，すばやくすべての褒美を集めるようになる。しかし，利根川教授と彼のチームは，餌を変えることで学習と記憶を司る脳の領域である海馬の特定の部分を遮断した変異マウスを創作した。その結果，これらの変異マウスはこれらのタスクができなかった。

3　これらの変異マウスを用いた実験で，研究者らはマウスの脳に電極を埋め込み，マウスが迷路を走ったときおよびその後の睡眠時の脳細胞の活動をモニターした（図2および図3）。研究者らは，シナプス経路として知られる海馬内の回路を調べた。マウスは，覚醒して走っている間に，すでに通り道がわかるようになっていた迷路を認識するための，活性化されたニューロン群〔パターン〕を脳内に形成した。走ったあとの睡眠中，特に徐波と呼ばれる深い睡眠段階で，走っている間に活性化された脳細胞の特定のニューロン・シーケンス〔群〕は，類似のシーケンスで「再現」された。しかし，変異マウスでは〔を用いると〕，徐波睡眠時のこの再現過程が阻害された。通常，マウスは，短期記憶の形成後，シナプス経路が機能しているときのみ，迷路についての長期記憶を形成することができた。

when their synaptic pathways **were functioning** after the formation of the short-term memories.

4 Although this replay during sleep had been speculated to be important for converting the recent memory **stored** in the hippocampus to a more permanent memory stored in the neocortex, it had never been demonstrated. Professor Tonegawa and his team demonstrated that this pathway is essential for **the transformation** of a recent memory, formed within a day, into **a remote memory** that still exists at least six weeks later. They concluded that **the synaptic pathway-mediated replay** of the hippocampal memory sequence during sleep plays a crucial role in the formation of a long-term memory.

>>> 解 説

1. that 以下の主語は，part of the process of turning A into B「A を B に変換するという過程の一部は」の形で，long-term memories まで。述語動詞は occurs 「起こる」。
2. these tasks「これらのタスク」とは，複雑な迷路を走り抜け，チョコレート味の褒美を集めるという作業を指すが，下線部(b)の直前の文がその理由となる。
3. 2・3 の実験結果をふまえて 4 をまとめる。

「短期記憶は，睡眠中に脳内ニューロンが活性化して再現され，長期記憶として蓄積される」というテーマは，入試で注目されるテーマの１つである。脳のニューロンに関する類題テーマとして，「脳のニューロンの活性化を可視化した実験」や，「睡眠とストレス」「痛みと脳」なども入試で取り上げられている。

ANSWER

1. 一時的な短期記憶が永続的な長期記憶に変換される過程の一部は，睡眠中に起こるのではと，専門家は長い間疑念を抱いてきた。
2. 変異マウスでは，食餌を変えることで，学習と記憶を司る脳の領域である海馬を遮断したから。
3. 海馬の働きを阻害された変異マウスは，睡眠中に短期記憶を再現できず，タスクを成し遂げることができなかったことから，長期記憶の形成ができなかった。このことから，長期記憶の形成に短期記憶を睡眠中に再現することが重要となる，と結論づけた。

④　この睡眠中の再現は，海馬に蓄積された最近の記憶〔短期記憶〕を，新皮質に蓄積される，さらに永続的な記憶〔中期記憶・長期記憶〕に変換するため（※ convert *A* to〔into〕*B*「*A* を *B* に変換する」）に重要であると考えられていたが，これまで立証されていなかった。利根川教授と彼のチームは，このシナプス経路は，1 日以内に形成された最近の記憶〔短期記憶〕を少なくとも 6 週間後にも存在する遠隔記憶〔≒長期記憶〕に転換するために，重要であることを立証した。彼らは，睡眠中に海馬記憶のシーケンス〔活性ニューロン群〕をシナプス経路が仲介し再現することが，長期記憶の形成において重要な役割を果たすと結論づけた。

3

大脳辺縁系（Cerebral Limbic System）

大脳の各葉と間脳の中間に位置し，
脳の高次精神機能と原始的な感情を
混合・統合するネットワーク。

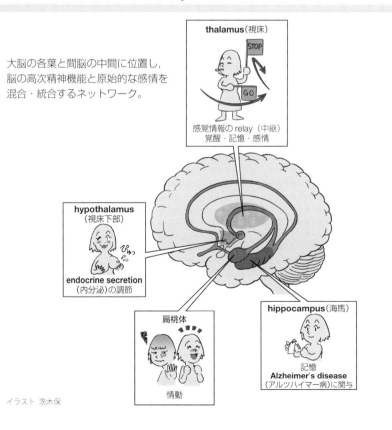

thalamus（視床）
STOP
GO
感覚情報の relay（中継）
覚醒・記憶・感情

hypothalamus
（視床下部）
endocrine secretion
（内分泌）の調節

扁桃体
情動

hippocampus（海馬）
記憶
Alzheimer's disease
（アルツハイマー病）に関与

イラスト　茨木保

64

プラスα ② 前頭側頭型認知症

順天堂大学（医学部）　　　　　目標 1 分 40 秒　239 語

[1]　Today, there is new hope for people with Mr. Karger's disease. "About a quarter of **frontotemporal dementia cases are genetic**," said Dr. Grossman, who directs the University of Pennsylvania's Frontotemporal Degeneration Center. In frontotemporal dementia —— in contrast to Alzheimer's disease —— we often know **which gene is causing the condition** and **which toxic molecule is accumulating** inside the brain. "This allows us to build rational treatments," Dr. Grossman said.

[2]　This summer, the biotechnology company Alector announced early results for a drug that was given to people with frontotemporal dementia **caused by mutations in a gene** called progranulin. **People with the mutated gene** have **abnormally low levels of** progranulin protein, but those who **received the drug** saw levels increase **to a normal range**.

[3]　Two more **trials** are underway for **people with a different genetic mutation** that **causes amyotrophic lateral sclerosis** (**A.L.S.**) but can also cause frontotemporal dementia. All three studies seem to **validate an idea** that has been bubbling up through the wider community of neurologists for several years: **Molecularly targeted therapeutics** may be the future of dementia care. Some neurologists wonder if dementia should be treated like cancer.

[4]　"Because frontotemporal dementia is often **familial**, we can get people into a trial **before they have symptoms**," Dr. Grossman said. "By **sequencing genes from a blood sample**, we know which family members are probably going to **get the disease**. If we can **slow down progression** in those people, it's virtually a cure."

© The New York Times

3

1 今日ではカーガー氏の病気をもつ人々に新たな希望がある。「前頭側頭型認知症例のおよそ４分の１は遺伝性のものです」とグロスマン博士は語った。博士はペンシルベニア大学前頭側頭型変性症センターの所長である。前頭側頭型認知症は――アルツハイマー病とは対照的に――どの遺伝子が病態を引き起こしているか，また，どの有毒分子が脳内で蓄積しているかが，わかる場合がある。「そのおかげで合理的な治療を構築することができるのです」とグロスマン博士は語った。

2 この夏，バイオテクノロジー企業のアレクターは，プログラニュリンと呼ばれる遺伝子変異によって引き起こされた前頭側頭型認知症の患者に投与した薬剤の初期結果を発表した（※ give には「処方する」という意味はない。薬の処方ができるのは医師のみ）。変異遺伝子をもつ人はプログラニュリンタンパク質値が異常に低いが，その薬剤を服用した人は正常値までの増加が認められた（※ see levels increase「レベルが上昇するのがわかる」see *A do* 知覚動詞の用法）。

3 筋萎縮性側索硬化症（ALS）を引き起こし，前頭側頭型認知症も引き起こす可能性のある，異なる遺伝子変異をもつ人々に対して，さらに２度の試験が行われている（※ trial「試験」trial は「検査」という意味ではあまり用いない）。こうした３つの試験は，広く神経学関係者の間で数年間わきあがっていた考えを実証するように思える。分子標的治療が将来の認知症治療になる可能性がある。神経学者の中には，認知症は癌のように治療すべきではないかと考える人もいる。

4 「前頭側頭型認知症は家族性の場合が多いため，症状が出る前に試験をすることができます」とグロスマン博士は語った。「血液サンプルの遺伝子配列を決定することによって，家族の誰がその病気にかかる可能性があるかがわかります（※ sequence（動詞）「～の配列を決定する」）。そうした人たちの（病気の）進行を遅らせることができれば，事実上の治療になります」

プラスα ③ 精神疾患の原因はなにか

旭川医科大学（医学部医学科）　　　　　　　　目標3分　326語

1　Each different approach to **mental disorders** emphasizes one kind of cause and a **corresponding kind of** treatment. Doctors who look for **hereditary factors and brain disorders** recommend drugs. Therapists who blame early experience and mental conflicts recommend **psychotherapy**. Clinicians who focus on learning suggest **behavior therapy**. Those who focus on **distorted thinking** recommend **cognitive therapy**. Therapists with a religious orientation suggest **meditation** and prayer. And therapists who believe most problems **arise from family dynamics** usually recommend, predictably, family therapy.

（中略）

2　Four decades of research by thousands of smart scientists, supported by billions of dollars, has still not found **a specific brain cause for** any of the major mental disorders, except for those such as **Alzheimer's disease and Huntington's chorea** in which **brain abnormalities** have long been obvious. For other mental disorders, we still have no **lab test or scan** that can **make a definitive diagnosis**.

3　This is as astounding as it is disappointing. **The brains of people with bipolar illness and autism** must somehow be different from those of other people. But brain scans and **autopsy** studies have **identified** only small differences. They are real, but small and inconsistent. It is hard to say which are causes and which are results of the disorders. None comes close to **providing a definitive diagnosis** of the sort **radiologists** provide for **pneumonia** or **pathologists** provide for cancer.

4　Hope for diagnosis based on genetics has also collapsed. **Having schizophrenia, bipolar disorder, or autism** depends almost entirely on what genes a person has, so most of us engaged in **psychiatric research** at the turn of the millennium thought **the specific genetic culprits** would soon be found. However, **subsequent studies** have shown that there are no common **genetic variations** with large effects on these disorders. Almost all specific variations increase the risk by 1 percent or less. This is the most important —— and most discouraging —— discovery in the history of psychiatry. What it means, and what we should do next, are big questions.

[From Good Reasons for Bad Feelings by Randolph M. Nesse, Dutton]

3

1　精神疾患別の対応は，1種類の原因とそれに応じた治療に重きを置く。遺伝的因子や脳の障害と考える医師は，薬を勧める。幼少期の経験や心の葛藤に原因があるとするセラピストは，心理療法を勧める。学習を重視する臨床医は，行動療法を勧める。認知〔思考〕のゆがみを重視する人は，認知療法を勧める。宗教的な志向をもつセラピストは，瞑想や祈りを勧める。そしてほとんどの問題は家族力動が原因で起こると考えるセラピストは通常，予想通り家族療法を勧める。(中略)

2　何十億ドルのサポートを受けている何千人もの優秀な科学者による40年にわたる研究で，脳の異常がずっと以前から明らかになっているアルツハイマー病やハンチントン病以外の，主要な精神疾患の特定の脳の原因はいまだに発見できていない。それ以外の精神疾患については，いまだに確定診断をすることができるラボ検査やスキャンがないのである。

3　これは驚くべきことで，残念なことである。双極性障害や自閉症の患者の脳は，他の人たちの脳とはいくぶん異なるに違いない。しかし，脳スキャンや検死解剖の研究では，わずかな違いのみを同定している。それらは実際に存在するが，わずかで一貫性がない。どれが障害の原因で，またどれが結果かを述べるのは難しい。肺炎に対する放射線科医や，癌に対する病理学者の診断のような確定診断を行うことはとうていできない（※ come close to *doing*「〜することに近づく」 of the sort 〜「〜のような」）。

4　遺伝学に基づく診断への期待もなくなっている。統合失調症や双極性障害，自閉症になることは，その人がもっている遺伝子によってほぼ決まるため，21世紀への時代の変わり目に精神医学の研究に携わっていた私たちの大半は，特定の遺伝的要因がすぐに発見されるだろうと考えていた。しかし，その後に続く研究で，これらの疾患に大きな影響を与える共通の遺伝子変異はないことが示唆されている。ほとんどすべての特定の変異は1％以下でリスクを増加させる。これは，精神医学の史上で最も重要であり，そして最も落胆する発見である。この発見が意味すること，そして私たちが次にすべきこと，それが大問題である。

68

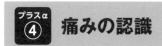
痛みの認識

東京慈恵会医科大学（医学部医学科）　　　　　　　🕐 目標 4 分 30 秒　494 語

1　The perception of pain is so fundamental to our survival that it affects our brains in profound ways. There is not one single **pain center**; instead, the whole brain lights up like a Christmas tree when pain is perceived. In the short term we are immediately prompted to protect **the painful area**, to remove it from the source of the pain and often to cease all use of **the affected area** while we examine it. In the longer term, our subconscious behavior is altered. If we hit our head on a specific low beam or handle, next time we'll duck. An experience of pain that lasts for long, continuous periods may affect our emotions and attitudes. We may develop depression and become less active. Alternatively, a severe experience of pain and a conscious awareness of exactly what led to that pain may result in the development of **an aversion** to anything resembling the cause. We call that aversion fear. The aversion may become a long-term subconscious memory that lasts far longer than your memory of the event that caused it. You may no longer remember the time you fell off the high wall and painfully **twisted your ankle** as a child, but **your fear of heights** may still be with you.

3

1　痛みの認識は，我々の生存に必須であるがゆえ，脳に奥深く影響している。唯一の疼痛中枢があるのではない。その代わり，痛みを認識したとき，クリスマスツリーのように，脳全体がライトアップする。短期的には，疼痛領域を保護し，疼痛の原因から疼痛を取り除いて〔鎮痛をし〕，疼痛を調べている間，往々にして患部の使用をすべて停止するよう即座に促す。長期的には，潜在意識の行動〔無意識に行動〕を変える（※ここは，「無意識に行動が変えられる」という受動態を能動態で訳すと自然）。低い梁や取っ手に頭をぶつけた場合，次回はかがむようになる。長く継続的に続く痛みを経験すると，感情および行動に影響を及ぼすだろう。鬱を経験するかもしれないし，活動をより控えるようになるかもしれない。または，痛みの強烈な経験およびその痛みにつながった原因への意識によって，痛みの原因に似ているいかなるものに対しても嫌悪感を感じるようになるかもしれない〔または，痛みの経験が強烈であれば，その痛みの原因を意識し，原因に似たいかなるものに対しても嫌悪感が生まれるかもしれない〕。その嫌悪感を恐怖と呼ぶ。その嫌悪感は，それを引き起こした出来事自体の記憶より長く継続する，長期的潜在記憶となる場合がある。子供の頃に高い壁から落ち，足首をひどくくじいたときのことは覚えていないかもしれないが，高所への恐怖はつきまとう可能性がある。

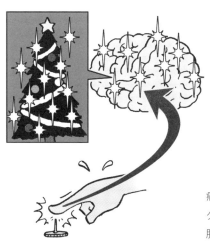

痛みを認識したとき，
クリスマスツリーのように
脳全体をライトアップする

イラスト　茨木保

2   We don't always perceive pain. Even when the nerve cells are sending us pain signals, there are times when it is more important for us simply to run away, rather than roll about on the ground in agony. So there are regions of the brain that actively inhibit our perception of pain, sometimes for just a few minutes, sometimes for several days. But there are also areas of the brain that **do the reverse**, and make us **hypersensitive to pain**. When we're safe and recovering, such heightened sensations might, for example, encourage us to avoid using the painful part while it heals.

3   Astonishingly, there used to be considerable confusion about when we first start experiencing pain. A hundred years ago it was widely accepted that **newborn babies** simply did not perceive pain at all, because their brains had not developed sufficiently. Perhaps rather cruelly by today's standards, for decades many 'pin-prick' experiments were conducted on sleeping infants in attempts to understand the onset of pain perception. Much confusion was caused in those early experiments by the seeming **lack of sensitivity** of babies straight after birth, which turned out to be because the mothers had received **anesthetics** while giving birth, and the babies received a small dose via their umbilical cords. Today (as anyone with children can affirm), it is well understood that a baby in pain will show clear discomfort. Crying, wriggling, fisting, large muscle movements, accompanied by clear respiratory and hormonal changes and erratic sleep, are all clear signs of pain. But those early scientifically flawed experiments sadly resulted in a culture that disregarded the pain of babies for much too long, despite the true scientific findings.

[From The Undercover Scientist: Investigating the Mishaps of Everyday Life by Peter J. Bentley, Random House Books]

② 　我々は必ずしも，疼痛を認識するとは限らない。神経細胞が疼痛シグナルを送っているときでさえ，我々が苦しみにもがき地面に転げまわるより，単に（疼痛から）逃避することがさらに重要な場合がある。疼痛の認識を積極的に遮る脳の領域があり，遮る時間は，ほんの数分のときもあれば，数日続くときもある。しかし，反対の作用をし，疼痛に対して**過敏**にする脳の領域もまたある。（損傷から）無事で回復していると，痛みの感作性が高まると，たとえば，回復期に，疼痛を感じないようにする場合がある〔疼痛部分を用いることを避けるよう促す〕。

③ 　驚いたことに，（生まれて）初めて疼痛を感じ始めるとき（の考え方）についてかなり混乱があった。百年前，**新生児**は疼痛を単に全く認識しないと，広く考えられていた。それは，新生児の脳が十分に発達していないという理由からであった。疼痛の認識がいつから始まるかを理解しようと，おそらく今日の水準では，かなり残酷に，ということになるが，数十年間にわたり，睡眠中の乳児に「ピンで刺す」検査が多く行われていた。初期の実験において，新生児の誕生直後の，一見感受性が欠如していると考えられたことによって，多くの混乱が起こっていた。その感受性の欠如は，母親が出産時に**麻酔**を受けており，乳児もへその緒を通して，少量の麻酔を受けたという理由からだと判明した。今日（子供のいる人はだれでも確信できるが），痛みを感じている乳児が明らかな不快感を示すことは，十分に理解されている。明らかな呼吸の変化およびホルモンの変化，不規則な睡眠を伴い，泣いたり，体をよじったり，握りこぶしをつくったり，大きく筋肉が動いたりすることすべては，疼痛の明らかなサインである。しかし，悲しいことに，初期の科学的に欠陥のあった実験により，真実の科学的な所見があったにもかかわらず，乳児の疼痛が，長きにわたりあまりにも無視されるという文化が生まれてしまった。

プラスα ⑤ 認知の中間領域

⏰ 目標 6 分　521 語

1 Memory researchers have shone light into a **cognitive limbo**. A new memory —— the name of someone you've just met, for example —— is held for seconds in so-called **working memory**, as your **brain's neurons** continue to fire. If the person is important to you, the name will over a few days enter your **long-term memory**, preserved by permanently **altered neural connections**. But where does it go during the in-between hours, when it has left your standard working memory and is not yet **embedded in** long-term memory?

2 A research team shows that memories can be resurrected from this limbo. Their observations point to a new form of working memory, which they dub prioritized long-term memory, that exists without **elevated neural activity**. Consistent with other recent work, the study suggests that information can somehow be held **among the synapses that connect neurons**, even after conventional working memory has faded. (*Science*, 14 March 2008, p.1543).

3 "This is a really fundamental finding —— it's like the dark matter of memory," says Geoffrey Woodman, **a cognitive neuroscientist** at Vanderbilt University in Nashville who was not involved with the work. "It's hard to really see it or measure it in any clear way, but it has to be out there. Otherwise, things would fly apart."

1 記憶研究者たちが認知上の中間領域〔短期記憶から長期記憶へ転送するための機構〕に着目している。新たな記憶，例えば，会ったばかりの人の名前は，脳のニューロンが発火し続けている間，いわゆる作業記憶に数秒間保持される（※ as S V「～している間」）。その人があなたにとって重要ならば，その名前は数日間に長期記憶となり，永久的に改変された神経結合によって保持される。しかし，中間の時間，標準的な作業記憶から移行し，長期記憶に固定化されていない間は，それ〔その記憶〕はどこへ行くのだろうか。

2 ある研究チームは，記憶は中間領域から思い出すことは可能であると示唆している。かれら〔研究チーム〕の観察は，新型の作業記憶を指摘する。それは優先的長期記憶と呼ばれ，神経活動が上昇せずに存在している。最近の他の研究と一致するが，この研究は，従来の作業記憶が消滅した後でさえ，ニューロンをつないでいるシナプス間隙に，情報をとりあえず保存している可能性がある（※受動態を能動態で訳す）と示唆している。

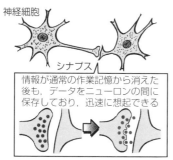

神経細胞

シナプス

情報が通常の作業記憶から消えた後も，データをニューロンの間に保存しており，迅速に想起できる

イラスト 茨木保

Information can somehow be held **among the synapses that connect neurons**, even after **conventional working memory** has faded.

3 「これは実に抜本的な所見です。つまり，記憶のダークマター〔直接観測できないもの〕のようなものです」と，その作業に関与していなかったナッシュビル州ヴァンダービルト大学所属の認知神経科学者 Geoffrey Woodman 氏は述べる。「何らかの明瞭な方法でこれを観察したり測定したりするのは非常に困難ですが，必ず存在していなくてはならない。さもなければ，すべてが飛び散って〔ばらばらになって〕しまいます」

4 Cognitive neuroscientist Nathan Rose and colleagues at the University of Wisconsin (UW) in Madison initially had **subjects** watch a series of slides showing faces, words, or dots moving <u>in one direction.</u> They <u>tracked</u>(V1) the **resulting neural activity** using **functional magnetic resonance imaging (fMRI)** and, with the help of a **machine learning algorithm**, showed they could <u>classify</u>(V2) **the brain activity** associated with each item.

5 Then <u>the subjects</u>(S) viewed(V1) the items in combination —— a word and face, for example —— but **were cued to**(V2) focus on just one item. At first, **the brain signatures** of both items showed up, as measured in this round with **electroencephalography** (EEG). But neural activity for **the uncued item** quickly dropped to baseline, as if it had been forgotten, whereas the EEG signature of **the cued item** remained, a sign that it was still in working memory. Yet subjects could still quickly **recall** the uncued item when <u>prompted to</u> remember it a few seconds later.

6 Rose, who recently left UW for the University of Notre Dame in South Bend, Indiana, and his colleagues then <u>turned to</u> transcranial magnetic stimulation (TMS), a **noninvasive method** that uses rapidly changing **magnetic fields** to <u>deliver</u> a **pulse of electrical current** <u>to</u> the brain. They(S) had(V1) subjects perform the same cued memory task, then applied(V2) a **broad TMS pulse** just after the signature of the uncued memory item had faded.

4　マジソン州ウィスコンシン大学の認知神経科学者 Nathan Rose とその同僚らは，最初に顔や単語の一連のスライドや，一方向に動く点を被験者たちに見せ，機能的磁気共鳴画像法（fMRI）を用いて，その結果生じる神経活動を追跡し(V1)，機械学習アルゴリズムの助けを借り，各項目に関連する脳の活動を分類できる(V2)ことを示唆した。

5　次に被験者ら(S)は，例えば，単語と顔といった組み合わせで項目を見た(V1)が，1つの項目だけに注視するように促された(V2)（※ be cued to *do*「〜するよう指示を与えられる」）。最初，脳波検査（EEG）で計測すると，両項目についての脳シグネチャー（特徴的な脳活動所見）が現れた。しかし，注視していない項目の神経活動は，まるで忘れられたかのように，基線まで急速に低下し，一方注視した項目の EEG シグネチャーは残っていたが，つまりそれ〔注視した項目の EEG〕が，作業記憶にあった，と示唆した〔サインだった〕（※ baseline「基線（正常値）」）。それでも，被験者らは，数秒後に想起するよう促されると，注視していない項目を迅速に想起することができた。

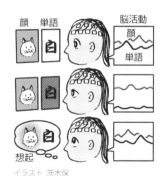

注視していない項目　⇨単語
注視した項目　　　　⇨顔

イラスト 茨木保

6　ウィスコンシン大学からインディアナ州サウスベンドのノートルダム大学へ最近移籍した Rose と同僚らは，次に経頭蓋磁気刺激（TMS）すなわち，非侵襲性の方法にとりかかった。その方法は，急速に変化をする磁場を用いて，電流パルスを脳に送る（※ deliver *A* to 〜「*A* を〜に送る」）。彼らは(S)被験者らに同様の注視した記憶作業をしてもらい(V1)（※ have 人 *do*「人に〜してもらう」），それから注視しない記憶項目のシグネチャーが消えた直後に，広範囲に TMS パルスを施行した(V2)。

TMS によって脳の局所で神経細胞を活性化
磁場
磁場
電流パルス
電流パルス
イラスト 茨木保

7 The appropriate neural activity for that "forgotten" item spiked, showing the memory was **reactivated into** immediate consciousness from its **latent state**. What's more, when the TMS directly targeted the brain areas that were **initially active** for the uncued item, the reactivation response was even stronger.

8 The study doesn't address how **synapses** or other **neuronal features** can hold this second level of working memory, or how much information it can store. "It's a primitive early step in understanding how we bring things into mind," says UW cognitive neuroscientist Bradley Postle, a study co-author.

[From Energy pulses reveal possible new state of memory, Science Vol.354 Issue 6316 2 Dec. 2016 by Jessica Boddy, American Association for the Advancement of Science (AAAS)]

7 その「忘れた」項目に対する適切な神経活動が再燃し，その記憶が潜伏状態から即時意識へと再活性化されたことが示唆された（※ latent state「潜伏状態」）。さらに，TMS が注視しなかった項目に対して初めに活性化した脳の領域を直接標的にした場合，再活性反応はさらに増強した。

8 この研究は，どのようにしてシナプスやその他のニューロンの特徴がこの 2 次レベルの作業記憶を保持できるか，または，どれくらいの情報を貯蔵できるのかは言及していない。「これは，我々が物事をどのように思い出すかを理解することのごく初期の段階です」とウィスコンシン大学の研究の共著者である認知神経科学者 Bradley Postle は述べている（※ primitive「初歩的な」）。

記憶の保存場所

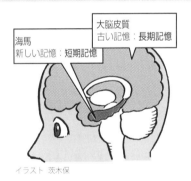

イラスト 茨木保

記憶の過程は短期記憶・作業記憶（認識）から長期記憶となる。短期記憶（短時間保管された記憶）は，ワーキング・メモリー（作業記憶）によって処理され，必要と判断された情報は短期記憶から長期記憶へ送られる。

テーマ理解

Chapter 4 ≫ 呼吸器系／感染症
The Respiratory System

知っておきたい医系用語

● 感染菌
- ☐ **infectious agent**「感染菌」
- ☐ **strain**「菌株」
- ☐ **source of infection**「感染源」
- ☐ **infected people**「感染者」

● 感　染
- ☐ **infectious disease ／ contagious disease**「感染症」
- ☐ **pandemic ／ epidemic ／ plague**「世界的に大流行した感染症」
- ☐ **outbreak**「アウトブレイク」地域内における感染症の集団発生。
  - ◆ contain the outbreak「アウトブレイクを制御する」
- ☐ **incubation period**「潜伏期」[ìnkjubéiʃən píəriəd]
- ☐ **infect**「～を感染させる」
- ☐ **transmit**「～を伝播させる」
- ☐ **develop ／ contract ／ come down with ～**「（病気）にかかる」

● 感染症
- ☐ **SARS : Severe Acute Respiratory Syndrome**「重症急性呼吸器症候群」
- ☐ **respiratory system**「呼吸器系」[réspərətɔ̀:ri sístəm]
- ☐ **AIDS : acquired immunodeficiency syndrome**「後天性免疫不全症候群」
- ☐ **HIV : human immunodeficiency virus**「ヒト免疫不全ウイルス，エイズウイルス」
- ☐ **highly pathogenic avian influenza**「高病原性トリインフルエンザ」
- ☐ **Spanish Lady**「スパニッシュ・レディー」過去最大の犠牲者を出したインフルエンザ名。
- ☐ **chronic pneumonia**「慢性肺炎」
- ☐ **polio**「ポリオ」◆ eradicate polio「ポリオを撲滅する」
- ☐ **smallpox**「天然痘」

☐**BSE : bovine spongiform encephalopathy**「牛海綿状脳症」
（≒**mad cow disease**「狂牛病」）

☐**encephalic**「脳の」［ènsəfǽlik］

☐**rabies**「狂犬病」

☐**West Nile virus**「西ナイルウイルス」

● 治　療

☐**prevent**「～を予防する」（≒**control**／**contain**「～を制御する」）

☐**treat**「～を治療する」

☐**diagnose**「～を診断する」［dáiəgnòuz］

☐**follow-up**「～を追跡調査する」

☐**manage**「～を管理する」

☐**medical checkup**「健康診断」

☐**vaccine**「ワクチン」［vǽksi(:)n］

☐**vaccination**／**inoculation**「予防接種」［væ̀ksinéiʃən／inὰkjuléiʃən］

● 抗原抗体反応

☐**antigen-antibody response**［**reaction**］「抗原抗体反応」

☐**allergen**「アレルゲン」［ǽlərdʒən］アレルギーを引き起こす原因となる物質。

☐**be allergic to** ～「～にアレルギーである」

☐**histamine**「ヒスタミン」くしゃみ，鼻水などのアレルギー症状の原因物質。
◆ Mast cells secrete histamine.「肥満細胞はヒスタミンを分泌する」

☐**mucus**「粘液」　◆ swollen mucus membrane「腫れた粘膜」

● 症　状

☐**inflammation**「炎症」

☐**sneezing**「くしゃみ」

☐**runny nose**「鼻水」

☐**recurrence**［rikə́:rəns］／**reemergence**／**relapse**「再発」

☐**subsequent**「続発性の」

☐**persistent**「継続性の，しつこい」

☐**asthma**「喘息」

☐**atopy**「アトピー」

呼吸器系（The Respiratory System）

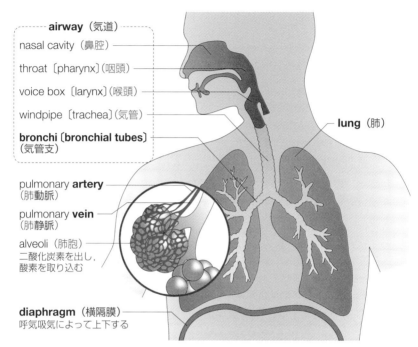

airway（気道）
nasal cavity（鼻腔）
throat〔pharynx〕(咽頭)
voice box〔larynx〕(喉頭)
windpipe〔trachea〕(気管)
bronchi〔bronchial tubes〕
（気管支）

lung（肺）

pulmonary **artery**
（肺動脈）
pulmonary **vein**
（肺静脈）
alveoli（肺胞）
二酸化炭素を出し，
酸素を取り込む

diaphragm（横隔膜）
呼気吸気によって上下する

Respiration : We receive our supply of **oxygen** by **extracting** it from the air we breathe into our lungs. A normal pair of **lungs** contains about a billion tiny **air sacs** where blood **is purified**, supplied with oxygen, and sent on its way to the rest of the body. When we breathe out, we **exhale** carbon dioxide gas and a lot of other waste materials. We eliminate **carbon dioxide** from our lung. The air in most cities **is contaminated**, containing **pollutants** such as **carbon monoxide**, **sulfuric acid**, **hydrochloric acid**, benzene, methane, and ammonia.

　呼吸：我々は，肺に吸い込む空気から酸素を抽出することで，酸素が供給されている。正常な一対の肺には10億の空気の袋（※肺胞）があり，そこで血液は，浄化され，酸素が供給され，身体の他の部位へと送り出される。息を吐くとき，我々は二酸化炭素と他の多くの老廃物を吐き出す。二酸化炭素を肺から除く。多くの都市の空気は汚染されていて，一酸化炭素，硫酸，塩酸，ベンゼン，メタン，アンモニアのような汚染物質を含む（※他にも，アスベストなどが問題となる）。

感染症（Infection）

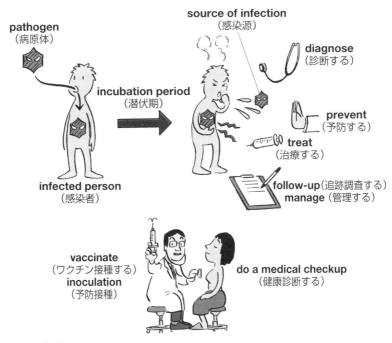

source of infection
（感染源）

pathogen
（病原体）

incubation period
（潜伏期）

diagnose
（診断する）

prevent
（予防する）

treat
（治療する）

follow-up（追跡調査する）
manage（管理する）

infected person
（感染者）

vaccinate
（ワクチン接種する）
inoculation
（予防接種）

do a medical checkup
（健康診断する）

イラスト 茨木保

---

highly pathogenic avian influenza（高病原性トリインフルエンザ）

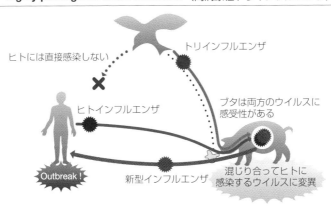

ヒトには直接感染しない

トリインフルエンザ

ブタは両方のウイルスに
感受性がある

ヒトインフルエンザ

混じり合ってヒトに
感染するウイルスに変異

Outbreak！

新型インフルエンザ

今後の懸念：トリインフルエンザウイルスが人に直接感染するウイルスに**mutate**（突然変異）し，その結果 **pandemic**（世界的な大流行）に発展する可能性が懸念されている。

82

いろいろな感染症（Infectious diseases）

1918 ～ 1919 年のいわゆる "Spanish Lady" or "Spanish Flu"（「スパニッシュ・レディー」すなわち「スペイン風邪」）の pandemic（世界的大流行）は，10 億人が infected（感染し），14 世紀の bubonic plague（腺ペスト），16 世紀の smallpox（天然痘），および現在起こっている HIV / AIDS（ヒト免疫不全ウイルス：human immunodeficiency virus / エイズ：acquired immunodeficiency syndrome「後天性免疫不全症候群」）の世界的 epidemic（大流行）さえ超える，既知の病気でもっとも devastating（悲惨な）ものとなった。

Spanish Lady
過去最大の犠牲者を出したインフルエンザ名

highly pathogenic avian influenza
（高病原性トリインフルエンザ）

smallpox
（天然痘）

outbreak

イラスト 茨木保

トリインフルエンザの outbreak

BSE：bovine spongiform encephalopathy（牛海綿状脳症）は，体内にある正常型の prion protein（プリオン蛋白質）が，異常型に変異した病原体により引き起こされる。mad cow disease（狂牛病）とも呼ばれる。人に移ると，CJD：Creutzfeldt-Jakob disease（クロイツフェルト・ヤコブ病）になる。

4

HIV（ヒト免疫不全ウイルス）

免疫系のヘルパーT細胞に感染
し，死滅させる。

AIDS（後天性免疫不全症候群）

免疫不全のため，**susceptible
to infection**（易感染性）となる。

BSE（牛海綿状脳症）
mad cow disease（狂牛病）

prion protein（プリオン蛋白
質）の感染により，脳がスポン
ジ状に変性する。

polio

oral live polio vaccine
（経口生ポリオワクチン）

ワクチン未接種者

イラスト　茨木保

長文読解 ☆★☆☆

8 喘息

順天堂大学（医学部） 496 語

[1]　**Asthma** seems to be increasing throughout most of the developed world, yet medical experts remain unsure about **its causes**. Nearly every statement we might make about asthma can be challenged, including the claim that it is getting worse. One study says that **asthma cases** have increased by 60 percent in the past ten years and that asthma-related deaths have tripled. Yet another study claims that this supposed increase is just an illusion. According to this argument, modern people are simply more aware of asthma, more ready to go to the doctor **with mild cases**, and more prepared to define as asthma something that would once have been called a cold.

[2]　Still, the greater probability is that asthma problems are actually getting worse and that the cause is **pollution**. But what kind of pollution? Smoke has long been suspected of being **a leading cause of asthma**. Yet most of us today inhale far less smoke than our ancestors did, with their wood fires and poorly constructed chimneys, so it seems unlikely that smoke, alone, can have caused the recent increase. More than smoke, it seems a more common trigger for asthma is the common **dust mite's droppings**. These creatures **thrive in** modern heated indoor homes, where they live in carpets and bedding. Thus, modern homes may account for much of the increase of asthma.

[3]　But many other factors are also at work. One theory holds that people who wash too much as children or who encounter less dirt in everyday life **are more likely to develop asthma**; that **hygiene**, not lack of it, is the problem. A study of 14,000 children in Britain showed that those who washed their hands five times a day or more and bathed twice a day had a 25 percent **chance of having asthma**, while those who washed their hands less than three times a day and bathed every other day had only about half that **risk of asthma**. The theory is that dirt contains **bacteria**, which stimulate one part of the **immune system**. Our immune systems, the theory goes, are set up in such a way that they expect to be stimulated by soil bacteria early in childhood; when they are not, the result is an unbalanced system which is more likely to develop asthma. According to this theory, our bodies may need **small doses of** dirt to keep them healthy.

[4]　The other big factor in asthma, and one which still remains a mystery, is

🍃同様のテーマが出題されたことのある大学

兵庫医科大(医)・獨協医科大(医)

4

①　先進国世界のいたるところで喘息が増加しているようであるが，医療専門家はいまだにその原因を確信していないままである。喘息についてのほとんどの説明に問題がありうるが，喘息が悪化しているという主張もそれに含まれる。ある研究によると，喘息症例は過去10年間に60パーセント増加し，喘息に関連した死亡数は3倍になっているとされる。しかし，このような推定による増加は，単なる錯覚であると主張する別の研究もある。この論によると，現代人は単に以前よりも，喘息の認識度が増し，軽症で医者に行こうとし，以前は風邪と呼ばれていたであろうものを喘息として定義しようとするだけである。

②　それでも喘息問題は事実上悪化しており，その原因は汚染であるという可能性が高まっている。しかし，どのような種類の汚染であろうか。煤煙が喘息の主要原因ではないかと長い間，疑われてきた。しかし，薪や貧弱な作りの煙突によって煙を多く吸った先祖より，今日の多くの人々は煙を吸うことがずっと少ない。したがって，煤煙だけが最近の増加を引き起こしている要因であるということにならないだろう。喘息の引き金は，煤煙よりも，よくいるチリダニの糞であることが多いだろう。これらの生物は，近代的な暖房のついている室内で繁殖する。そこで，カーペットや寝具に生息する。このように，近代住宅が，喘息の増加の主要原因だろう。

③　しかし，他の多くの要因も作用している。子供のころに身体を洗いすぎたり，日常生活で埃にあまり接触しなかったりする人々は，喘息になりやすいとする理論もある。すなわち，清潔を欠くことではなく，清潔であること（※ hygiene「衛生」）が問題であるというのである。イギリスの子供14,000名を対象とした研究は，1日に5回以上手を洗い，1日に2回入浴する子供は，喘息になる可能性が25パーセントであるが，手洗いが1日に2回以下で，1日おきに入浴する子供は，喘息のリスクが約半分であったことを示した。この理論によると，埃は細菌を含み，それが一部の免疫系を刺激する。我々の免疫系は，子供時代の初期に，土壌の細菌に刺激されることを前提として作られていると，この理論は論じている。そうでない場合は，免疫系がバランスを欠いて，喘息になりやすくなるという結果となる。この理論によると，我々の身体は，健康に保つために少量の埃が必要であるだろう。

④　喘息の他の主要な要因で，依然として謎であるのは，遺伝である。人が喘息を発

heredity. Clearly a person's **genetic background** plays a major role in determining his or her **probabilities of developing asthma**. Medical researchers are hopeful that the recent **mapping of the human genetic structure** will eventually lead to genetic-based cures of asthma. But such a cure still seems many years away. For now, most doctors and patients are concentrating on improving the environmental conditions which <u>are associated with</u> asthma. This seems to be the most cost-effective approach, and it connects with other health and social benefits as well.

>>> 解 説

💡攻略ポイント

5択問題が6問なので3問ずつ設問に目を通し，内容を頭に入れて長文を読み始め，段落を特定して選択肢の内容を言い換えている箇所を見つけよう。

設問 **1 ~ 3** の要点は，
1.「ある専門家が，最近喘息が増加してきているというのは錯覚だという理由は…」
2.「汚染と喘息の関係点は…」
3.「喘息に関して，現代の家の問題点は…」

1.「なぜ，ある専門家たちは，最近喘息が増加してきているというのは錯覚だと述べるのか」①を参照して，
(a)「汚染レベルが実際に以前よりも下がっているから」
(b)「単に喘息に対する人々の意識が高まり，その報告が多くなっているかもしれないから」⇒ *l.* 6 (this supposed increase is just an illusion「推定による増加は単なる錯覚である」) 以下に述べられている理由 (*ll.* 6-9) と一致。
(c)「喘息についてのあらゆる説明に対して異論があるから」
(d)「過去10年間で喘息症例が60パーセント増加したから」
(e)「専門家らが喘息の原因を確信していないままであるから」
2.「この記事では汚染と喘息の関係点をどう主張しているか」②を参照して，
(a)「喫煙の減少が喘息の減少をもたらした」
(b)「薪と貧弱な作りの煙突が喘息の主な原因である」
(c)「汚染は喘息の原因を十分に説明するものではない」⇒ *ll.* 3-6 と一致。
(d)「喫煙は喘息のもっとも一般的な要因である」
(e)「煤煙が喘息の主な原因である」
3.「喘息に関して，現代の家の問題点は何か」②を参照して，

現する可能性を決定するのに，遺伝的背景が明らかに重要な役割を果たしている。近ごろのヒトの遺伝子構造のマッピング（※染色体上の遺伝子の位置を調べること）が，最終的に遺伝子に基づく喘息の治療につながるだろうと医学の研究者は期待している。しかし，そのような治療はまだ何年も先のようである。現在，多くの医師と患者は，喘息に関係する環境条件の改善に注目している。これは，もっとも費用対効果の高い方法であり，他の健康上の利益ならびに社会的利益につながる。

4

(a)「煤煙が多すぎる」

(b)「喘息の罹患率を下げる」

(c)「近代的な会計システムを用いている」

(d)「狭すぎる」

(e)**「小さな虫によいすみかを提供する」** ➡ *ll.* 7-8と一致。

設問 **4**〜**6** の要点は，
 4.「衛生と喘息の関係は…」
 5.「**3**の主張は…」
 6.「**4**の主張は…」

4.「ある専門家は衛生と喘息の関係についてどう考えているか」**3**を参照して，

(a)「手を洗うことが喘息の原因である」

(b)「喘息予防のためにもっと風呂に入るべき」

(c)**「埃に十分接していないと喘息になりやすい」** ➡ *ll.* 1-3 と一致。

(d)「埃に接すると喘息になりやすくなる」

(e)「喘息予防のために衛生計画をやめるべきである」

5.「**3**ではどんな主張がなされているか」

(a)「イギリスの子供は喘息になりやすい」

(b)**「免疫系は細菌にさらして刺激されるべき」** ➡ *ll.* 9-11「我々の免疫系は，子供時代の初期に，土壌の細菌に刺激されることを前提として作られている」と一致。

(c)「細菌を含むので埃と土は避けるべきである」

(d)「免疫系は少量の細菌を作り出す」

(e)「喘息になるためにバランスのとれた免疫系が必要である」

6.「**4**ではどんな主張がなされているか」

(a)**「今日，環境条件の改善は，喘息に対応する上で重要な方法である」** ➡ *ll.* 6-9 と一致。

88

(b)「遺伝は喘息を引き起こすもっとも重要な要因である」

(c)「環境問題は喘息を引き起こすもっとも重要な要因である」

(d)「遺伝に基づいた治療が今日もっとも効果的な喘息の治療方法である」

(e)「遺伝子構造のマッピングにより喘息の治療法を見つけることができた」

　➡ ④ の内容は「喘息の発現に遺伝がかかわっているのは明らかであり，遺伝子治療に期待が寄せられるが，実現はまだ先のことであり，現在は環境の改善が効果的」というものなので，(b)～(e)は不一致。

ANSWER　　1 —(b)　　2 —(c)　　3 —(e)
　　　　　　　　4 —(c)　　5 —(b)　　6 —(a)

4

速読・速解法！

病気についてよく用いられる必須フレーズ
医学関連文で使用頻度の高いフレーズは一語として読めるようにしておこう。

「〜の患者」
☐ A patient who suffers from incurable disease「不治の病の患者」
☐ A patient with diabetes mellitus「糖尿病患者」

「(病気)にかかる」
☐ 人 contracts a cold「風邪をひく」
☐ 人 comes down with the flu「インフルエンザにかかる」
☐ 人 suffers from a disease「病気を患う」

「(病気・症状)が発現する，現れる」
☐ (病気・症状) affects 人
　◆ COVID-19 affects the elderly severely.
☐ (病気・症状) develops / occurs / appears
☐ 人 develops (病気・症状)
appear と occur は人が主語とならない。(×人 appears / occurs (病気・症状))

90

プラスα
⑥ 小児喘息

順天堂大学（医学部）　　　　　　　　　🕐 目標 4 分　445 語

[1] Researchers from Tufts University **pooled data** from five previous **epidemiological studies** to investigate **the prevalence of asthma** in children in the Boston neighborhoods of Chinatown and Dorchester. Among children born in the United States, low socioeconomic status (SES) and **exposure to pests** (mice and cockroaches) were both associated with **having asthma**. Neither association was present in children born outside of the United States.

[2] "In earlier studies, we found that country of birth to be associated with **asthma risk**, which led us to the current analyses. Our current **findings** may help bring a new perspective to asthma research as they highlight the importance of studying foreign-born children. Much of the existing research **follows** U. S.-born children from birth to see if, and potentially why, they **develop asthma**. It might add to our understanding of **what causes asthma** if we knew why foreign-born children seem to be less likely to develop asthma," said Doug Brugge, senior author and professor of **public health** and **community medicine** at Tufts University School of Medicine.

[3] "Pooling data from these studies gave us a larger sample size and allowed us to **conduct** additional **analyses**. We found that, in addition to an association with **place of birth**; both low SES and exposure to pests are associated with asthma in U. S.-born children but not in foreign-born children," said Mark Wooding, senior lecturer in the department of public health and community medicine at Tufts University School of Medicine.

[4] "While this type of epidemiological study cannot **establish causation**, our findings may be explained by the fact that certain **pathogens** common in the developing world are nearly nonexistent in the U. S. If exposure to such pathogens confers some sort of protection against developing asthma, foreign-born children may be **less susceptible** than children born in the U. S.," Brugge said.

[5] This idea, called the "**hygiene hypothesis**," suggests that children born in less-developed countries may have early exposure to **intestinal worms, viruses** and **bacteria** that affect **immunity** and **make them more resistant to** asthma than U. S.-born children.

[6] The studies were conducted from 2002 to 2007, **sampling** a total of 962

4

1　タフツ大学の研究者らは，チャイナタウンとドーチェスターというボストン郊外の小児喘息の広がりを調査するため，先行する疫学研究 5 回のデータを収集した。米国で生まれた小児は，低い社会的・経済的状態（SES）と有害生物（ネズミとゴキブリ）に暴露されることがともに喘息にかかること<u>と関連があった</u>。米国外で生まれた小児にはいずれも関連はなかった。

2　「初期の研究で，私たちは出生国が喘息リスクと関連していることがわかり，それが現在の分析につながりました。私たちの現在の所見は，喘息の研究に対して新たな見解をもたらす一助となるかもしれません。それらの所見は，外国生まれの小児を研究することが重要であることを強調するからです。既存の研究の多くは，米国生まれの小児が喘息を発症するかどうか，そしてなぜ喘息を発症する潜在的な可能性があるのかを調べるために，米国生まれの小児を誕生のときから追跡調査しています。もし私たちが外国で生まれた小児がなぜ喘息にかかりにくいかがわかれば，喘息の原因について，さらに理解を深められるかもしれません」と第一著者でありタフツ大学医学部の公衆衛生および地域医療学科教授ダグ゠ブラッグは述べた。

3　「これらの調査のデータ集積をしたことにより，より大規模な標本を収集することができ，私たちはさらなる分析を行うことができました。出生国との関連ばかりでなく，低い SES と有害生物への暴露がともに，米国生まれの小児の喘息と関連していること，また，外国生まれの小児は関連していないことがわかりました」とタフツ大学医学部の公衆衛生および地域医療学科准教授マーク゠ウッディングは述べた。

4　「このようなタイプの疫学研究は因果関係を確立することはできませんが，私たちの所見は，発展途上国に多い特定の病原体が米国にはほぼ存在していないという事実によって説明されるのかもしれません。もしそのような病原体に暴露されることが，喘息に対してある種の予防になるとすれば，外国生まれの小児は米国生まれの小児と比較し，喘息にかかりにくい可能性があります」とブラッグは述べた。

5　「衛生仮説」と呼ばれているこの概念は，開発途上国生まれの小児は，米国生まれの小児よりも，免疫に影響を及ぼし，喘息に対してさらに抵抗性を高める腸内寄生虫，ウイルスおよびバクテリアに早くから暴露されている可能性があることを示唆している。

6　その研究は 2002 年から 2007 年まで実施され，4 歳から 18 歳までの子供合計

children ages 4 to 18. There did not initially appear to be **a significant relationship** between pest exposure and asthma; but when the researchers took birthplace into account, they found that U.S.-born children who were exposed to pests were 60 percent more likely to have asthma than U.S.-born children not exposed to pests. Pest exposure **had no** statistically **significant impact on asthma risk** in foreign-born children. Similarly, U.S.-born children with low SES **were two times more likely to have** asthma than U.S.-born children without low SES, while low SES has no statistically significant effect on asthma risk in foreign-born children.

[From What can country of birth tell us about childhood asthma?, Tufts Now on October 25, 2010]

962 人をサンプリングした。当初は，有害生物に暴露されることと喘息との間に有意な関係があるようには見えなかった。しかし，出生国を考慮すると（※ take *A* into account「*A* を考慮すると」），有害生物に暴露された米国生まれの小児は有害生物に暴露されなかった米国生まれの小児と比較し，60 パーセント喘息にかかりやすいことがわかった。有害生物に暴露されることは，外国生まれの小児の喘息のリスクに統計学的に有意に影響を及ぼさなかった。同様に，SES が低い米国生まれの小児らは，SES が低くない米国生まれの小児より 2 倍喘息にかかりやすかった。一方，SES の低さは外国生まれの小児の喘息のリスクに統計学的に有意に影響を及ぼしてはいない。

小児喘息の話題として興味深いテーマを扱った記事。

4

Chapter 5 》 免疫系
The Immune System

知っておきたい医系用語

● 免疫細胞
- white blood cell「白血球」
- macrophage「マクロファージ」[mǽkrəfèiʒ]
- lymphocyte「リンパ球」[límfəsàit] 骨髄（bone marrow）でつくられる。
- lymphatic vessel「リンパ管」[limfǽtik vésl]
- spleen「脾臓」

● 免疫系
- immune system「免疫系」　　　　□ immune response「免疫応答」

□ natural immunity「自然免疫」 マクロファージ，NK（ナチュラルキラー）細胞が異物を攻撃	
□ adaptive immunity「適応免疫」 （＝acquired immunity「獲得免疫」）	□ cellular immunity「細胞性免疫」 キラーT細胞が抗原を直接攻撃
	□ humoral immunity「体液性免疫」 B細胞が抗体産生（抗原抗体反応を担う）

● 抗原抗体反応
- antigen「抗原」
  - ◆ capture antigen「抗原を捕捉する」　　◆ present antigen「抗原を提示する」
- antibody「抗体」　　　　　　　　　□ invader「侵入者」
- foreign substance「異物」　　　　　□ receptor「受容体」

● 情報伝達物質
- hormone「ホルモン」　　　　　　　□ cytokine「サイトカイン」[sáitəkàin]

● 内分泌系
- endocrine gland「内分泌腺」
- pituitary gland「脳下垂体」
- hypothalamus「視床下部」

リンパ系（Lymphatic System）

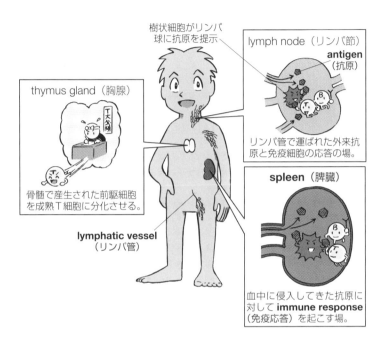

樹状細胞がリンパ球に抗原を提示

lymph node（リンパ節）
antigen（抗原）

リンパ管で運ばれた外来抗原と免疫細胞の応答の場。

thymus gland（胸腺）

骨髄で産生された前駆細胞を成熟 T 細胞に分化させる。

lymphatic vessel（リンパ管）

spleen（脾臓）

血中に侵入してきた抗原に対して **immune response**（免疫応答）を起こす場。

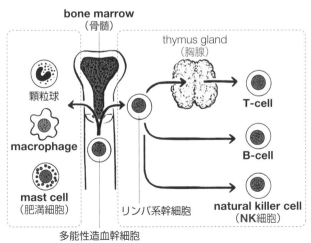

bone marrow（骨髄）

thymus gland（胸腺）

顆粒球

macrophage

mast cell（肥満細胞）

リンパ系幹細胞

T-cell

B-cell

natural killer cell（NK細胞）

多能性造血幹細胞

自然免疫（Natural Immunity）

natural〔innate〕immunity（自然免疫）
感染の際，最初に働く，生まれつき備わっている免疫。

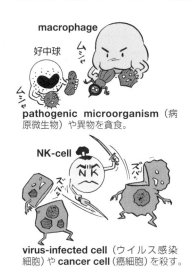

macrophage

好中球

pathogenic microorganism（病原微生物）や異物を貪食。

NK-cell

virus-infected cell（ウイルス感染細胞）や **cancer cell**（癌細胞）を殺す。

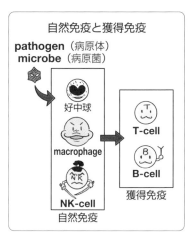

自然免疫と獲得免疫

pathogen（病原体）
microbe（病原菌）

好中球

macrophage

NK-cell

自然免疫

T-cell

B-cell

獲得免疫

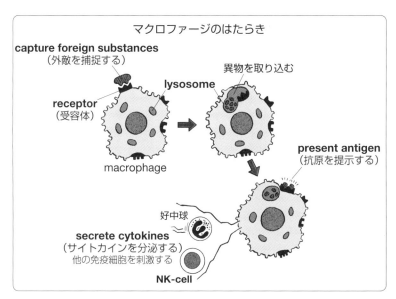

マクロファージのはたらき

capture foreign substances
（外敵を捕捉する）

lysosome

異物を取り込む

receptor
（受容体）

macrophage

present antigen
（抗原を提示する）

好中球

secrete cytokines
（サイトカインを分泌する）
他の免疫細胞を刺激する

NK-cell

獲得免疫（Acquired Immunity）

acquired〔adaptive〕immunity（獲得〔適応〕免疫）
病原体侵入のあと，免疫細胞が抗原を認識して獲得される免疫。

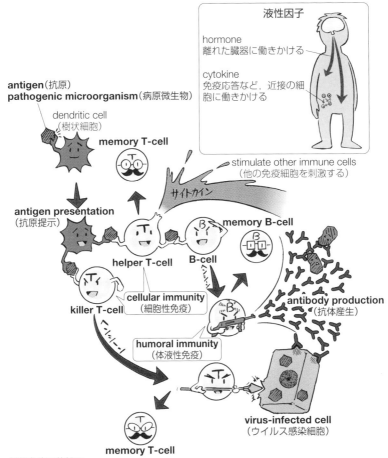

5

獲得免疫の仕組み

樹状細胞がヘルパーＴ細胞に抗原を提示して刺激する。抗原と反応したＢ細胞は同じ抗原に反応するヘルパーＴ細胞から刺激を受け，抗体産生細胞となる。さらに，**activated**（活性化した）したヘルパーＴ細胞が産生したサイトカインがＢ細胞を刺激し，**induce antibody production**（抗体産生を促す）【体液性免疫】。サイトカインはマクロファージなどの **phagocytosis**（貪食作用）も促す。また，活性化したキラーＴ細胞はウイルス感染細胞を直接攻撃して殺す【細胞性免疫】。活性化したＴ細胞やＢ細胞の一部は **memory cell**（記憶細胞）となって潜伏し，抗原が再侵入したときにいち早く免疫反応に応じる。

イラスト 茨木保

長文読解 ☆☆★★★

9 アレルギー

藤田医科大学（医学部） 688 語

[1] In 1893 Emil von Behring was busy investigating **the properties of diphtheria toxin, the biochemical by-product of diphtheria bacteria** that is [あ]responsible for the disease of the same name. This toxin **acts as** a kind of poison to **normal tissues**. A few years earlier von Behring and his colleague Shibasaburo Kitasato had performed an experiment that showed that **immunity to diphtheria** was [い]due to **antitoxin elements**, "**antibodies**," in the blood. What von Behring did not expect to find in his studies on diphtheria toxin —— but to his surprise did find —— was this: some animals given a *second* dose of toxin too small to injure an animal when given **as a *first* dose**, nevertheless had **drastically exaggerated harmful responses to the tiny second dose.** In some cases **the response to** the puny second dose was so overwhelming as to cause death. Von Behring (A)coined the term '**hypersensitivity**' (*Überempfindlichkeit*, in German) to describe this **exaggerated reaction** to a small second dose of diphtheria toxin. This experimental **finding** was so odd relative to the rest of immunological science at the time that it was essentially ignored for about ten years.

[2] In 1898, Charles Richet and Jules Hericourt reported the same finding, this time with **a toxin** derived from **poisonous eels**. It too was noted and then ignored. Then in 1902 Paul Portier and Richet published **an experimental result** that caught the sustained attention of other immunologists. They reported the same **exaggerated response to** a second small dose of poison derived from **marine invertebrates**. [う]What distinguished their report of the same phenomenon von Behring first described nine years earlier was their careful and detailed description of **the hypersensitive response** as an observable form of cardiovascular shock. Richet and Portier worked in France rather than in Germany, unlike von Behring, and a good deal of political tension and professional animosity existed between those two leading centers of **immunological research**. The French scientists weren't about to use a term like 'hypersensitivity' (A)coined by a German, so they called the exaggerated response *anaphylaxis* (to highlight its harmful aspects as contrasted with *prophylaxis*, the medical term for 'protection').

[3] During the next decade a host of prominent immunologists systematically

🎓同様のテーマが出題されたことのある大学

東京女子医科大(医)・東邦大(医)・愛知医科大(医)

1　1893 年，エミール゠フォン゠ベーリングは，同じ名前の病気の原因であるジフテリア菌の生化学副産物，ジフテリア毒素の特性の研究に忙しかった。この毒素は正常組織へ一種の毒として作用する。その数年前に，フォン゠ベーリングと彼の同僚である北里柴三郎は，ジフテリアに対する免疫が，血中の抗毒素要素である「抗体」に起因していることを示す実験を行っていた。フォン゠ベーリングがジフテリア毒素に関する自らの研究で発見すると考えていなかったものの予想外に発見したことは，以下の通りであった。「1 度目」の投与としてならその動物に損傷を与えないほどの少量の毒素を，「2 度目」として投与された動物は，その 2 度目の少量投与に対して，著しい副反応を示した。ある症例では，2 度目の微量の投与量に対する副反応は，死を引き起こすほど著しかった。フォン゠ベーリングは，ジフテリア毒素の 2 度目の少量投与に対するこの過剰反応を表すのに，「過敏症」（ドイツ語で *Überempfindlichkeit*）という用語を作り出した。この実験による所見は，当時の他の免疫科学と比較し奇妙なものであったので，およそ 10 年間，本質的に無視された。

2　1898 年，シャルル゠リシェとジュール゠エリクールが同じ所見を報告したが，今回は有毒ウナギに由来する毒素を伴う所見であった。それも注目されたあと，無視された。その後，1902 年，ポール゠ポルティエとリシェは，他の免疫学者の注目を長らく浴びた実験結果を発表した。また，海洋無脊椎動物に由来する 2 度目の少量の毒に対する，同様の過剰反応について報告した。フォン゠ベーリングが 9 年前最初に記載したのと同じ現象についての彼らの報告を際立つものにさせたのは，観察できる心臓血管系のショックとして，過敏反応を細心かつ詳細に記載したことである。リシェとポルティエは，フォン゠ベーリングとは異なり，ドイツではなくフランスで研究したのだが，それら 2 つの主要な免疫学研究の中心地の間には，かなり多くの政治的緊張があり，専門性の見解で相反していた。フランスの科学者たちは，ドイツ人によって作り出された「過敏症」のような学術用語を用いようとはしなかったので，彼らはその過剰反応を（「予防」を表す医学用語である「プロフィラキシー」と対照的に，その有害な面を強調するために）「アナフィラキシー」と呼んだ（※ call *A B*「*A* を *B* と呼ぶ」）。

3　その後 10 年間で，多数の著名な免疫学者が，質と量の両面で，系統的にアナフ

investigated **the nature of anaphylaxis**, both its qualitative and its quantitative aspects. In 1903 Maurice Arthus **performed the experiments** that would result in the discovery of the phenomenon <u>named [ぇ]after</u> him: **The Arthus reaction is a characteristic skin lesion** formed by **the intradermal injection** of certain kinds of proteins. In 1906 Clemens von Pirquet and Bela Schick studied ⟨B⟩**serum sickness**, the unfortunate phenomenon whereby a small percentage of persons given **standardized diphtheria or tetanus shots**, which do not harm a majority of recipients, nevertheless become extremely sick from the shots. They argued that **the observational evidence** pointed to **an immunological cause** of serum sickness. To have a convenient way of referring to any medical condition in which otherwise harmless or beneficial substances paradoxically produce illness in certain persons who come into contact with them, von Pirquet and Schick ⟨A⟩coined the term *allergy* (from the Greek *allos ergos*, altered working). In the same year, Alfred Wolff-Eisner published a textbook on **hay fever** in which he presented **the evidential case** for hay fever being **a form of hypersensitivity** <u>traceable to</u> **the immune system**. In 1910 Samuel Meltzer made the same kind of case for asthma as a form of immunological hypersensitivity somehow **localized in the lung tissues**.

④ Notice in this account of the early days of modern immunology how a surprising observational mystery is first [お]noted, then perhaps [か]ignored for a bit, and eventually [き]set upon with experimental frenzy. Not all observational mysteries are happily resolved in such a way (some are ignored permanently); but in <u>a large number of</u> cases the course **a given area of science** takes does seem *evidence driven* in a way many other forms of knowledge gathering are not driven by observational evidence. ⟨C⟩Scientific claims deliberately run a risk: the risk of being shown to be false. Some philosophers of science have seen in this at-risk status <u>an important contrast with</u> other forms of human belief such as political ideology, theological doctrines, and so on.

≫≫ 解 説

◎攻略ポイント

設問ごとの〝キーワード〟に目を留めながら，読み進めよう。

1. [あ] be responsible for 〜「〜（病気）の原因である」
   medi 類語：contribute to 〜

ィラキシーの特性を調査した。1903 年，モーリス゠アルチュスが実験を行ったが，その実験は，彼の名前にちなんだ現象を発見する結果となった。アルチュス反応とは，ある種の蛋白質を皮内注射することによって形成される特徴的な皮膚の病変である。1906 年，クレマン゠フォン゠ピルケとベラ゠シックは，標準化したジフテリアや破傷風の予防接種を受けた人のうち少数にみられた不幸な現象，つまり血清病について研究した。その血清病というのは，その予防注射を受けた大多数の人には害がないが，数パーセントが極めて重篤な血清病になる。観察研究から得られるエビデンスから血清病の免疫学的な病因を指摘できると彼らは論じた。無害な，または恩恵をもたらす物質が，その物質に接触すると，特定の人において，逆説的に病気を引き起こす病態について言及するための便宜的方法として〔を得るため〕，フォン゠ピルケとシックは，ギリシア語の「変化した (*allos*)」と「能力 (*ergos*)」由来の「アレルギー」という言葉を作った。同年，アルフレッド゠ウォルフ゠アイスナーは，花粉症〔枯草熱〕についてのテキストを出版し，その本で，免疫系に由来する一種の過敏症である花粉症のエビデンスに基づく症例を提示した。1910 年，サミュエル゠メルツァーは，同種の喘息の症例を，肺組織に局在する一種の免疫学的過敏症と主張した（※ make a case「主張する」）。

5

④　近代免疫学の当初のこの説明で，どのようにして，驚くべき観察上の謎が最初は注目され，それからおそらく少し無視され，そしてついには熱狂的に実験に取り組まれたかについて注目してほしい。観察上の謎のすべてが，運よくそのような方法で解決されるというわけではない（永遠に無視されるものもある）。しかし，多くの場合，科学のある分野がたどる道〔コース〕は，多くのその他の知識集積が観察研究から得られるようなエビデンス由来ではないのと異なり，「エビデンス由来である」ように思える。科学的な主張は，意図的にリスクを冒している。つまり，虚偽であることを示されるというリスクである。科学哲学者の中には，このリスクのある状態の中に，政治イデオロギーや神学教義などのような，他の形態の人間信条との重要な対比を見ている者もいる。

　　[い] due to ~「~が原因で」
　　medi due to ~, caused by ~, because of ~ は医学英語でよく用いられる表現。
2．① *ll*. 8-10 参照。要旨：「初回投与量は害を与えないほどの少量で，2 度目の投与量は同様に少量を投与したが，過剰な副反応を示した」
3．coin「~を創り出す」の意。よって(3)が正解。

4． 並べかえると(5) what (1) **distinguished** (3) their report of the same phenomenon (4) **von Behring** (2) first described nine years earlier となる。「フォン゠ベーリングが9年前最初に記載したのと同じ現象についての彼らの報告を際立つものにさせたのは」(3)と(4)の間に that を補うとわかりやすくなる。phenomenon （that） von Behring …

5． name after 〜「〜にちなんで名付ける」 熟語として覚えよう。

6． まずは serum sickness「血清病」についての記載箇所を見つけよう。下線部直後のコンマは同格を表すので，the unfortunate … from the shots の部分が，血清病の説明となっている。よって(4)が正しい。

7． (a)〜(c)の選択肢の内容に先に目を通す。(a)「少し無視された」 (b)「注目された」 (c)「熱狂的に実験に取り組まれた」 ② *ll.* 2-3 It too was noted and then ignored. を参照すると，[お]には(b)，[か]には(a)が入る。③ *ll.* 1-3より［き］には(c)が入る。

8． コロン以下は a risk の説明となっている。

9． 内容真偽の問題は，本文の順に問われていることが多いので，最後に解くのではなく，解きながら該当箇所を読み進めてもよい。

(1)① *ll.* 4-10 参照。北里柴三郎という名前に目を留める。北里柴三郎との共同研究のあとに，フォン゠ベーリングは過敏症を発見したので，不一致。

(2)① 最終文および③ *ll.* 1-3 の内容と一致するので正解。

(3)② *l.* 9 以降の内容と一致するので正解。

(4)③ 最終文参照。喘息についても，「免疫学的過敏症」と記載されており，不一致。

(5)④ 最終文参照。選択肢では科学と政治イデオロギーの対象の違いを比較させているが，本文に書かれているのは「間違いを指摘されるリスク」に関する対比。よって不一致。

> 英文レベルはやや上級。アレルギーの発見を紹介した良テーマ。内容把握を確認する良問である。

ANSWER

1．[あ]—(4)　[い]—(2)
2—(8)
3—(3)
4．2番目：(1)　4番目：(4)
5—(1)
6—(4)
7—(3)
8．科学的な主張は，意図的にリスクを冒している。つまり，虚偽であることを示されるというリスクである。
9—(2)・(3)

アレルギー（Allergy）

allergen,
antigen
（抗原）

IgE-antibody
（IgE 抗体）

アレルゲンと IgE 抗体が
結びつくと肥満細胞からヒ
スタミンが放出される。

血管透過性亢進

mast cell
（肥満細胞）

histamine

平滑筋収縮

hay fever（花粉症）

inflammation（炎症）
粘膜膨張

pollen
（花粉）

sneezing（くしゃみ）
runny nose（鼻水）

wheezing（喘鳴）

atopy

asthma（喘息）

itchy
（かゆい）

breathing difficulty
（呼吸困難）

shortness of breath
（**SOB**：息切れ）

イラスト　茨木保

☆☆★☆☆

10 ピーナッツアレルギー患者の増加

🎓 日本大学（医学部）   670 語

1 A generation ago, **peanut allergies** seemed to be a rare occurrence. Today, they're getting much more attention in the news —— with stories popping up all the time of children with severe and **life-threatening reactions** to peanuts. So what's going on here?

2 Peanut allergies are still relatively rare —— **affecting** about 1 to 2 percent of children in the United States. But some studies have indeed found evidence that the number of reported nut allergies is increasing over time.

3 That said, it's tough to disentangle this from **broader trends**. Allergies on the whole have been increasing, says Wesley Burks, an allergy expert and chair of pediatrics at UNC School of Medicine. Peanut allergies seem, for the most part, to be part of this broader mysterious trend.

4 Meanwhile, scientists have recently done a surprising flip on what they think causes peanut allergies. Up until recently, many medical experts thought that exposure to peanuts in **the womb** or in early life was the trigger. Now, they're not so sure and have some evidence that a lack of exposure to peanuts might cause allergies. Here's a guide to what researchers know so far on the topic.

5 Until recently, most experts recommended that **pregnant and nursing mothers** should avoid eating peanuts altogether. They assumed that exposure to peanuts early in life was what was causing peanut allergies.

6 Parents followed the advice —— but peanut allergies continued to rise in the United States anyway. So, in 2008 the American Academy of Pediatrics released a report stating that there wasn't any evidence to support restricting mothers' and babies' diets.

7 Since then, there's been more research on the topic. In 2014, a study came out in the Journal of the American Medical Association that observed a correlation between mothers eating more nuts being less likely to have children with peanut and tree-nut allergies. The study was quite large, involving 8,205 children, 140 of whom had nut allergies.

8 But this was just a **correlational observation**, not a **controlled experiment**. A newer, ongoing study led by Gideon Lack of King's College London should

1　一世代前，ピーナッツアレルギーは極めて稀にしか起こらないと思われていた。今日，ピーナッツアレルギーはニュースでさらに大きな注目を集めている。つまり，ピーナッツに対して深刻で生命を脅かす反応を起こした小児らについての常に流れているニュースである。何が起こっているのか。

2　ピーナッツアレルギーは依然として比較的まれで，米国の小児のおよそ1～2％が発症している。しかし，報告されたナッツアレルギー数は経時的に増加しているというエビデンス（※ evidence「エビデンス」：カタカナ表記）を事実認めている研究もある。

3　その研究によると，より幅広い傾向からこれ〔ピーナッツアレルギー〕を区別することは難しい（※ disentangle *A* from *B*「*A* を *B* と区別する」）。アレルギーの専門家でノースカロライナ大学医学部の小児科医長であるウェスレー゠バークスは，「アレルギーは全体として増加してきている」と言う。ピーナッツアレルギーの大半は，このより幅広い謎の傾向の一部であるようである。

4　その一方で，最近，科学者らは，ピーナッツアレルギーを引き起こすと考えるものについて驚くべき反論をしている。最近まで，多くの医療専門家は，子宮の中，あるいは幼少期にピーナッツへ暴露されることが引き金になると考えていた。今日は，彼らはそれほど確信をもっておらず，ピーナッツへの暴露の不足がアレルギーを引き起こすかもしれないというエビデンスももっている（※ exposure to ～「～への暴露」）。このテーマについて，現在研究者らがわかっていることへのガイドがここにある。

5　最近まで，専門家の多くは，妊娠中あるいは授乳中の母親にピーナッツを全く食べないよう推奨した。彼らは幼少期のピーナッツへの暴露（すること）がピーナッツアレルギーを引き起こしていると想定した。

6　保護者はその忠告に従った。しかし，米国ではピーナッツアレルギーがとにかく増加し続けた。そのため，2008 年に米国小児科学会は母親と乳児の食事の制限をすることを支持するいかなるエビデンスもないと記述した報告を公表した。

7　それ以来，このテーマについてより多くの研究がある。たくさんナッツを食べる母親は，ピーナッツと木の実アレルギーの子供をもつ可能性が低いという相関関係を観察した研究が 2014 年に米国医師会の学会誌に掲載された。その研究は大規模で小児 8,205 例が参加し，そのうち 140 例がナッツアレルギーをもっていた。

8　しかしこれは単に相関的な観察であり，コントロール試験ではなかった。キングス・カレッジ・ロンドンのギデオン゠ラックが率いる新たな継続中の研究が，よりよ

provide better answers. The experiment enrolled 640 children at high risk of developing peanut allergies and **randomly assigned** some of them to eat peanuts three times a week and some of them to never eat peanuts at all for their first three years of life. The researchers will then look at which kids develop peanut allergies by age five.

9 Lack is also leading a separate study of 1,303 families to test out what happens when babies are exposed to several foods while they're still being breastfed.

10 It could turn out that peanut allergies develop in utero, through breast milk, or by eating peanuts. These studies should help find out.

11 Another possible culprit? Peanut dust. Peanuts are such a fundamental part of many Americans' diets that peanut dust is found in our homes, and there's evidence that some children with a **specific genetic profile** are susceptible to developing peanut allergies through **skin exposure**.

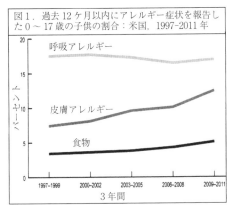

図 1．過去 12 ケ月以内にアレルギー症状を報告した 0 ～ 17 歳の子供の割合：米国，1997-2011 年

呼吸アレルギー

皮膚アレルギー

食物

1997-1999　2000-2002　2003-2005　2006-2008　2009-2011
3 年間

12 If researchers can figure out what causes peanut allergies, then they may be able to give parents better advice to prevent more children from developing them in the first place.

13 But what about those who are already allergic? Are they doomed to **peanut-butter-free-existence** for the rest of their lives?

14 Maybe not. Right now, the best advice for those with peanut allergies is to avoid foods with peanuts and to be trained how to use **an adrenaline pen** in the rare case of **an anaphylactic shock**.

15 But scientists are also developing treatments that might reduce how allergic children are. In the past decade or so, researchers started compiling good evidence that by very carefully exposing children to tiny bits of peanut, they could very slowly work up children's tolerance.

16 Patients eat **tiny doses of peanut** or use **a peanut patch worn on the skin**,

い解答を出すはずである。その実験にはピーナッツアレルギーを発現するリスクが高い小児 640 例が参加しており，そのうちの何人かは週に 3 回ピーナッツを食べ，何人かは 3 歳までは全くピーナッツを食べないように無作為に振り分けられる。それから研究者らは，どの小児が 5 歳までに，ピーナッツアレルギーを発現するかを調べるだろう。

⑨　ラックはまた家族 1,303 例を対象に別の試験を指揮し，乳児がまだ母乳の授乳期間中に，数種の食べ物に暴露された時，何が起こるかを実際に試験した（※ expose「暴露する」）。

⑩　ピーナッツアレルギーは子宮内で，母乳を通して，またはピーナッツを食べることによって，発現することが明らかになる可能性がある（※ develop は，人も病気も主語になる。S develop the disease「S が病気を発症する」 The disease develops「病気が発症する」）。これらの研究は発見の助けとなるはずである。

⑪　他に（ピーナッツアレルギーの）原因はあるだろうか（※ culprit「犯人」 病気の原因のたとえに用いられる）。ピーナッツの粉末。ピーナッツは米国人大半の食事に欠かせないものであるので，ピーナッツの粉末は家の中に見られ，特定の遺伝子プロファイルをもつ小児は，皮膚暴露によって，ピーナッツアレルギーを発現しやすいというエビデンスがある（※ susceptible to 〜「〜にかかりやすい」）。

⑫　研究者らが，ピーナッツアレルギーを引き起こすもの〔ピーナッツアレルギーの原因〕を理解できれば，さらに多くの小児らがピーナッツアレルギーをまず発現しないよう予防するために，保護者によりよい助言を与えられるかもしれない（※ give A better advice to do「〜するために A によりよい助言を与える」）。

⑬　しかしすでにアレルギーのある人についてはどうだろうか（※ what about（名詞）「〜はどうだろうか」）。彼らは残りの人生を，ピーナッツバターを食べないよう運命づけられるのだろうか。

⑭　おそらくそうではない。現在，ピーナッツアレルギーをもつ人への最善の助言は，ピーナッツの含まれる食品を避け，アナフィラキシーショックの稀なケースで，アドレナリン注射製剤をどのように用いるかを訓練することである（※ be to do「〜することである」不定詞の名詞的用法）。

⑮　しかし科学者らはまた，小児アレルギーを低減する治療法も開発している。ここ 10 年くらいの間，研究者らは極めて注意深く小児にほんの少量のピーナッツを暴露することによって，極めてゆっくりと小児の（ピーナッツ）耐性を高めることができるという十分なエビデンスを積み上げ始めた。

⑯　患者らはごく少量のピーナッツを食べるか，肌に貼るピーナッツパッチを用いる。

and medical professionals stand ready to jump in with **an adrenaline shot** in case of a severe reaction. Over time, as the dose increases, the body learns that the peanut is not the enemy.

>>> 解 説

💡攻略ポイント

選択肢が本文の内容に合っていても，設問文の内容に合わないものがあるので注意しよう。

1.「③で，this broader mysterious trend とは」
①「ピーナッツアレルギーの減少」
②「すべてのアレルギーの割合が減少」
③**「すべてのアレルギーの割合が増加」** ➡ ③ *ll.* 1-2 Allergies on the whole … に「アレルギーは全体として増加している」とあるので，正解。
④「ピーナッツアレルギーの増加」

✓速読攻略

設問 2～4 は④～⑧に関する質問。設問 2 と 4 の選択肢を頭に入れ，解答を探しながら⑧まで読もう。設問 3 は語彙の問題。

2.「④～⑦によると，妊婦間のピーナッツ消費に関する，現在の医療の立場は」
①**「彼女たちが食べたいのならピーナッツを食べることができる」** ➡ ⑦ *ll.* 3-4 mothers eating …．「より多くナッツ類を食べた母親の子供は，ピーナッツや木の実アレルギーを発症する可能性が低かった」とある。質問がピーナッツ消費についてなので，正解。
②「彼女たちは木の実を食べることができる」
③「彼女たちはピーナッツを食べることはできない」
④「彼女たちはたくさんピーナッツを食べ過ぎてはならない」

3.「⑦で，correlation の意味に最も近いのは」
①「二分，両分」
②「同一性」
③「不平等，不均衡」
④**「相関関係」** ➡正解。

4.「⑦と⑧で，米国医師会の学会誌の 2014 年の研究の限界は」

そして医療専門家らが重篤な反応の場合，アドレナリン注射で即時対応するために待機している。時間の経過とともに，（ピーナッツの）用量が増加するにつれ，体がピーナッツは敵ではないと学ぶのである。

① 「それはピーナッツアレルギーを発症する危険性が高い小児 640 例を参加させた」➡ 8 *l.* 2 A newer, ongoing study … より，別の研究についての説明であり不一致。

② 「それは小児 8,205 例が参加した」➡ 被験者数は一致するが，質問に対する答えではない。

③ 「それはナッツをよりたくさん食べる母親の方がナッツアレルギーの子供をもつことが少ないという相関関係に気づいた」➡ 7 の内容とは一致するが，質問に対する答えではない。

④ **「それはコントロール試験ではなかった」**➡ 8 *l.* 1 this was just … と一致するので，正解。

5. 「Figure 1 で，1997 年から 2011 年までの食物アレルギーの割合の増加は」

① 「劇的な増加」

② 「わかりにくい増加」

③ **「わずかな増加」**➡ Figure 1 から，正解。

④ 「反比例した増加」

☑✔速読攻略

設問 6 と 7 は 11 に関する質問。選択肢を頭に入れ，解答を探しながら 11 を読もう。

6. 「11 で，culprit の意味に最も近いのは」

　直前文でピーナッツアレルギーの原因でありうるものとして breast milk（母乳），eating peanuts（ピーナッツを食べること）をあげているので，culprit は，

① 「アレルギー」

② **「原因」**➡ 正解。

③ 「罪人」

④ 「もの」

7. 「11 で，ピーナッツの粉末について適切でないものは」

① 「それは米国人がピーナッツを大量に食べるために一般的である」➡ 11 *ll.* 2-3

Peanuts are such a fundamental part of …と一致。

② 「それは米国の家庭では滅多に見られない」 ➡ ⑪ *ll.* 1-4 に不一致なので，正解。

③ 「それは特定の遺伝子をもつ子供に影響するかもしれない」

④ 「それは皮膚接触でアレルギーの発現に至る場合がある」

➡③・④は，⑪ *ll.* 5-8 some children with a … と一致。特定の遺伝子をもつ小児が皮膚接触でアレルギーを発現しやすい場合もあると述べられている。

8. 「⑬ において，peanut-butter-free-existence の意味は」

medi ～ free「～のない」

① 「ピーナッツバターを自由に食べられる」

② 「ピーナッツバターは何のアレルギー反応も引き起こさない」

③ 「ピーナッツバターはお金がかからない」

④ 「ピーナッツバターを決して食べない」 ➡正解。

9. 「⑮ の内容を最も反映しているものは」

☑✐速読攻略

選択肢を頭に入れ，解答を探しながら ⑮ を読もう。

① 「過去数十年において，科学者らと患者らは，ピーナッツ少量摂取により起こるアナフィラキシーショックを，アドレナリン注射製剤を用いて予防するために協力した」 ➡不記載。

② 「過去数年において，科学者たちは，アレルギーにもかかわらず，なぜアレルギーの小児が少量のピーナッツを食べたがるのかが不確かであった」 ➡不記載。

③ 「最近，研究者らは，少量のピーナッツの断片を患者に暴露するといった，アレルギーの新規治療法を研究している」 ➡ ⑮ *ll.* 2-3 researchers started compiling …と一致するので，正解。

④ 「科学者らはアレルギーの小児らが，自分たちがもっているピーナッツアレルギーの本当の性質を理解するために少し体を鍛えることについて新たな研究を行っている」 ➡不記載。

10. 「この記事に最も適切なタイトルは」

① 「ピーナッツの収穫高の増加」 ➡不記載。

② 「低アレルギー性のピーナッツレシピ」 ➡不記載。

③ 「ピーナッツアレルギーの症状とは何か」 ➡まれな症状としてアナフィラキシーショックについて触れられているが，症状全般については記載なし。

④ 「なぜピーナッツアレルギーが増えているか」 ➡正解。

覚えておきたい医系頻出熟語

- [ ] **be susceptible to ～**「～にかかりやすい」
- [ ] **be vulnerable to ～**「～にもろい」
  - ◆ be vulnerable to cancer「癌になりやすい」
- [ ] **be subject to ～**「～にかかりやすい，～になる」
- [ ] **be immune to ～**「～に免疫がある」
- [ ] **be allergic to ～**「～にアレルギーがある」
- [ ] **secondary to ～／ subsequent to ～**「～に続発する」
  - ◆ heart failure secondary to hypertension「高血圧に伴う心臓疾患」
- [ ] **in response to ～**「～に反応して」
  - ◆ in response to a stimulus「刺激に反応して」

5

免疫系

順天堂大学（医学部）　　　　　　　　　　　目標1分30秒　229語

1 Every tissue and organ in the body is controlled by a complex interaction among the chemicals **in the bloodstream** and **the hormones** created by our **endocrine glands**. This mixture is controlled by the "**master gland**," **the pituitary gland**. The output of hormones from the pituitary gland, in turn, is controlled by both chemicals and **nerve impulses** from the neighboring part of the brain, called **the hypothalamus**. **Nerve fibers** enter the hypothalamus from nearly all other regions of the brain, and so intellectual and emotional processes occurring in the brain affect the body.

2 **The immune system** consists of more than a dozen different types of **white blood cells**. They are divided into two main types. One group, called **B cells**, produces **chemicals that eliminate poisons** made by disease organisms. The other group, called **T cells**, destroys **invading bacteria and viruses**. The immune system, then, is controlled by the brain, either indirectly through hormones in the blood, or directly through the nerves and nerve chemicals. One theory about the cause of cancer states that cancer cells are developing in our bodies all the time but are normally destroyed by white blood cells. Cancer according to this theory, appears when the immune system becomes weakened and can no longer fight off the cancer cells. Thus, anything that upsets the brain's control of the immune system makes it easier for cancer to develop.

[From Love, Medicine and Miracles by Bernie S. Siegel, Harper Perennial]

1　身体のどの組織も器官も，血中の化学物質と，内分泌腺によって作り出されるホルモンの，複雑な相互作用によって制御される。この混合作用は，「マスター腺」（脳下垂体）によって制御されている。脳下垂体からのホルモンの産生量は，化学物質と，視床下部と呼ばれる脳の隣接部位からの神経インパルスの，両方によって制御される。神経線維は，脳のその他のほとんどすべての領域から視床下部に入る。その結果，脳の中で起こるさまざまな知的・感情的プロセスが身体に影響する。

2　免疫系は，12を超えるタイプの白血球細胞からなる。それらは2つの主要なタイプに分けられる。1つのグループはB細胞と呼ばれ，病原体によって作られる毒素を排除する化学物質を産生する。もう一方のグループはT細胞と呼ばれ，侵入した細菌やウイルスを破壊する。したがって，免疫系は，血中のホルモンを通して間接的に，または神経とその化学物質を通して直接的に，脳によって制御される。癌の原因についてのある理論は，癌細胞は常に体内で産生されているが，正常では白血球によって破壊されると論じる。この理論によると，免疫系が弱まり，もはや癌細胞を撃退できないときに，癌が出現する。このように，脳による免疫系の制御を乱すものは何であれ，癌の発現を容易にする。

5

Chapter 6 ≫ 癌
Oncology

知っておきたい医系用語

● 癌（ガン）
☐ **cancer**「癌」   ☐ **cancerous cells**「癌細胞」
☐ **malignant tumor**「悪性腫瘍」［məlígnənt t(j)úːmər］
☐ **growth**「成長したもの，腫瘍」   ☐ **mass**「塊（癌をさすこともある）」
☐ **breast cancer**「乳癌」   ☐ **lung cancer**「肺癌」
☐ **oncogene**「癌遺伝子」［ánkədʒìːn］   ☐ **oncology**「腫瘍学」
☐ **tumor suppressor gene**「腫瘍抑制遺伝子」異常細胞を死なせる遺伝子。
☐ **apoptosis**「アポトーシス」個体をよりよい状態に保つための自発的な細胞死。
☐ **telomere**「テロメア」細胞核にある染色体の末端領域で，細胞の寿命を決める。
☐ **replicate**「〜を複製する」（≒ **copy**，**duplicate**）
☐ **reproduce**「〜を再生する，〜を生殖させる，〜を複製する」

● 癌因子
☐ **carcinogen**「発癌物質」［kɑːrsínədʒən］
☐ **radiation**「放射線」 ◆ exposure to radiation「放射線への暴露」
☐ **free radical**「フリーラジカル，活性酸素」
☐ **menopause**「更年期」［ménəpɔ̀ːz］
☐ **period**「月経」（≒ **bleeding**「出血」（cf. breeding「飼育」））
☐ **estrogen**「エストロゲン（女性ホルモン）」

● 癌の転移
☐ **spread**「転移，拡大」（≒ **metastasis**「転移」）
☐ **surrounding cells**「周辺細胞」   ☐ **anticancer drug**「抗癌剤」

● 罹　患
☐ **incidence** (**rate**)「罹患率」   ☐ **morbidity**「罹患率」
☐ **history**「病歴」   ☐ **past history**「既往歴」
☐ **family history**「家族歴」家族や近親者の病歴。

癌の発生（The Development of Cancer）

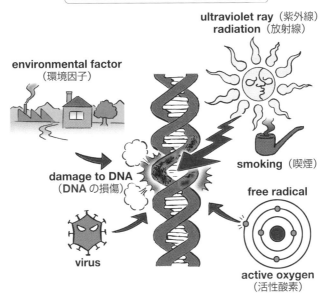

risk factors for cancer（癌の危険因子）

environmental factor（環境因子）

ultraviolet ray（紫外線）
radiation（放射線）

smoking（喫煙）

damage to DNA（DNAの損傷）

free radical

virus

active oxygen（活性酸素）

6

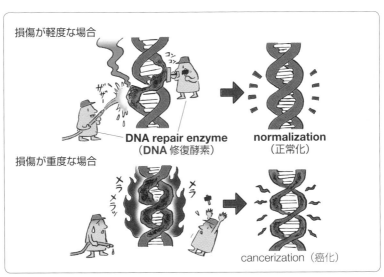

損傷が軽度な場合

DNA repair enzyme（DNA修復酵素）

normalization（正常化）

損傷が重度な場合

cancerization（癌化）

癌の特徴（Features of Cancer）

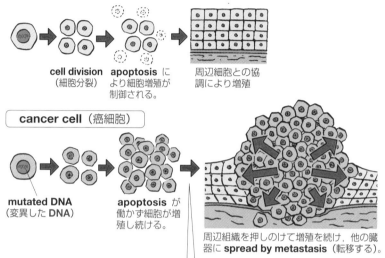

normal cell（正常細胞）

cell division
（細胞分裂）

apoptosis に
より細胞増殖が
制御される。

周辺細胞との協
調により増殖

cancer cell（癌細胞）

mutated DNA
（変異した DNA）

apoptosis が
働かず細胞が増
殖し続ける。

周辺組織を押しのけて増殖を続け，他の臓
器に **spread by metastasis**（転移する）。

telomerase expression（テロメラーゼの発現）
cellular lifespan（細胞の寿命）が **extend**（延長する）される

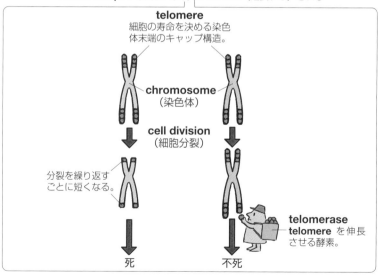

telomere
細胞の寿命を決める染色
体末端のキャップ構造。

chromosome
（染色体）

cell division
（細胞分裂）

分裂を繰り返す
ごとに短くなる。

telomerase
telomere を伸長
させる酵素。

死

不死

癌の転移（Metastasis of Cancer）

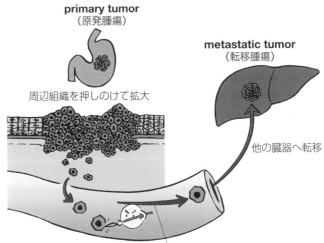

primary tumor
（原発腫瘍）

metastatic tumor
（転移腫瘍）

周辺組織を押しのけて拡大

他の臓器へ転移

immune cell（免疫細胞）をすり抜ける

リンパ行性転移⇨**lymphatic vessel**（リンパ管）を通じて転移
血行性転移⇨**blood vessel**（血管）を通じて転移

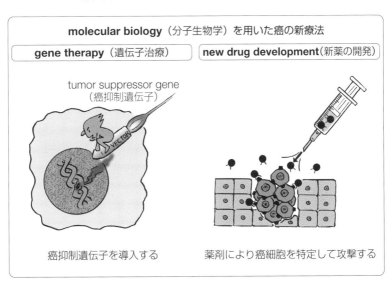

molecular biology（分子生物学）を用いた癌の新療法

gene therapy（遺伝子治療）　**new drug development**（新薬の開発）

tumor suppressor gene
（癌抑制遺伝子）

VECTOR

癌抑制遺伝子を導入する　薬剤により癌細胞を特定して攻撃する

☆★☆☆☆

11 癌治療

🎓 日本大学 (医学部)　　　　　　　　　　　　　　　407 語

1 There will probably never be a cure for all cancers but a considerable amount of progress has been made recently. In the early 1970s, United States President Richard Nixon declared war on cancer. The U.S. has since then given nearly 70 billion dollars to its National Cancer Institute. This does not include money spent by drug companies and charities in researching ways of combating the disease. Yet despite the vast sums spent, **the mortality rate of cancer** has increased from 163 per 100,000 people in 1971 to 194 per 100,000 in 2001. By contrast, deaths from other major diseases such as **heart attacks and strokes** have fallen in that period.

2 Fortunately, behind these numbers lies some good news. Researchers are finding new ways of treating cancers so that while there may not be any "magic bullet" discovered for cancer within the next 10 or 20 years, over the long term, cancer may be more treatable so that it becomes more like **a chronic condition** than **a fatal diagnosis**.

3 Cancer is connected with the fact that our bodies are constantly reproducing cells. Cancer is basically **the unregulated growth of unhealthy cells**, many of which grow into **tumors**. Current **cancer therapies** simply attack all cells which are reproducing. This means that both healthy and unhealthy cells are killed. This causes **side effects** such as **dizziness** and **fatigue**. However, recently developed **anticancer drugs** target only **cancerous cells**. They work at the molecular level and don't kill healthy cells which are **dividing**. This **approach** looks very promising and may produce treatments which are effective and have fewer side effects. However, all patients are different and there are many different kinds of cancer so a doctor needs to match the appropriate drug to the patient.

4 Many anticancer drugs are very poisonous to the body so researchers have developed vehicles to deliver these to **the cancerous areas** using **variants of bacteria and viruses**. For example, **injecting a modified cold virus** into the body could kill cancer cells or even carry **radioactive materials** to the cancerous area. Most important, however, is **early detection**. Even a small tumor can contain a billion cancerous cells so **scanning** a patient's body with MRI or other techniques is an essential part of diagnosis. Such scanning

1　おそらく，すべての癌に対する治療法などないだろうが，最近，癌治療はかなり進歩してきている。1970 年代の初頭，米国大統領リチャード゠ニクソンは，癌に対して宣戦布告をした。それ以来，米国は，国立癌研究所におよそ 700 億ドルの資金を投じてきている。この額には，製薬会社や慈善団体がこの病と闘う方法を研究する費用は含まれていない。しかし，この巨額の資金が費やされたにもかかわらず，癌死亡率は，1971 年の 10 万人中 163 例から 2001 年の 10 万人中 194 例へと増加してきている。これとは対照的に，心臓発作や脳卒中のような，その他の主要な疾病による同期間の死亡は，減少している。

2　幸運なことに，このような数字の背後には，よいニュースもある。研究者たちが癌の新しい治療法を発見しているので，この先 10 年または 20 年以内に癌の「特効薬」は発見されないかもしれないが，長期的には，癌の治療はさらに容易になり，死の診断というより慢性疾患のようなものになる。

3　癌は，我々の身体が常に細胞を再生し続けているという事実に関連している。癌は基本的に，不健康な細胞の抑制できない増殖で，その多くは腫瘍になる。現在の癌療法は，単に再生している細胞すべてを攻撃する。これは，健康な細胞と病気の細胞の両方が死ぬことを意味する。これにより，めまいや疲労感などの副作用を引き起こす。しかし，最近開発された抗癌剤は，癌性細胞のみを攻撃目標にする。それらは分子レベルで作用し，分裂している健康な細胞は殺さない。この方法は非常に有望であり，効果的で副作用がさらに少ない治療法をつくるだろう。しかし，すべての患者は異なり，多くの異なる癌があるため，医師は，患者に適切な薬剤を合わせる必要がある。

4　抗癌剤の多くは身体に非常に有毒であるため，研究者らは，細菌やウイルスの変異株を用いて癌病巣に抗癌剤を輸送する，運搬体を開発してきている。たとえば，変異させた風邪のウイルスを身体に注射することで，癌細胞を殺したり，放射性物質を癌病巣に運んだりすることさえできるだろう。しかし，もっとも重要なことは，早期発見である。小さな腫瘍にさえ，10 億の癌性細胞が含まれている可能性があるため，患者の身体を MRI〔磁気共鳴影像法〕などの技術を用いてスキャニングすることは，診断の不可欠な部分である。そのようなスキャニング技術を用いて，発現しているわ

120

techniques can reveal even a small number of cancer cells developing so this may mean that more people will be diagnosed with cancer but will result in a better chance of treating it.

>>> 解 説

設問 1 ～ 4 の要点は,
 1.「他の病気による死亡数と比較して，癌による死亡数は…」
 2.「新しく開発された癌治療と以前の癌治療との違いは…」
 3.「医師が癌患者に治療を処方する際，注意を要する理由は…」
 4.「将来，さらに多くの人が癌と診断される可能性が高くなる理由は…」

1.「他の病気による死亡数と比較して，癌による死亡数はどのくらいか」
 ⇒ 1 *ll.* 6-9 をまとめる。
2.「新しく開発された癌治療は以前の癌治療とどのように違うか」
 ⇒ 3 *ll.* 3-7 をまとめる。
3.「医師が癌患者に治療を処方する際，注意を要するのはなぜか」
 ⇒ 3 最終文参照。
4.「将来，さらに多くの人が癌と診断される可能性が高いのはなぜか」
 ⇒ 4 最終文参照。

ずかな癌細胞でさえ検知することができる。したがってこれは，さらに多くの人が癌と診断されたとしても，癌治療率の増加をもたらすだろう，ということを意味する。

6

ANSWER

1．2001 年までの 30 年間で，その他の病気による死亡数が減少しているのに対し，癌による死亡率は，10 万人中 163 例から 194 例へ増加している。

2．以前の癌治療は健康な細胞と癌性細胞の両方を攻撃していたので，癌細胞と健康な細胞の両方が死に，めまいや疲労感などの副作用があったが，新しく開発された抗癌剤は癌性細胞のみを攻撃するので，効果的で副作用がより少ない。

3．患者は異なり，多様な癌があるので，それぞれの患者に合う薬を見つける必要があるから。

4．MRI などのスキャニング技術のおかげで，少数の癌細胞の発現も見つけることができるようになり，癌がより早期に発見できるようになるから。

12 癌細胞の体組織への浸潤

東京慈恵会医科大学（医学部医学科）　　　　　　　　　　　486 語

[1]　**The worst cancer cells** don't sit still. Instead they **metastasize** —— **migrate from** their **original sites** and establish new tumors in other parts of the body. Once **a cancer spreads**, it is harder to (A)**eliminate**. A study by developmental biologists offers a fresh clue to how cancer cells (1)acquire the ability to **invade other tissues** —— **a prerequisite for metastasis**. It reveals that **invasion** requires cells to stop **dividing**. Therefore, the two (B)processes —— invasion and **proliferation** —— are mutually exclusive. The finding could inform cancer therapies, which typically target rapidly proliferating cancer cells.

[2]　David Matus of Stony Brook University and David Sherwood of Duke University turned (C)to a **transparent worm** to **elucidate** this invading process. During the **worm's normal development**, a cell known as **the anchor cell** breaks through a structure called **the basement membrane**, which initially separates **the uterus** from the vulva. The process is similar to how human cancer cells invade basement membranes to enter **the bloodstream**, which carries them to **distant sites**. So biologists have adopted *Caenorhabditis elegans* as a metastasis model organism, which they can easily **image** and **genetically manipulate**.

[3]　After turning on and off hundreds of genes in *C. elegans*, Matus's team found a gene that **regulated anchor cell invasion**. When it was turned off, the anchor cell failed to invade the basement membrane. But the anchor cell also did something unexpected: it began to divide. Conversely, when the researchers **inhibited cell proliferation**, the anchor cell stopped dividing and began to invade again. Further experiments showed that **halting** cell division was both necessary

1　最も悪性な癌細胞はじっと一カ所にとどまらない。その代わりに，それらは転移する，つまり，もとの発生部位〔原発巣〕から移動して，他の部位に新しい腫瘍を形成する。いったん癌が広がると，それを消滅させるのはより困難になる。発生生物学者による研究は，癌細胞が，どのようにして，転移の前提条件である他の組織に浸潤する能力を獲得するかについての新しい手がかりを提供している。研究では，癌細胞が他の組織に浸潤するには，細胞分裂を止める必要があることを明らかにしている。それゆえに，浸潤と増殖という2つの過程は相互排他的である（※共存しないという意味）。この所見は，癌治療の情報を提示するだろうが，その治療は急激に増殖する癌細胞を典型的に標的にしている。

2　ストーニーブルック大学のデイヴィッド゠メイタスとデューク大学のデイヴィッド゠シャーウッドは，この浸潤の過程を解明するために透明な線虫を選んだ（※ turn to ～「～を方法として選ぶ」）。線虫が正常に発達している間，アンカー細胞として知られる細胞が，生殖孔と子宮を分ける基底膜と呼ばれる構造を貫通する。その過程はヒト癌細胞が，基底膜に浸潤して血流に入り，遠位部へと移動するのと似ている。それゆえ，生物学者たちは転移のモデル生物として，「カエノラブディティス・エレガンス」という線虫を採用した。それらを簡単に画像化でき，遺伝子操作ができる。

3　「C.エレガンス」の何百もの遺伝子のスイッチを入れたり切ったりした後，メイタスのチームはアンカー細胞の浸潤を制御している遺伝子を発見した。その遺伝子を非活性化した〔スイッチを切った〕時，アンカー細胞は基底膜へ浸潤することができなかった。しかしアンカー細胞はさらに予想外のことをした。すなわち，分裂し始めた。逆に，研究者たちが細胞増殖を阻害すると，アンカー細胞は分裂を止め，再び浸潤し始めた。追加の実験により，細胞分裂を止めることが浸潤の必要十分条件である

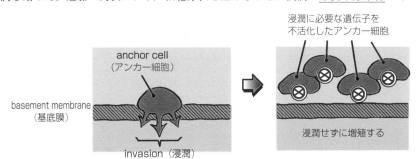

anchor cell
（アンカー細胞）

basement membrane
（基底膜）

invasion（浸潤）

浸潤に必要な遺伝子を
不活化したアンカー細胞

浸潤せずに増殖する

イラスト 茨木保

124

and sufficient for invasion. Although (2)anecdotal observations by pathologists have suggested this either/or situation might be the case, the new study is the first to **uncover the genetic mechanism** that explains why these two processes(S) must be(V) mutually exclusive. The results were published in October in the journal *Developmental Cell*.

4 The study also explains the long-standing but mysterious observation by cancer biologists that **the invading front** of many tumors does not contain dividing cells; instead the invasive cells(S) lead(V1) the dividing cells behind them and push forward into(V2) healthy tissue as the tumor grows in size. "This research changes how we think about cancer at some level," Matus says. "We think of cancer as a disease of uncontrolled cell division, and in fact, many **cancer drugs** are designed to **target** these dividing cells. But our study suggests that we need to figure out how to target these nondividing cells, too, as these are the ones that are invasive."

5 Before the (3)insight makes its way into **cancer treatments**, however, it will need further testing. "Now we can take that simple model and go to more complex systems —— like **breast cancer tumors**," says Andrew Ewald, a cancer cell biologist at Johns Hopkins University. **Metastatic breast cancer** alone (D)accounts for about 40,000 deaths every year in the U.S., but **the five-year survival rate** is nearly 100 percent if caught before the cancer spreads.

>>> 解 説

☑速読攻略

設問 1・2 は，1 題につき 1 分で解くようにしよう。また，1 では設問 3，2 では設問 4，3 では設問 5 の選択肢を頭に入れ，解答を探しながら，読み進めよう。この東京慈恵会医科大学の英文は，段落の最初にその段落の要点が述べられ，設問の解答が得られることが多くなっている。

1.
(A)空所を含む部分は「一度癌が広がると，(　　) のはより困難になる」という意味。

ことが示唆された。病理学者らによる事例観察から，この二者択一の状況が事実であると示唆されてきたが，新しい研究は，なぜこれらの２つの過程が(S)互いに排他的なのか(V)〔なぜ増殖と浸潤が同時に起きないか〕を説明する遺伝子メカニズムを初めて明らかにした（※ be the case「事実である」 構文説明：the genetic mechanism that（関係詞）「遺伝子メカニズム」が先行詞。関係詞 that 以下について，why S V は　名詞節の目的語。「なぜ S が V するかを説明する」）。この研究の結果は 10 月に雑誌『ディベロップメンタル・セル』に掲載された。

④ この研究はまた，癌生物学者たちが長期にわたり謎であった観察について説明もする。それは，多くの腫瘍の浸潤最前線は，分裂細胞を含まない。つまり，その代わりに腫瘍が大きくなるにつれて，浸潤細胞が(S)分裂細胞を前線の (them) 背後へと追いやり(V1)，健康な組織へと侵攻していく(V2)（※ as the tumor grows in size「腫瘍が増大するにつれ」）。「この研究によってあるレベルで私たちの癌についての考え方が変わります」とメイタスは言う。「私たちは癌を制御不可能な細胞分裂の疾患だと考えていますし，実際，多くの癌治療薬は，そうした分裂細胞を標的にしてつくられています（※ think of A as ～「A を～として考える」）。しかし私たちの研究は，分裂しない細胞が浸潤するので，分裂しない細胞に対しても，いかに標的にするかを理解する必要があるということを示唆しています（※ as these are the ones that are invasive の these は分裂しない細胞を指す。分裂しない細胞 (these) が浸潤するので，分裂する細胞に加えて，分裂しない細胞も標的治療の対象にする必要があるという意味)」

⑤ しかし，この発見が癌治療に応用される前に，さらなる試験が必要となるだろう（※ make its way「進む〔応用する〕」）。「さて，こうした簡潔なモデルをとりあげ，例えば乳癌のようなさらに複雑なシステムへと進むことができます」とジョンズ・ホプキンズ大学の癌細胞生物学者アンドリュー゠エワルドは述べる。転移性の乳癌だけで米国で毎年死亡例が約４万を占める。しかし，癌が広がる前に発見できれば，５年生存率はほぼ 100 パーセントである。

6

1. exclude「～を除外する」　2. reject「～を拒絶する」
3. discard「～を廃棄する」　**4. eliminate「消滅させる，無くす」**⇒正解。
(B)空所を含む部分は「２つの（　）つまり，浸潤と増殖」という意味。
1. processes「過程」⇒正解。　2. discoveries「発見」
3. methods「方法」　4. dilemmas「ジレンマ」
(C) turn（　）
1. turn on ～「～を作動させる」　2. turn out ～「～と判明する」
3. turn away ～「～を拒む」　**4. turn to ～「～を方法として選ぶ」**⇒正解。

(D)空所を含む部分は「転移性乳癌だけで毎年米国での死亡例が約 4 万（　　）」という意味。

> 1. **accounts for ～**「～の原因となる，～を占める」⇒正解。account for ～は，単に「数になる」ではなく（cf. count for ～「数となる」），「原因となる，～を占める」という意味合いが含まれる。
>
> 2. takes up ～「～の場所をとる」
>
> 3. gives up ～「～をあきらめる」
>
> 4. comes from ～「～が由来である」

2.

(1) acquire the ability to ～「～する能力を得る」という意味。

> 1. **attain「～を獲得する」**⇒正解。　　2. experience「～を経験する」
>
> 3. reach「～に到達する」　　　　　　　4. proceed「進行する」

(2) anecdotal observations「事例観察」　anecdotal は「個人の見解に基づき，裏付けに乏しい＝事実に基づかない」という意味。

> 1. scientific「科学的な」⇒反対の意味。　2. mysterious「神秘的な」
>
> 3. statistical「統計の」⇒反対の意味。　**4. subjective「主観的な」**⇒正解。

(3) insight「重要な発見」　ここでは，「癌細胞の増殖」を従来の「分裂細胞が浸潤する」という見解から，「分裂しない細胞も浸潤する」という新たな解釈を示したので，発見という意味が，3 の「awareness」より的確となる。

> 1. conclusion「結論」
>
> 2. **discovery「発見」**＝productive insight ⇒正解。
>
> 3. awareness「自覚，認識」＝a deep understanding of a complex situation
>
> 4. research「調査」

3.「この研究の目的は何か」

> 1.「癌細胞が転移するのを防ぐ方法を発見するため」
>
> 2. **「癌が体の新しい部分に移動する方法を明らかにするため」**⇒ [1] *ll.* 4-5 how cancer cells … と一致しているので，正解。
>
> 3.「癌細胞が分裂する仕組みを明らかにするため」
>
> 4.「癌細胞が増殖するのを防ぐ方法を発見するため」

4.「科学者たちはどのようにして研究を行ったのか」

> 1.「彼らは癌細胞の転移の過程をまねするために線虫のアンカー細胞を改良した」⇒不記載。
>
> 2.「彼らは癌細胞がどのように広がるのかを観察するために，透明な線虫の基底膜

に癌細胞を注入した」➡不記載。

3. 「彼らは成長している線虫のある細胞がどのように体のある部分から別の部分へと移動するよう誘導するかを観察した」➡ ②*l.3* the anchor cell breaks through … と一致しているので，正解。

4. 「彼らは人間の癌細胞と同様に，ある線虫のアンカー細胞が基底膜を浸潤するということに気づいた」➡設問 4 に対する答えではない。

5. 「科学者たちが発見したことは何か」
科学者たちが発見したことは分裂を止めると増殖が始まる。分裂と増殖は排他的である（同時に起こらない）ということ。

1. 「アンカー細胞は分裂する間は体内を転移することはできない」➡ ③*l.5* the anchor cell stopped …に一致しているので，正解。

2. 「ある特定の遺伝子をはたらかせなかったら，癌細胞の転移を防ぐことができる」➡不記載。

3. 「癌細胞は浸潤か分裂のどちらかに特化しているが，両方を行うことはできない」➡不記載。

4. 「アンカー細胞と癌細胞は体内で同じように振る舞うことはない」➡不記載。

6

☑速読攻略

設問 **6** の英作文は，将来の治療法について述べられている ④ と ⑤ を参照して，5 分以内でまとめよう。時間内に解けるまで繰り返して練習し，あらかじめ時間配分の感覚を養っておこう。

6. 「将来の癌の治療法は，より効果的になるようにどのように変えられるべきか。自分の文を用いて英語で答えなさい」④・⑤ をまとめる。

解答例）

Until now, dividing cancer cells have been targeted, but cancer cells do not divide while they are metastasizing, so we should also find treatments that target non-dividing cells. If cancer can be discovered before it spreads, we can hope that the survival rate will rise.

「これまでは，分裂している癌細胞を標的にしてきたが，癌細胞は浸潤している間は，分裂をしないので，分裂をしていない癌細胞を標的にする治療を見つけるべきだ。癌がひろがる前に発見できれば，生存率の上昇が期待できる」

ANSWER 1. (A)—4 (B)—1 (C)—4 (D)—1 2. (1)—1 (2)—4 (3)—2
3—2 4—3 5—1 6. 解答例参照

128

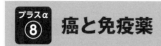

🎓 順天堂大学（医学部）　　　　　　　　　⏱ 目標9分　920語

1　A "whole new era" for cancer treatment is upon us, according to experts. Two new studies published in *the New England Journal of Medicine* **provide further evidence** that **immunotherapy** —— the use of drugs to **stimulate immune response** —— is highly effective against the disease.

2　Recently presented at the 2015 American Society for Clinical Oncology annual meeting, one study revealed that **a drug combination of ipilimumab and nivolumab** (an immune therapy drug) **reduced tumor** size in almost 60% of **individuals with advanced melanoma** —— the deadliest form of skin cancer —— compared with (only 19% for) ipilimumab alone, while another study found nivolumab reduced **the risk of lung cancer death** by more than 40% .

3　Nivolumab is **a drug already approved by** the Food and Drug Administration (FDA) **for the treatment of metastatic melanoma** in patients who **have not responded to** ipilimumab or other medications. It is also approved for the treatment of non-small cell lung cancer (NSCLC) that has **metastasized** during or after chemotherapy.

4　According to cancer experts, however, the results of these latest studies indicate that nivolumab and other immune therapy drugs could one day become **standard treatment** for cancer, **replacing chemotherapy**.

5　Prof. Roy Herbst, chief of medical oncology at Yale Cancer Center in New Haven, CT, believes this could happen in the next 5 years. "I think we **are seeing a paradigm shift** in the way oncology is being treated," he told The Guardian. "**The potential for long-term survival**, effective cure, is definitely there."

Nivolumab plus ipilimumab reduced tumor size by at least a third for almost 1 year

6　Nivolumab belongs to **a class of drugs** known as "checkpoint **inhibitors**." It works by **blocking the activation of PD-L 1 and PD-1** —— proteins that help cancer cells hide from **immune cells**, avoiding attack.

7　In a phase 3 trial, Dr. Rene Gonzalez, of the University of Colorado Cancer Center, and colleagues **tested the effectiveness** of nivolumab combined with

1　専門家によれば，癌治療の「完全に新しい時代」が近づいている。『ニュー・イングランド・ジャーナル・オブ・メディシン』誌に発表された2つの新しい研究は，免疫反応を刺激する薬を用いる免疫療法は癌に対して有意に効果があるというさらなるエビデンスを提供した。

2　最近，アメリカ臨床腫瘍学会の2015年度年次学会で発表された研究によると，イピリムマブ単独投与で，もっとも致死率の高い型の皮膚癌である進行性メラノーマ患者の19％に腫瘍の縮小が見られたのと比べ，イピリムマブとニボルマブ（免疫治療薬の1つ）の併用〔投与〕では，患者のおよそ60％において，腫瘍が縮小したことが明らかになった。一方，別の研究では，ニボルマブは肺癌の死亡リスクを40％以上低減させることがわかった。

3　ニボルマブは，イピリムマブや他の薬剤に対して反応を示さなかった患者の転移性メラノーマの治療に対して，アメリカ食品医薬品局（FDA）によってすでに認可された医薬品である。ニボルマブはまた，化学療法中または化学療法後，転移した非小細胞肺癌（NSCLC）の治療に対しても承認されている。

4　しかし，癌の専門家によれば，これら最新の研究の結果は，ニボルマブと他の免疫治療薬は，いつか化学療法に取って代わり，癌の標準的治療になる可能性を示唆している。

5　コネティカット州ニューヘイブンのエール大学癌センター医療腫瘍学の主任ロイ゠ハーブスト教授は，免疫治療薬が化学療法に取って代わる治療は，今後5年以内に生じる可能性があると考える。「我々は，腫瘍学の扱われ方においてパラダイムシフト（※規範と考えられていた概念の変化のこと）を見ていると考えています」と彼はガーディアン紙に語った。「長期生存への可能性，つまり効果的な治療法は確実にすぐそこまで来ています」

ニボルマブとイピリムマブの併用により，ほぼ1年間で腫瘍の大きさは少なくとも三分の一小さくなった

6　ニボルマブは「免疫チェックポイント阻害剤」として知られる薬剤クラスに属している。（免疫細胞の）攻撃を避け，癌細胞が免疫細胞から隠れる助けをする蛋白質のPD-L1とPD-1活性を阻害することにより作用する。

7　コロラド大学癌センターのルネ゠ゴンザレス医師と彼の同僚らは，第Ⅲ相試験〔フェーズⅢ〕において，事前に治療を受けなかった進行性メラノーマ患者（ステー

ipilimumab —— a drug that **stimulates immune cells** to help fight cancer —— or **ipilimumab alone** in 945 **patients with advanced melanoma** (stage Ⅲ or stage Ⅳ) who had received no prior treatment.

8 While 19% of patients who received ipilimumab alone experienced a reduction in tumor size for a period of 2.5 months, the tumors of 58% of **patients who received nivolumab plus ipilimumab** reduced by at least a third for almost a year.

9 Commenting on these findings, study co-leader Dr. James Larkin, of the Royal Marsden Hospital in the UK, told BBC News: "By **giving these drugs together** you are effectively taking two brakes off **the immune system** rather than one, so the immune system is able to **recognize tumors** it wasn't previously recognizing and **react to** that and destroy them." "For **immunotherapies**, we've never seen **tumor shrinkage** rates over 50% so that's very significant to see. This is **a treatment modality** that I think is going to have a big future for **the treatment of cancer**."

10 Dr. Gonzalez and colleagues also demonstrated **the effectiveness of another immune therapy drug** called pembrolizumab in **patients with advanced melanoma**.

11 While 16% of 179 **patients treated with chemotherapy** alone experienced no **disease progression** after 6 months, the team found that **disease progression was halted** for 36% of 361 patients treated with pembrolizumab after 6 months.

12 Dr. Gonzalez notes that while a combination of nivolumab and ipilimumab **shows greater efficacy** against advanced melanoma than pembrolizumab, it also **presents greater toxicity**. Around 55% of patients treated with nivolumab plus ipilimumab had **severe side effects**, such as fatigue and colitis, with around 36% of these patients **discontinuing treatment**.

13 Dr. Gonzalez says such treatment may be better for patients whose cancer does not involve **overexpression** of the PD-L 1 protein.

14 "Maybe PD-L 1-negative patients will benefit most from the combination, whereas PD-L 1-positive patients could use a drug targeting that protein with equal efficacy and less toxicity," he adds. "In metastatic melanoma, all patients and not just those who are PD-L 1-positive may benefit from pembrolizumab."

ジ 3 またはステージ 4）945 名において，癌と闘う免疫細胞を刺激する薬剤イピリム
マブとニボルマブとの併用投与とイピリムマブ単独投与の有効性を試験した。

8　イピリムマブを単独投与した患者の 19 ％は，2.5 カ月間で腫瘍サイズの縮小を
経験したのと比較し，ニボルマブとイピリムマブを併用投与した患者の 58 ％の腫瘍
は，およそ 1 年間に，少なくとも三分の一縮小した。

9　イギリスのロイヤル・マースデン病院の共同リーダーの研究者ジェームズ゠ラー
キン医師は，これらの所見について BBC ニュースに対し「これらの薬を併用投与す
ることで，免疫系を効果的に 1 カ所ではなく 2 カ所活性化する〔ブレーキを外す〕の
です。したがって免疫系は，以前に認識していなかった腫瘍を認識することができ，
腫瘍に反応し，腫瘍を破壊することができます」と述べた。「免疫療法に関して，
50 ％を超える腫瘍の縮小率はこれまで認めたことはなく，これは非常に有意なことで
す。免疫療法は，癌治療に将来有望になると考えている治療方法です」

10　ゴンザレス医師と彼の同僚らはまた，進行性メラノーマ患者において，ペンブロ
リズマブと呼ばれる別の免疫治療薬の有効性を示した。

6

11　そのチームは，化学療法のみを受けた患者 179 名中 16 ％が 6 カ月後，病気の進
行が認められなかったのと比較し，ペンブロリズマブで治療した患者 361 名中 36 ％
が 6 カ月後，病気の進行が停止したことを認めた。

12　ゴンザレス医師は，ニボルマブとイピリムマブの併用はペンブロリズマブと比較
し，進行性メラノーマに対しさらに高い有効性を示すが，またさらに高い毒性も示す
と記している。ニボルマブとイピリムマブを併用投与した患者の約 55 ％は，疲労や
大腸炎といった重篤な副作用があり，これらの患者の約 36 ％は治療を中止した。

13　ゴンザレス医師は，このような治療は癌に PD-L 1 蛋白質の過剰発現を伴わない
患者に対して，さらに恩恵があるだろうと述べている。
14　「おそらく PD-L 1 陰性の患者は，併用投与がもっとも効果があるでしょう。一方，
PD-L 1 陽性の患者は，その蛋白質を標的とし，同等の有効性がありさらに毒性が少
ない薬剤を使用することが可能でしょう」と彼はつけ加えた。「転移性メラノーマに
おいては，PD-L 1 陽性の患者だけでなくすべての患者は，ペンブロリズマブが効果
的でしょう」

Nivolumab almost doubled patient survival from NSCLC

[15] In another study, Dr. Julie Brahmer, director of the Thoracic Oncology Program at the Johns Hopkins Kimmel Cancer Center, and colleagues **tested the effectiveness** of nivolumab against **standard chemotherapy** with the drug docetaxel among 260 patients with NSCLC.

[16] All patients had been treated for the disease previously, but **the cancer had returned and spread.**

[17] The team found that patients who received nivolumab had longer overall survival than **those treated with standard chemotherapy,** at 9.2 months versus 6 months.

[18] At 1 year after treatment, the researchers found nivolumab almost doubled patient survival. Around 42% of patients who received nivolumab were alive after 1 year, compared with only 24% of patients who received chemotherapy.

[19] The study results also demonstrated a longer **period of halted disease progression** for patients who received nivolumab **compared with those who had chemotherapy,** at 3.5 months versus 2.8 months.

[20] Overall, the researchers **estimated** that, compared with patients who received chemotherapy, those who received nivolumab were at 41% lower **risk of death from NSCLC.**

[21] Commenting on these findings, Dr. Brahmer says: "This solidifies immunotherapy as a treatment option in lung cancer. In the 20 years that I've **been in practice,** I consider this a major milestone."

[22] While both studies show **promise for the use** of immunotherapy in cancer treatment, experts note that such treatment would be expensive. The use of nivolumab plus ipilimumab for the treatment of advanced melanoma, for example, would cost at least $200,000 per patient.

[23] As such, researchers say it is important that future research determines which cancer patients would be most likely to benefit from immunotherapy.

[From Immunotherapy heralds 'new era' for cancer treatment, Medical News Today on June 3, 2015 by Honor Whiteman]

ニボルマブ投与により NSCLC の患者の生存はほぼ 2 倍になった

15 別の研究では，ジョンズ・ホプキンズ大学キンメル癌センターの胸部腫瘍学プログラムの責任者ジュリー゠ブラーマー医師とその同僚らが，NSCLC を患っている患者 260 名においてドセタキセルという薬剤を用いた標準的化学療法に対して，ニボルマブの有効性を試験した。

16 すべての患者は，その病気に対して以前に治療を受けていたにもかかわらず，癌が再発し広がっていた。

17 その研究チームは，ニボルマブを投与した患者は，全生存期間 9.2 カ月で，標準的化学療法で治療された患者の生存期間 6 カ月と比較し，さらに長いことを認めた。

18 治療 1 年後，研究者らは，ニボルマブが患者の生存率をほぼ 2 倍にしたことを明らかにした。化学療法を受けた患者の 24%のみが生存したのと比較し，ニボルマブを投与した患者の約 42%が 1 年後も生存した。

19 この研究結果は，また，病気の進行停止期間は，化学療法を受けた患者の 2.8 カ月と比較し，ニボルマブを投与した患者は 3.5 カ月とさらに長くなることを明らかにした。

20 全体として，化学療法を受けた患者と比較し，ニボルマブを投与した患者は NSCLC 起因の死亡リスクが 41%低いと研究者らは推定した。

21 ブラーマー医師はこれらの所見にコメントし，「このことにより，肺癌における治療の選択肢として免疫療法が強固なものとなります。私が診察してきた 20 年で，私はこれを非常に画期的な出来事と考えています」と述べる。

22 2 つの研究はともに癌治療における免疫療法の使用が有望であることを示しているが，専門家は，このような治療は高価になるだろうと注意する。たとえば，進行性メラノーマの治療に対してニボルマブとイピリムマブを併用すると，患者 1 人あたり少なくとも 20 万ドル必要だろう。

23 そのようなわけで，今後の研究では，どの癌患者が，免疫療法からもっとも恩恵を得る〔免疫療法が効果的である〕可能性が高いかを決定することが重要だと研究者たちは述べている。

6

実験データに基づいた薬剤の有効性について記載した医療ニュース記事である。数語を塊で読む演習により，速読が期待できる。医学関連文では，受動態を能動態で訳すことが多い。

134

プラスα ⑨ 抗癌剤オプジーボ

東北医科薬科大学（医学部）　　　　　　　⏰目標1分25秒　214語

1　The big news right now in the medical world is the development of **anti-cancer drugs** that use **the body's natural immune system** to **fight off tumors**. In Japan, the most famous of these drugs is probably Opdivo, created by the relatively minor Ono Pharmaceutical Co. **in collaboration with** Bristol-Myers Squibb Co.

2　Opdivo was approved for **treating a certain type of lung cancer** by the Ministry of Health, Labor and Welfare, which means **national health insurance** will pay for treatments. (中略)

3　Consequently, Opdivo, which was originally **developed to treat skin cancer**, is giving hope to **lung cancer patients** in Japan. (中略)

4　After telling the story of one 74-year-old **lung cancer sufferer** who saw no **positive results from chemotherapy** but whose **tumors shrank** after beginning treatment with Opdivo, the program presented a physician, Dr. Hideo Kunito of the Red Cross Hospital, who warned that widespread use for such expensive drugs will "destroy Japan's medical system." (中略)

5　The main problem is that doctors are still learning how to use the drug, and at present **the dosages** are mostly guesswork. Sometimes the tumor shrinks and sometimes it gets bigger, which means doctors may **increase dosages**. But since the drug is only effective 30 percent of the time at most, it makes it even more difficult to determine **how much to administer**.

[The Japan Times, August 13, 2016]

1　最近の医学界の重大ニュースは，腫瘍を撃退する自然免疫系を用いる（活性化する）抗癌剤の開発である。日本では，抗癌剤でおそらく最も有名なのは，オプジーボだろう。それは，比較的マイナーな小野薬品工業（株）がブリストル・マイヤーズスクイブ社と共同で開発した。

2　オプジーボは　厚生労働省によって，ある種の肺癌を治療するのに承認され，つまり，そのことは，国民健康保険によって，治療費が支払われることを意味する。(中略)

3　オプジーボは，元は皮膚癌を治療するために開発されたが，結果的に日本では肺癌患者に希望を与えている。(中略)

4　74歳の肺癌患者が，化学療法では何の良い結果も得られなかったが，オプジーボを用いて治療を開始した後，腫瘍が収縮した，という話をした後，その番組は，日本赤十字社医療センターの國頭英夫内科医を迎え，彼は，「高価な薬の広範な使用は日本の医療制度を破壊する」と警告した（※ positive「陽性」 cf. negative「陰性」）。(中略)

5　その主要な問題は，医師らがその薬の使い方をまだ学習中であり，現時点で，その投与量はたいてい，推量である，ということである。腫瘍は収縮する場合もあるし，拡大する場合もあるが，それは，医師が投与量を増やす可能性がある，ということを意味する。しかし，その薬は最大でも30％の確率でしか有効でないため，投与量を決定するのを，さらに困難にさえする（※構文説明：since S V「～なので」of the time「～の確率で」）。

Chapter 7 ≫ 循環器系・心臓血管系／生活習慣病
The Circulatory / Cardiovascular System
Life-Style Disease

知っておきたい医系用語

● 循環器系
- [ ] **circulatory system**「循環器系」[sə́ːrkjulətɔ̀ːri sístəm]
- [ ] **blood flow**「血流」(＝**bloodstream**)
- [ ] **blood circulation**「血液循環」
- [ ] **pump blood**「血液を押し出す」
- [ ] **heartbeat**「鼓動」
- [ ] **heart rate**「心拍」
- [ ] **blood filtration**「血液の濾過(ろか)」
- [ ] **blood type**「血液型」

● 生活習慣病
- [ ] **hypertension**「高血圧」(＝**high blood pressure**)
- [ ] **arteriosclerosis**「動脈硬化」[ɑːrtiəriouskliəróusis]
- [ ] **cardiovascular disease**「心疾患」[kàːrdiəvǽskjulər diziːz]
- [ ] **stroke**「脳卒中」
- [ ] **heart failure**「心不全」
- [ ] **kidney failure**「腎不全」
- [ ] **complication**「合併症」

動脈破裂（脳卒中など）までの経過
fatty deposit ⇨ **blood clot** ⇨ **aneurysm rupture** ⇨ **hemorrhage**
　脂肪蓄積　　　　血塊　　　　動脈瘤の破裂　　　　出血

● 臓器移植

☐ **organ transplant**「臓器移植」

☐ **rejection response**「拒絶反応」

☐ **interspecies transplantation**「異種移植」（＝**xenotransplant**）

☐ **homotransplantation**「同種移植」［hòumoʊtrænstéiʃən］

☐ **transfusion**「輸血」

☐ **donor**「臓器提供者」

☐ **recipient**「臓器被提供者」

● 血清脂質

☐ **LDL ［low-density lipoprotein］ cholesterol**「低比重リポ蛋白〔悪玉〕コレステロール」

☐ **HDL ［high-density lipoprotein］ cholesterol**「高比重リポ蛋白〔善玉〕コレステロール」

☐ **triglyceride**「トリグリセリド〔中性脂肪〕」

☐ **calorie**「カロリー」

☐ **obesity**「肥満」

7

循環器系（The Circulatory System）

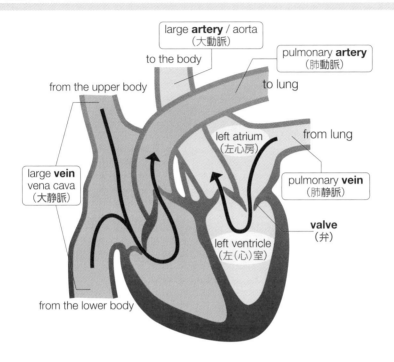

large **artery** / aorta
（大動脈）

to the body

pulmonary **artery**
（肺動脈）

from the upper body

to lung

left atrium
（左心房）

from lung

large **vein**
vena cava
（大静脈）

pulmonary **vein**
（肺静脈）

valve
（弁）

left ventricle
（左（心）室）

from the lower body

血圧（Blood Pressure）

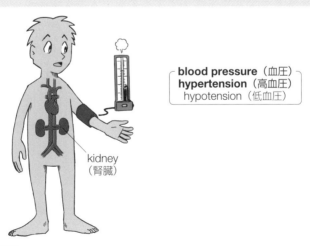

blood pressure（血圧）
hypertension（高血圧）
hypotension（低血圧）

kidney
（腎臓）

動脈硬化（Arteriosclerosis）

　Arteriosclerosis occurs when **a plaque accumulates（builds up），narrowing the lumen of the artery**. When this occurs in the coronary arteries, **blood flow to the heart** is reduced, which can cause *chest pain*（*angina*）. As the coronary arteries continue to narrow, the plaque may **rupture** and **a blood clot** rapidly forms, a condition called **thrombosis**. Then, the coronary artery **becomes completely blocked, resulting in a life-threatening condition** called **a heart attack**（medically known as **a myocardial infarction**）.

　動脈硬化は，粥腫（プラーク）が蓄積し，血管内腔を狭小化して，起こる。これが冠状動脈で起きると，心臓への血流が減少し，「胸痛（狭心症）」を引き起こす。冠状動脈が狭くなり続けると，プラークが破裂し，血栓が急速に形成され，その状態を血栓症という。それから，冠動脈が完全に閉塞し，心臓発作（医学用語で心筋梗塞）という生命に危険を及ぼす病態に至る。

7

動脈硬化の発生

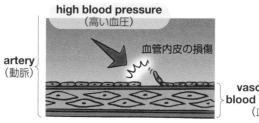

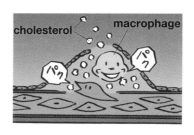

atherosclerosis
（粥状硬化／アテローム硬化）

イラスト　茨木保

動脈硬化の治療

intervention（インターベンション）
従来の内科的な薬物療法でも外科的な手術でもない治療法。たとえば，皮膚にあけた小さな穴からカテーテルと呼ばれる細い管状の器具を挿入して，患部を治療する。

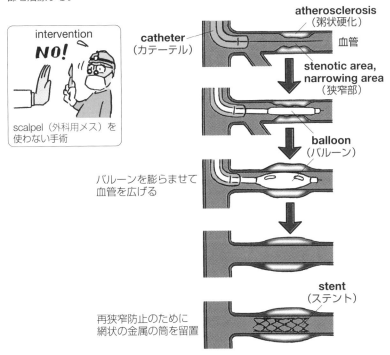

intervention
NO!
scalpel（外科用メス）を
使わない手術

catheter
（カテーテル）

atherosclerosis
（粥状硬化）

血管

**stenotic area,
narrowing area**
（狭窄部）

balloon
（バルーン）

バルーンを膨らませて
血管を広げる

stent
（ステント）

再狭窄防止のために
網状の金属の筒を留置

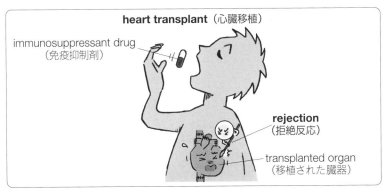

heart transplant（心臓移植）

immunosuppressant drug
（免疫抑制剤）

rejection
（拒絶反応）

transplanted organ
（移植された臓器）

イラスト　茨木保

速読訓練 ☆☆★★☆

13 ACLY の立体構造の解明

久留米大学（医学部医学科） 464 語

1 Columbia University scientists have demystified **a metabolic enzyme** that could be the next major **molecular target** in cancer treatment. The team has successfully determined the 3D strucure of human ATP-citrate lyase (ACLY) —— which plays a key role in cancer cell (1)proliferation and other cellular processes —— for the first time.

2 **The findings** represent a first step in better understanding the enzyme in order to create effective molecular targeted (2)therapies for patients. While previous experiments have succeeded with fragments of the enzyme, the current work reveals the full structure of **human ACLY at high resolution.**

3 ACLY is a metabolic enzyme that controls many processes in the cell, including **fatty acid synthesis** in cancer cells. By inhibiting this enzyme, the researchers hope to **control cancer growth.** In addition, the enzyme has other roles, including **cholesterol biosynthesis,** so **inhibitors against this enzyme** could also be useful toward (3)controlling **cholesterol levels.**

4 Targeted therapy is an active area of cancer research that involves identifying specific molecules in cancer cells that help them **grow, divide and spread.** By targeting these changes or **blocking** their effects with **therapeutic drugs**, this type of treatment **interferes with** the (4)progression of cancer cells.

5 Earlier this year, another group of researchers presented results of **a phase 3 clinical trial** for bempedoic acid, **an oral therapy for the treatment of patients with high cholesterol.** The drug, a first-generation ACLY inhibitor, was shown to reduce **low-density lipoprotein (LDL) cholesterol** by 30% when taken alone and an additional 20% in combination with statins.

6 ACLY has been found to **be over-expressed** in several types of cancers, and experiments have found that "turning off" ACLY leads cancer cells to stop growing and dividing. Knowledge of the complex molecular architecture of ACLY will point to the best areas to focus on for inhibition, paving the way for targeted drug development.

7 The scientists performed **an imaging technique** known as **cryogenic electron microscopy (cryo-EM)** to **resolve** the complex structure of ACLY.

1 コロンビア大学の科学者らは，癌治療の次の主要な分子標的となりえる代謝酵素を解明している。研究チームは，癌細胞の増殖やその他の細胞プロセスで重要な役割を果たす，ヒト ATP- クエン酸リアーゼ（ACLY）の立体構造を，初めて決定することに成功している。

2 この所見は，患者に対する効果的な分子標的治療を開発するために，酵素をより理解する第一歩である。従来の実験では，酵素の断片で成功している〔酵素の断片が解明されていた〕が，最近の研究によって，ヒト ACLY の全構造〔立体構造〕が高解像度で明らかになった（※ high resolution「高解像度」）。

3 ACLY は，癌細胞の脂肪酸合成といった，細胞内の多くのプロセスを制御する代謝酵素である（※ including「～といった，～などの」）。研究者らは，この酵素を阻害することで，癌の増殖を抑制することを期待している（※ control「～を制御する」 growth「増殖」）。加えて，ACLY はコレステロールの生合成などの他の役割ももっているため，この酵素（ACLY）に対する阻害薬はコレステロール値を制御するのにも役立つ可能性がある。

4 標的治療は，癌細胞の増殖，分裂，拡大を手助けする特定の分子を同定することを含む癌研究の活発な一分野である。癌細胞のそのような変化を標的にしたり，治療薬でその作用を阻止したりして，この種の治療は癌細胞の進行に干渉する（※ progression「進行」 ※構文説明：blocking の前に by が省略されている）。

5 今年初め，別の研究グループが，高コレステロール患者の治療用の経口治療薬である（※ acid と an の間にあるカンマは「すなわち」という意味）ベンペド酸についての第 3 相臨床試験の結果を発表した（※ clinical trial〔study〕「臨床試験」）。第一世代の ACLY 阻害薬であるこの薬は，単剤投与で低密度リポタンパク質（LDL）コレステロールを30％低下させ，スタチンとの併用投与でさらに 20％低下させることが示唆された（※ when taken alone「単剤投与時」 in combination with ～「～と併用して」）。

6 ACLY は数種類の癌で過剰発現することがわかっており，実験によって，ACLY を「停止させる〔無効にする〕」ことが，癌細胞の増殖と分裂の停止につながることが認められている（※ lead A to do「A が～することにつながる」）。ACLY の複雑な分子構造を知ることで，阻害に対して最も注目すべき領域が指摘され，標的治療薬の開発への道を開くだろう。

7 科学者らは，ACLY の複雑な構造を解明するために，クライオ電子顕微鏡法（クライオ EM）として知られる画像技術を用いた。クライオ EM によって，電子顕微鏡

144

Cryo-EM allows for **high-resolution imaging** of frozen biological (5)specimens with **an electron microscope**. A series of **2-dimensional images** are then computationally reconstructed into accurate, detailed **3D models** of intricate biological structures like proteins, viruses, and cells.

⑧ A critical part of **the drug discovery process** is to understand how the compounds work <u>at the molecular level</u>. This means determining the structure of the compound <u>bound to</u> the target, <u>which in this case is ACLY</u>.

⑨ The cryo-EM results revealed an unexpected mechanism for effective inhibition of ACLY. The team found that a significant change in the enzyme's structure is needed for the inhibitor to **bind**. This structural change(S) then indirectly blocks(V) **a substrate** from binding to ACLY, averting **enzyme activity** from occurring as it should. This (6)novel mechanism of ACLY inhibition could provide a better approach for developing drugs to treat cancer and metabolic disorders.

>>> 解 説

☑速読攻略

設問 1 は, 空欄のある段落ごとに内容を確認し, 単語を選ぼう。

設問 2 は, 文の内容真偽問題。選択肢(a)~(h) の要点に下線を引くなどして, 要点を頭に入れて英文を読もう。

選択肢(a)~(h) の要点は,

(a) 「ACLY は, 重要な働き」

(b) 「研究の目的は新薬の試験」

(c) 「LDL を 30 ～ 50% 減少させる」

(d) 「酵素の構造は変えられない」

(e) 「ACLY を高解像度で見られない」

(f) 「ACLY の構造の解明が研究目的でない」

(g) 「増殖する癌細胞の特定は難しい」

(h) 「新薬の開発には, 極めて微細な化学構造の解明が必要」

設問 1 の解答を探すと同時に, 設問 2 の問題を解いていこう。

を用いて，凍結した生体標本を高解像度で可視化できる。そして，一連の2次元画像は，コンピュータによって，タンパク質，ウイルス，細胞のような複雑な生物学的構造の正確で詳細な3次元モデルへ再構成される。

⑧　非常に重要な薬剤開発プロセスは，化合物が分子レベルでどのように作用するかを理解することである（※ be to *do*「～することである」不定詞の名詞的用法）。これは，標的，この場合は ACLY，に結合する化合物の構造を決定することを意味する。

⑨　クライオ EM の結果から，ACLY を効果的に阻害する予想外のメカニズムが明らかになった。研究チームは，阻害薬が結合するのには，酵素の構造に有意な変化が必要であることがわかった（※ significant change「有意な変化」 inhibitor「阻害薬」）。この構造変化により (S)，本来起こるべき酵素の活性を変化させ，基質が ACLY に結合するのを間接的に阻害する (V)（※ substrate「基質」 avert enzyme activity「酵素活性を変化する」）。この ACLY 阻害の新奇なメカニズムは，癌や代謝障害の治療薬を開発するためのよりよい方法を提供する可能性がある。

7

1.

(1)

(a)「宣言」

(b)「不足」

(c)「増殖」 ➡ 正解。癌細胞は増殖するという予備知識から，正解の選択肢を選ぼう。

(d)「不足，希少」

①の要点：酵素 ACLY の3D構造の解明について記載。⇨設問**2**(a)は正解。(b)・(f)は不正解。

(2)

(a)「土台」 cf. basis「基底」

(b)「髄」

(c)「衛星」

(d)「治療」 ➡ 正解。標的にするのは治療である。

②の要点：ACLY の構造の解明について記載。⇨設問**2**(e)・(f)は不正解。

(3)

(a)「作る」

(b)「抑制する」 ➡ 正解。③ *l.2* の inhibiting「阻害する」と一致している。

(c)「刺激する」

(d)「切り替える」

3の要点：ACLY は，癌細胞の脂肪酸合成を阻害する。

(4)

(a)「**進行**」➡正解。

(b)「低下，悪化」

(c)「具体化」

(d)「分類」

4の要点：癌細胞増殖を手助けする特定の分子を解明し，標的治療はその増殖分裂（つまり進行）を抑える。⇨設問 **2**(g)は不正解。

5の要点：ACLY 阻害薬は，LDL（悪玉コレステロール）を 30% 削減し，スタチン（薬）との併用で 50% 減少できる。⇨設問 **2**(c)は正解。

6の要点：ACLY を阻害すると，癌の増殖を止めることができることから，新薬開発が期待できる。⇨新薬試験が目的ではないので，設問 **2**(b)は不正解。

(5)

(a)「病原菌」

(b)「義務」

(c)「病気」

(d)「**標本**」➡正解。生物学的標本を用いるという予備知識が必要。

7の要点：高解像度画像を用いて ACLY の構造解明をする。⇨設問 **2**(e)・(f)は不正解。

(6)

(a)「重要でない」

(b)「**新奇な**」➡正解。ACLY 阻害に対して，9 *l.* 1 の unexpected と類似表現。

(c)「素朴な」

(d)「時代遅れの」

8と9の要点：ACLY 阻害薬の解明が新薬開発につながる。⇨設問 **2**(h)は正解。

2．

(a)「**ACLY は癌細胞の産生に非常に重要な役割を果たす**」➡1 *ll.* 3-4（ACLY）— which plays a key role in cancer cell proliferation と一致しているので，正解。

(b)「この研究の主要な目標は，新しい癌治療薬を試験することだった」➡この研究は ACLY の構造を解明するものである。治療薬につながる ACLY の構造の解明が目的。1の内容と不一致。

(c)「**一種の ACLY の阻害薬は LDL を 30～50% 減少させることができる**」➡「30%」の数字のある文を見つけ，前後を読もう。5 *ll.* 4-5 to reduce low-density lipoprotein … と一致しているので，正解。

(d)「酵素の構造は広範囲に変更することができない」➡不記載。

(e)「研究は，高解像度で ACLY を見ることができなかった」➡②*l.* 4 reveals the full structure … と不一致。

(f)「ACLY の構造を解明しようとすることは，研究者らの選択肢ではなかった」➡①*l.* 3 successfully determined … と不一致。

(g)「どの種の癌細胞が増殖し転移するか同定することは困難である」➡④*l.* 2 identifying specific molecules in cancer cells that … と不一致。

medi identify「～を同定する」　grow「増殖する」

(h)「**新薬を発見するには，研究者らが極小レベル（＝分子レベル）で化合物を見ることが必要である**」➡正解。⑧*ll.* 1-2 to understand how the compounds work at the molecular level. と一致。ACLY に結合する化合物の構造を決定するということ。

7

ANSWER　**1.** (1)—(c)　(2)—(d)　(3)—(b)　(4)—(a)　(5)—(d)　(6)—(b)
2 —(a)・(c)・(h)

148

プラスα ⑩ 心筋梗塞と D2B 時間

兵庫医科大学（医学部）　　　　　　　　　　目標2分　334語

1　A middle-aged man collapses with **a heart attack**. Paramedics arrive, and they do all the right things: **give him an aspirin** to chew, **place nitroglycerin under his tongue**, and **administer oxygen** through a face mask. Then they take him to a local hospital that doesn't **perform angioplasty** to **open blockages in the coronary arteries**. Angioplasty is **the best treatment for a heart attack** if performed expeditiously by experienced doctors. Instead, the man receives **a clot-dissolving drug** ―― **a thrombolytic** ―― which in his case doesn't work.

2　By the time the man **is transferred to our hospital** for angioplasty, it is too late. He is already **exhibiting signs of heart failure**. At this point there is little reason for us to open his blocked coronary artery because the part of his heart that is fed by the artery is already dead.

3　The story of this patient is one we encountered almost every day my first year at Long Island Jewish Medical Center: **a heart attack victim** taken by ambulance to a community hospital that isn't equipped to perform angioplasty. If the man had been brought to our hospital, which has **cardiac catheterization available** twenty-four hours a day, **the damage to his heart could have been averted**, adding years to his life. But it would have required a degree of coordination and oversight that many ambulance fleets in New York and across the country lack.

4　We discussed many such cases at hospital meetings on how to shorten door-to-balloon (D2B) time, the time between hospital arrival and **balloon angioplasty** for **patients having heart attacks**. In 1971, Eugene Braunwald, a cardiologist at Harvard Medical School, proposed a radical hypothesis: "Time is muscle." He postulated that **acute myocardial infarction** is a dynamic process and that **cardiac injury could be reduced** by **expeditious intervention**. Many studies since then have demonstrated that shorter D2B time is strongly associated with survival. However, a large number of heart attack victims are still not being treated within the guideline-recommended D2B time of ninety minutes or less.

[From Doctored: The Disillusionment of an American Physician by Sandeep Jauhar, Farrar, Straus and Giroux]

⬜1　ある中年男性が心臓発作で倒れる。救急隊員が到着すると，咀嚼服用アスピリンを投与し，ニトログリセリンを舌下投与し，マスクで酸素を供給するといった適切な処置を実施する。そして，彼らは，冠動脈の閉塞を開けるための血管形成術を行っていない地域病院に彼を搬送する。血管形成術は，経験豊富な医師が迅速に施行すれば，心臓発作の最善の治療である（※ treatment for（a heart attack）「（病名：心臓発作）の治療」）。その代わりに，この男性には血栓を溶かす薬——血栓溶解剤を投与するが（※受動態を能動態で訳す），この症例では効果がない。

⬜2　この患者が血管形成術を受けるために当院に搬送されるときには，手遅れである。患者はすでに心不全の兆候を示している。この時点で，冠動脈から（血液の）供給を受けている心臓の一部はすでに壊死しているため，閉塞した冠動脈を開く理由はほとんどない。

⬜3　この患者の話は，ロングアイランド・ジューイッシュ・メディカルセンターでの最初の年に，ほとんど毎日出くわした話である。つまり，救急車で，血管形成術を施行する設備のない地域病院に搬送された心臓発作による死亡である。この患者が 24 時間体制で心臓カテーテルが可能な我々の病院に運ばれていれば，心臓の損傷を低減し，寿命を延ばすことができたかもしれない。しかし，ニューヨークや全米で多くの救急隊に不足している，一定程度の調整と監視を必要としただろう。

⬜4　私たちは，ドア・トゥー・バルーン（D2B）時間，すなわち心臓発作患者の病院到着からバルーン血管形成術施行までの時間をいかに短縮するかについて，病院の会議で，このような多くの症例について議論した。1971 年，ハーバード大学医学部の心臓専門医であるユージン=ブラウンワルドは，「時は筋肉なり」と大胆な仮説を提唱した。彼は，急性心筋梗塞は動的な経過（※加速度的に悪化する）であり，迅速な介入によって心外傷を低減することができると推論した。多くの研究では，それ以来，D2B の短い時間が生存と強く関係があることを示した。しかし，多くの心臓発作による死亡者は，ガイドラインが推奨している D2B90 分以内にいまだ，治療されていない。

Chapter 8 ≫ 消化器系／生活習慣病
The Digestive System / Life-Style Disease

知っておきたい医系用語

● 免 疫
☐ **general immune system**「全身免疫系」
☐ **immune booster**「免疫促進剤」[imjúːn búːstər]
☐ **boost ／ enhance ／ elate**「～を高める，～を増加させる」
☐ **activate**「～を活性化する」
☐ **diminish ／ decline**「～を低減する」

● 細 菌
☐ **Helicobacter pylori**「ヘリコバクター・ピロリ」胃潰瘍や胃癌を引き起こす菌。
☐ **isolate**「～を分離する，～を隔離する」
☐ **identify**「～を同定する」　　　☐ **culture**「培養菌，培養」
☐ **solution**「溶液」　　　　　　　☐ **solvent**「溶媒」
☐ **solute**「溶質」

● 病 名
☐ **gastritis**「胃炎」[gæstráitis]　　☐ **ulcer**「潰瘍」(cf. tumor「腫瘍」)
☐ **diarrhea**「下痢」[dàiəríːə]（＝**loose stool**）
☐ **constipation**「便秘」[kànstipéiʃən]
☐ **indigestion**「消化不良」[ìndidʒéstʃən]

● 症 状
☐ **nausea**「吐き気」[nɔ́ːziə]
☐ **vomit**「嘔吐（する)」

● 物 質
☐ **digestive enzyme**「消化酵素」
☐ **antioxidant**「抗酸化物質」

消化器系（The Digestive System）

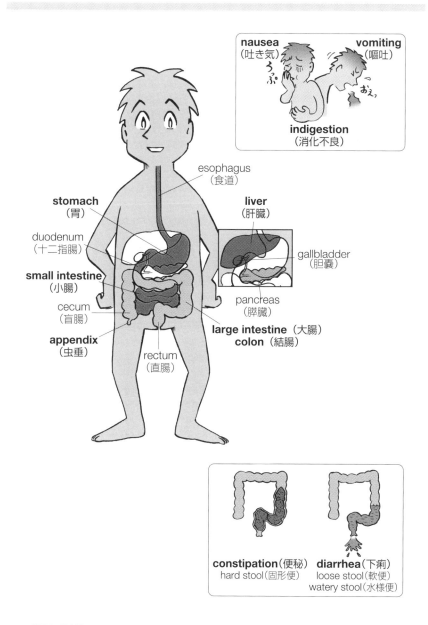

nausea
（吐き気）

vomiting
（嘔吐）

indigestion
（消化不良）

esophagus
（食道）

stomach
（胃）

liver
（肝臓）

duodenum
（十二指腸）

gallbladder
（胆嚢）

small intestine
（小腸）

pancreas
（膵臓）

cecum
（盲腸）

large intestine （大腸）
colon （結腸）

appendix
（虫垂）

rectum
（直腸）

8

constipation（便秘）
hard stool（固形便）

diarrhea（下痢）
loose stool（軟便）
watery stool（水様便）

イラスト　茨木保

長文読解

☆☆★☆☆

14 ピロリ菌と胃潰瘍

🎓 北里大学（薬学部）   747 語

[1] Doctors and medical researchers are often hesitant to abandon a long-established idea. So it was with the discovery that **gastric ulcers** can result from **bacterial infection**. Until the mid-1990s, doctors blamed **the acid build-up** that supposedly caused gastric ulcers on stress and eating spicy foods, calling the causes "hurry, worry, and curry." **The finding** in the 1970s that **drugs which block acid production** (1)relieve ulcers seemed to confirm **the hypothesis** that **excess acid** caused them. For decades, the standard treatment for ulcers in the stomach or small intestine used to be a mild-tasting diet, stress reduction, **acid blocking drugs**, or surgery. The idea that an ulcer was (2)instead due to a bacterial infection that could be easily, quickly, cheaply, and permanently cured seemed ridiculous.

[2] *Helicobacter pylori* —— the key to a cure for **gastric ulcer patients** —— **was identified** in the laboratory of J. Robin Warren at Royal Perth Hospital in western Australia. Warren, a pathologist who examined **gastric biopsies**, realized that spiral-shaped bacteria were always present in tissue that showed **signs of inflammation**. Convinced that his observation was significant, he inspired the interest of Barry Marshall, then a medical resident, and together they (3)set out to **isolate the source of the infection**. They tried, without success, to **grow the bacteria** from stomach biopsies for months —— until **the cultures** were accidentally left in **the incubator** over the Easter holidays. Easter weekend in 1982 was a long, 4-day break and, as a result, **the culture plates** on which they had been trying to grow the mysterious cells taken from a stomach were left 4 days longer than the usual 2 days. With the longer **incubation time**, they discovered (4)on their return a large growth of bacteria with **helix-shaped cells**. They called the new bug *Helicobacter pylori*.

[3] Isolating *Helicobacter pylori* was **significant**, but it still did not establish whether the bacteria were **the cause of the inflammation** or whether they occurred as a result of it. Barry Marshall proposed a way to help determine the choice between these two hypotheses. He knew he had a healthy stomach and had never had **gastritis** or an ulcer. If the bacteria caused the inflammation, they (5)would do so in him. So on a hot July day in 1984, Marshall decided to swallow **a solution** containing the bug. Marshall got sick. He had headaches,

1　医師や医療研究者は，従来の確立された考えを捨てることに，ためらいがちである。胃潰瘍が，細菌感染の結果として起こる可能性があるという発見についてもそうであった。1990年代半ばまで，医師は，胃潰瘍を引き起こすと考えられる酸の蓄積は，ストレスや辛い食べ物を食べることが原因である（※ blame *A* on *B*「*A*を*B*のせいにする」）として，それらの原因を「hurry, worry, curry（急ぐこと，心配事，刺激物）」と呼んだ。制酸剤が潰瘍を軽減するという，1970年代の所見が，過剰な酸が潰瘍を引き起こすという仮説を確定したようにみえた。数十年間，胃潰瘍や小腸潰瘍の標準的治療は，刺激の強くない食事，ストレスの軽減，制酸剤，または手術などであった。それに代わって，潰瘍は，容易に，迅速に，安く，そして永久に治癒しうる細菌感染によって起こるという考えは，ばかげたもののように考えられた。

2　「ヘリコバクター・ピロリ」（胃潰瘍患者の治療へのカギ）は，オーストラリア西部のロイヤルパース病院にある，J.ロビン＝ウォレンの実験室で同定された。胃生検（※組織の一部を採取して検査・診断すること）を行っていた病理学者ウォレンは，らせん形の細菌が，炎症の兆候を示す組織内に常在していることを認めた。自らの観察は重要であると確信し，彼は，当時研修医だったバリー＝マーシャルの興味を喚起し，協力してその感染源を分離し始めた。彼らは，何カ月も胃生検から細菌を増殖し（※ grow「〈細菌〉を増殖する」）ようとしたが，成功しなかった。そしてついに，培養菌が，イースター休暇期間中，偶然にも培養器に残された。1982年，イースターの週末は長く，4日間あった。その結果，彼らが胃から採取した，不思議な細胞を増殖させようとしていた培養皿は，通常の2日間よりも長く，4日間放置された。培養期がさらに長かったため，彼らが戻ってくると，らせん形の細胞をもった細菌が多く増殖しているのを発見した（※ incubation time「培養期」 cf. incubation period「潜伏期」）。彼らはその新しい微生物を，「ヘリコバクター・ピロリ」と名付けた。

3　「ヘリコバクター・ピロリ」を分離することは有意であった。しかし，その細菌が炎症の原因であるか，または炎症の結果として起こるのかは，まだ確立していなかった。バリー＝マーシャルは，これら2つの仮説のどちらを選択するかを決定するのに役立つ方法を提案した。彼は，自分の胃が正常で，胃炎や胃潰瘍になったことがないことがわかっていた。もし，その細菌が炎症を引き起こすならば，彼の身体でも炎症を起こすだろう。そこで，1984年7月のある暑い日に，マーシャルは，その菌を含む溶液を飲み込もうと決心をした。マーシャルは病気になった。彼は，頭痛，嘔吐，

vomiting, abdominal discomfort, and **irritability**. **Endoscopic examination** proved he had **acute gastritis**, which **cleared up** without treatment by the fifteenth day. A second volunteer who also took the suspect bacteria was ill for several months. A 2-month treatment using **an antibacterial agent** and bismuth was required to **eradicate the organism**. Other researchers, using laboratory animals, soon confirmed the (6)causative link between *Helicobacter pylori* and gastritis and then a link to ulcers, too. Studies also showed **an increased incidence of ulcers in persons infected with the bacteria.**

4 Most **patients with gastric ulcers** have the bacteria in their stomach, as do many other people without ulcers, (7)implying that additional factors such as stress are also needed for **ulcer formation**. In about 80% of the **infected people**, the infection seems not to produce any ill effects. Nevertheless, the bacteria produce a toxin —— a poison which damages **the cells of the stomach wall**. In susceptible people, the amount of this toxin reaches a level which overcomes (7)the **natural defenses** of the cells and **initiates** the formation of an ulcer.

5 It took the best part of a decade to convince doctors that these bacteria were really living in the stomach and could cause ulcers. (f)Skepticism was fuelled by the fact that all bacteria would normally be killed by the large amount of acid in the stomach. Yet it was eventually found that the *Helicobacter* bacteria (8)are protected from the acid partly because they live within the layer of **mucus** which the stomach secretes to protect itself against the acid, and partly because they produce **the enzyme**, urease. This enzyme converts urea, a chemical made by stomach cells, to ammonia which **neutralizes** the acidity in the mucus immediately surrounding the bacteria, creating **a non-acidic microzone** that protects the bacteria.

6 We now know that many ulcers result from bacterial infection. The realization that **antibiotics** can effectively cure stomach ulcers may be one of the most **significant** medical (9)breakthroughs in the 20th century. The *Helicobacter* story shows that, in a time of "big science" and "mega research projects", there is still opportunity for individual investigators to challenge accepted theories and change them, (10)with great benefits to society and science.

腹部の不快感，過敏性を経験した。内視鏡検査で，彼は急性胃炎であることがわかり，15日目までに，治療しないで治癒した。その疑わしい細菌を飲んだ第二のボランティアも，数カ月間病気になった。その有機体を根絶するには，抗菌剤と医薬用ビスマス化合物を用いた，2カ月の治療が必要であった。他の研究者は実験動物を用いて，すぐに「ヘリコバクター・ピロリ」と胃炎との因果関係を確認し，潰瘍との関係も確認した。試験は，その細菌に感染した患者は，潰瘍の罹患率が高いことも示した。

4　胃潰瘍の患者の大半は，胃にその細菌をもっており，それは潰瘍のない他の多くの人々も同様である。これは，ストレスのような付加的な要因も，潰瘍形成に必要だということを示唆している。感染者の約80パーセントにおいて，その感染はいかなる悪影響も起こさないように思われる。それでも，細菌は毒素（胃壁の細胞を損傷する毒）をつくる。影響を受けやすい人において，この毒の量は，細胞の自然防御力〔生体防御〕にまさるようになり，潰瘍を形成し始めるレベルまで達する（※ which は，overcomes と initiates の両方にかかる）。

5　これらの細菌が胃に実際に生息し，潰瘍を引き起こす場合があると医師に確信させるのに，およそ10年はかかった。すべての細菌が通常，胃の中の大量の酸によって殺されるという事実により，（ヘリコバクター菌が潰瘍の原因であるという理論に対する）疑念が増したのである。しかし，「ヘリコバクター」菌が酸から守られていることが，最終的に認められた。1つには，ヘリコバクター菌は，胃が酸から自身を守るために分泌する粘液の層の内部で生息しているため，もう1つは，それらがウレアーゼという酵素を産生するためである。この酵素は，胃の細胞によってつくられる化学物質である尿素を，その細菌の周りと接する粘液の酸性を中和するアンモニアに変えて（※ convert A to B「A を B に変える」），その細菌を守る非酸性のミクロゾーンをつくる。

6　潰瘍の多くは細菌感染から起こることが，現在，わかっている。抗生物質が効果的に胃潰瘍を治癒できるという認識は，20世紀におけるもっとも有意な医学的ブレイクスルーの1つであろう。「ヘリコバクター」の話は，「大科学」と「巨大研究プロジェクト」の時代に，個人の研究者が既成の理論に挑み，それを変えて，社会や科学に大いに貢献する機会の余地があることを示す。

>>> 解 説

攻略ポイント

設問 **1** の(1)〜(6)の空所補充の問題を解きながら，**3** まで目を通そう。

1. 空欄前後の流れから適切な語句を選ぶ。

(1)「制酸剤が潰瘍を（　　　）という所見が，過剰な酸が潰瘍を引き起こすという仮説を確定した」➡④ **relieve**「〜を軽減する」が正解（cf. The ulcer resolve.「潰瘍が寛解する（症状がなくなること）」）。

(2)前後を要約すると，「過剰な酸が潰瘍を引き起こすと考えられてきた。（　　　），潰瘍が細菌感染によって起こるという考えは，ばかげたもののように考えられた」➡② **instead**「その代わりに」が正解。

(3)「自らの観察は重要であると確信し，彼は，当時研修医だったバリー=マーシャルの興味を喚起し，協力してその感染源を分離し（　　　）」➡⑤ **set out**「始めた」が正解。

① stood out「目立った」　② turned out「判明した」

③ worked out 〜「〜を解き明かした」

(4)「イースター休暇で培養皿は4日間放置された。長い培養期のため，彼らは（　　　）細菌が多く増殖しているのを発見した」➡① **on their return**「戻ると」が正解。

(5)「もし，その細菌が炎症を引き起こすならば，彼の身体でもそうする（＝炎症を起こす）だろう」➡仮定法過去の② **would do so** が正解。

(6)「『ヘリコバクター・ピロリ』と胃炎との間の（　　　）関係」

① legitimate「正当な」

② **causative**「原因である」➡正解。

③ humble「質素な」

④ exclusive「排他的な」

⑤ ambiguous「あいまいな」

攻略ポイント

設問 **1** の(7)〜(10)は空所補充，**2** は下線部(ア)・(イ)の内容の言い換え。**4** 以降を読みながら設問を解こう。**3** は内容真偽。

(7)and it implies that …「（that 以下）を示唆する」を表す分詞構文を選ぶ。

➡① **implying** が正解。

(8)「すべての細菌が通常，胃の中の大量の酸によって殺されるという事実により，疑念が増した。しかし，『ヘリコバクター』菌が（　　　）ということが，最終

的にわかった」➡前に Yet「しかし」があるので，前の文と逆の内容になる．③
are protected from the acid「酸から守られている」が正解。

⑼「もっとも有意な医学的（　　　）」

①「統計」

②「対立」

③「規制」

④「推測」

⑤**「ブレイクスルー〔大発見〕」**➡正解。

⑽「個人の研究者が既成の理論に挑み，それを変える機会がある。それは（　　　）
を伴う」

①「患者と家族に重い負担」

②「一般人への軽微な影響」

③「挑戦者に少し不利な点」

④「社会や科学への大いなる利益」

⑤「研究者と医師に大きな利点」

➡④が内容と合う。

2. ㈎「細胞の自然防御力〔生体防御〕」とは免疫力のこと。

①「免疫応答を減らすことができる物質」

②「免疫応答を刺激する医薬品を用いた病気の治療」

③「微生物の増殖を抑制したり殺したりする医薬品」

④「感染リスクを制限する厳重な衛生」

⑤**「特定の感染や毒物に抵抗する免疫系の能力」**➡正解。

㈑該当箇所は，「（ヘリコバクター菌が胃潰瘍の原因であるという発見に対して，）
すべての細菌が通常，胃の中の大量の酸によって殺されるという事実により，
『疑念が増した』」という箇所。**「選択肢を縦に読む方法」**（⇨ p. 9）を用いて，各
選択肢の同じ言葉を省いて読む。

「ウォレンとマーシャルの発見／研究の…」

①「価値の認識が高まった」

②「妥当性の判断を保留した」

③「重要性について疑惑が強まった」

④「重要性を認識した」

⑤**「他の研究者に自然と疑念を抱かせた」**

➡①・②・④は反対のことを述べている。「通常，細菌は胃酸で死ぬ」という事
実が真実を見えにくくしたのだから，⑤と一致。

158

3. 内容に一致しないものを選ぶ問題。

(1)① 「ウォレンとマーシャルが『ヘリコバクター・ピロリ』の分離に成功したとき，彼らはその細菌が炎症組織に引き寄せられたのか，または胃の炎症を引き起こしたのか，確信がもてなかった」 ➡ ③ *ll.* 1-3 と一致。

② 「『ヘリコバクター・ピロリ』は，胃潰瘍になっていない人の体内にも，その病気になっている人の体内にも存在する」 ➡ ④ *ll.* 1-2 と一致。

③ 「ウォレンとマーシャルの『ヘリコバクター・ピロリ』の発見は，保守的な懐疑に対する科学的検知作業の勝利を表している」 ➡ ⑥ 最終文と一致。

④ 「ウォレンとマーシャルは，培養皿を意図的にいつもより長く培養器に入れることで，『ヘリコバクター・ピロリ』を初めてうまく培養した」 ➡ ② *ll.* 7-9 「偶然に（accidentally）培養器に残した」と不一致。

⑤ 「動物実験は，胃の病気で『ヘリコバクター・ピロリ』が果たす役割を，医学者が証明するのに役立った」 ➡ ③ *ll.* 12-14 と一致。

(2) 「ヘリコバクター・ピロリ…」

① 「…は胃の酸の環境で，粘液の中に隠れたり，その局部で胃酸を中和したりすることで生存する」 ➡ ⑤ *ll.* 4-10 と一致。

② 「…の発見の話は，科学の進歩は独創的な洞察力と，独立した研究者たちの忍耐によって得られることを示している」 ➡ ⑥ 最終文と一致。

③ 「バリー=マーシャルが…を自己投与したことは，本人の予想に反して，『ヘリコバクター・ピロリ』菌と胃潰瘍との関係を裏付けた」 ➡ ③ と不一致。ヘリコバクター・ピロリ菌と胃潰瘍が関連しているのは，*ll.* 3-4 の「2つの仮説」の1つなので，予想に反してではない。

④ 「胃潰瘍が細菌によって引き起こされるという考えは，以前は非常にばかにされていた」 ➡ ① 最終文と一致。

⑤ 「…は，通常，実験室で培養される他の細菌よりも，かなりゆっくりと増殖することをウォレンとマーシャルは発見した」 ➡ ② *ll.* 12-14 と一致。

ヘリコバクター・ピロリ菌の発見と胃潰瘍における役割の解明により，ウォレンとマーシャルは，2005年，ノーベル生理学・医学賞を受賞している。

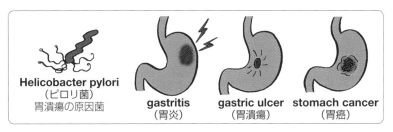

イラスト　茨木保

ANSWER	**1.** (1)—④	(2)—②	(3)—⑤	(4)—①	(5)—②
	(6)—②	(7)—①	(8)—③	(9)—⑤	(10)—④
	2. (ア)—⑤	(イ)—⑤			
	3. (1)—④	(2)—③			

☆☆★☆☆

15 腸チフスワクチン

🎓 慶應義塾大学（医学部）　　　　　　　　　　　　　　　642 語

[1]　**A new typhoid vaccine** works "fantastically well" and is being used to help stop an almost **untreatable strain of the infection**, doctors say. **Cases of the bacterial disease** fell by more than 80% in a trial reported in the *New England Journal of Medicine*. Experts said the vaccine was a game-changer and would reduce the "terrible toll wrought by typhoid".

[2]　Typhoid fever is caused by **highly contagious *Salmonella Typhi* bacteria** and **is spread** through **contaminated food** and water. (1)It is a disease of poverty, most common in countries with poor sanitation and a lack of clean water. **Symptoms include prolonged fever, headache, nausea, loss of appetite, and constipation**. It causes **fatal complications**, such as **internal bleeding**, in one in 100 people. Precise numbers on typhoid are hard to collect, but it affects between 11 million and 21 million people around the world each year and kills 128,000 to 161,000.

[3]　More than 20,000 children aged from nine months to 16 years took part in the trial in Kathmandu Valley, Nepal, where typhoid is a major **public-health problem**. Half of the children **were given the vaccine**, and the other half **received a placebo**. At the end of the first year of the study, **the rate of infections** was 81% lower in the group that had received the vaccine. "It works fantastically well in **preventing a disease** that affects some of the world's most **vulnerable children**," Prof. Andrew Pollard, from the University of Oxford, who has been involved in the trials, told BBC News. "The burden of typhoid is so huge that we're seeing families taking children into hospital to be treated and being plunged into poverty paying for the costs of investigation and **treatment with antibiotics**. The arrival of this vaccine to control the disease (2)is a pretty exciting moment."

[4]　The children in Nepal, as well as those taking part in other trials in Malawi and Bangladesh, will now **be followed up** to see how long protection lasts. Typhoid Vaccine Acceleration Consortium director Dr Kathleen Neuzil said the vaccine(S) could "reduce(V1) disease and save(V2) lives in populations that lack clean water and improved sanitation". A vaccine is particularly needed, because typhoid has, according to a World Health Organization report, acquired a

1　新しい腸チフスワクチンは「極めて有効」であり，ほぼ治療不可能な株の感染を止めるのを手助けするために用いられている，と医師は語る。『ニュー・イングランド・ジャーナル・オブ・メディシン』誌に報告された試験で，細菌性疾患の症例は，80％超低下した。専門家は，ワクチンは，ゲームチェンジャーであり，「腸チフスによる恐ろしい死亡者数」を低減するだろうと述べた（※ terrible toll = death toll「死亡者数」）。

2　腸チフスは極めて伝染性の強い「サルモネラチフス」菌によって引き起こされ，汚染された食物や水によって拡大する。腸チフスは，貧困の病気であり，非衛生的で，清潔な水が不足する国で最も多い病気である。この病気の症状は，長引く熱，頭痛，吐き気，食欲不振，便秘等がある（※ symptoms include ～「症状には～がある」）。内出血といった致命的な合併症が 100 例中 1 例に起こる。腸チフスの正確な数を収集するのは困難であるが，毎年，世界中で感染 1,100 万例から 2,100 万例で，死亡例が 12 万8,000 例から 16 万 1,000 例である。

3　生後 9 カ月から 16 歳までの 2 万人を超える小児が，ネパールのカトマンズ盆地での試験に参加した。そこでは（, where），腸チフスが主要な公衆衛生問題である。小児の半数にワクチンを投与し，残りの半数にプラセボを投与した（※受動態を能動態で訳す）。研究の初年度の終わりに，ワクチンを投与していたグループの感染率は81％低下した。「ワクチンは，世界で最も感染しやすい小児がかかる病気を予防するのに，驚くほど有効である」と，その試験に関与したオックスフォード大学のアンドリュー＝ポラード教授は BBC ニュースに述べた。「腸チフスのもたらす負担は極めて大きく，子供に治療を受けさせるために病院に連れて行き，検査費と抗生剤治療費を支払って貧困に陥る家族を知っている（※構文説明：see 人 *doing*「人が～しているのを見る」see は知覚動詞）。病気を制御するためのワクチンの到来は，極めて素晴らしいことだ」

4　マラウイとバングラデシュでの他の試験に参加した小児と同様に，ネパールの小児の感染防御がどれくらいの期間続くかを見るために，今後追跡調査が行われるだろう。Typhoid Vaccine Acceleration Consortium 代表のキャスリーン＝ノイツェル博士は，ワクチンは(S')「病気を低減し(V'1)，きれいな水と改善された衛生を欠く人々の命を救う(V'2)だろう」と述べた（※構文説明：clean water と improved sanitation の両方が lack の目的語で，「きれいな水と改善された衛生を欠いている」）。世界保健機関の報告書によれば，

162

"crazy amount" of **antibiotic resistance**, and the world is "reaching the limit" of current treatments. **Rapid urbanisation** in the developing world has left many countries unable to provide the most effective preventative measure —— clean water and flushing toilets. And while there are two typhoid vaccines already available, neither is licensed for children under the age of two, so the most vulnerable people are unprotected.

⑤ Pakistan has **an outbreak** of what is called **extensively drug-resistant (XDR) typhoid fever**. "Right now in Pakistan, a **strain of typhoid** has developed resistance to all but one of the antibiotics we use to treat the disease, threatening to take us <u>back to the days when</u> typhoid killed as many as one-fifth of the people that **contracted it**," Dr Seth Berkley, chief executive of Gavi, the Vaccine Alliance, told BBC News. It started in Hyderbad, in Sindh province, in November 2016 and more than 10,000 people have been infected. Gavi is paying for nine million children to be vaccinated, and Sindh province will now become the first region in the world to add the vaccine to routine childhood vaccinations.

⑥ Dr Berkley describes the new vaccine as a game-changer in the battle against typhoid, adding that it couldn't have arrived at a better time: "This vaccine should play a key role in <u>bringing this dangerous disease under control</u> and, once <u>introduced into</u> more countries' routine vaccination programmes, reducing the terrible toll wrought by typhoid worldwide." Prof. Pollard added, "It is really exciting to have a new intervention, in a very rapid space of time, that can not only prevent the disease but also help in the fight against antibiotic resistance."

腸チフスは，ワクチンが特に必要であり，それは，「極めて多量」の抗生物質耐性を獲得しており，世界が現在の治療の「限界に達している」ためである。発展途上国世界における急速な都市化の結果により，多くの国はきれいな水や水洗トイレといった，最も効果的な予防措置を提供できないままである。腸チフスワクチン2種類が利用可能であるが，どちらも2歳未満の子どもには認可されていないため，最も感染しやすい人に対して感染防御にならない（※ vulnerable (to a disease)「(病気に) かかりやすい」≒ suspectable (to a disease)）。

⑤　パキスタンでは，いわゆる広範囲薬剤耐性（XDR）腸チフスと呼ばれる感染症がアウトブレイクを起こしている。「現在パキスタンでは，一種の腸チフス株がその病気の治療に用いる一種類以外のすべての抗生物質に対して耐性を獲得してきており，腸チフスにかかった人のおよそ5分の1の多くの患者が死亡した時代に後戻りする脅威にさらされている」と Gavi ワクチンアライアンスの事務局長セス゠バークレー博士は BBC ニュースに語った（※ contract (a disease)「(病気に) かかる」）。この感染症は2016年11月にシンド州ハイデラバードで発生し，1万人を超える人が感染している。Gavi が小児900万人のワクチン接種費用を負担し，シンド州は小児定期予防接種にそのワクチンを追加する世界で初めての地域になるだろう（※ vaccinate「ワクチンを打つ」 vaccine「ワクチン」 vaccination「ワクチン接種」）。

⑥　バークレー博士は，新規ワクチンが腸チフスとの闘いにおけるゲームチェンジャーになると描写する。「ワクチンは最も良い時期に到来した」と述べている。「つまり，いったん，より多くの国々の定期予防接種計画へ導入されれば，このワクチンはこの危険な病気を制御し，世界中で腸チフスがもたらす恐ろしい死亡者数を減らすのに重要な役割をはたすだろう」と，ポラード教授は付け加えた（※構文説明：bringing …と reducing …は play a key role in にかかる。bring A under control「Aを制御する」）。「非常に迅速に，病気を予防するだけでなく，抗生物質耐性との闘いを助ける新たなインターベンション〔介入〕をすることは，本当に素晴らしいと思います」（※構文説明：not only A but also B「AだけでなくBも」 関係詞 that の先行詞は intervention となる）

>>> 解 説

✓速読攻略
設問 **1** は選択肢が段落順ではないので，フレーズがどの段落に記載されているかを判別しよう。

1. 「合致すると思うものには A，合致しないと思うものには B，内容が合致するかしないか判断できないものは C を記入せよ」

(ア)「2種類の腸チフスワクチンが試験中の新たなワクチンに加えて現在使用されている」⇒ **A**

4 最終文 there are two typhoid vaccines already available と一致。

(イ)「腸チフスは2株以上存在する」⇒ **A**

5 *ll.* 2-3 a strain of typhoid has developed… より，耐性菌が発現したことから2株以上あることがわかる。

(ウ)「ネパールでは腸チフス治療の費用をまかなえない家族がある」⇒ **A**

3 *ll.* 8-11 "The burden …と一致。

(エ)「多くの国では，健康保険は腸チフス治療を対象としていない」⇒ **C**　不記載。

(オ)「パキスタンには腸チフス治療のための有効な抗生物質はない」⇒ **B**

5 *l.* 3 all but one of the antibiotics …より一種類は有効なので不一致。

(カ)「パキスタンで，腸チフスが死因の約20%となった時期があった」⇒ **B**

5 *ll.* 4-5 typhoid killed as many as one-fifth of the people that …に「感染者の20%が死亡した」とあり，死因の20%ではないので，不一致。

(キ)「腸チフスは他の年齢集団と比べると幼児の致死性は低いと見られる」⇒ **B**

4 の最後に the most vulnerable people are unprotected とあり小児は感染しやすいので不一致。

medi be vulnerable to 〜「〜に弱い」 be vulnerable to stress「ストレスに弱い」 be suspectable to 〜「〜にかかりやすい」 be suspectable to infectious diseases「感染症にかかりやすい」（しばしば小児・高齢者・免疫力の低下した人，基礎疾患のある人）

2. 「空所(1)に入れる最も適切な文を選べ」

✓速読攻略
選択肢を頭に入れて，解答を探しながら **2** を読もう。

(A)「治療法がまだない病気である」

(B)「市場にワクチンがない病気である」

(C)「貧困のもたらす病気であり，非衛生的で，きれいな水が不足している国で最も

多い」➡ ②*ll.* 1-2 Typhoid fever … is spread through contaminated food and water. につながるので, 正解。

(D)「これはきれいな水で野菜を洗うなど衛生的な習慣によって広まりやすい病気である」➡非論理的で不記載。

3.「空所(2)に入れる最も適切な文を選べ」

☑️速読攻略
「病気を制御するこのワクチンの到来は」に続く内容について, 選択肢を頭に入れながら ③ を読もう。

③*ll.* 5-6 "It works fantastically well … から, プラス面の(B)か(C)で, (C)は将来起こることに対する期待の表現なので, (B)が正解となる。

(A)「私たち全員にとって危険なものである」➡マイナス面。

(B)**「極めて素晴らしい瞬間である」**➡正解。

(C)「私たちがとても楽しみにしているものである」

(D)「計画していなかったことである」➡マイナス面。

4.「(1)～(3)の英文を完成させるのに最も適切な選択肢を選べ」

(1)「腸チフスは」 ② を参照。

 (a)**「死に至る可能性がある病気である」**➡ ②*ll.* 5-6 It causes fatal …に,「内出血のような致死性の合併症を引き起こすことがある」とあるので, 正解。

 (b)「症状は頭痛や吐き気で便秘は起こらない」➡ ②*ll.* 4-5 Symptoms include prolonged … and constipation. より, 不一致。

 (c)「遺伝病である」➡細菌性なので遺伝病ではない。不一致。

 (d)「汚れた下水を通して急速に広まるウイルス性の病気である」➡不一致。bacterial（細菌性）と viral（ウイルス性）とは異なるので注意。

(2)「新しい腸チフスワクチンの有効な期間は少なくとも」 ③ を参照。

 (a)「1 カ月」

 (b)「3 カ月」

 (c)**「1 年」**➡ ③*l.* 4 At the end of the first year of the study…より, 正解。

 (d)「3 年」

(3)「腸チフスの感染拡大が続く主な理由は」 ④ を参照。

 (a)「起因菌はさまざまな経路から感染する可能性がある」

 (b)**「高度の衛生を今なお達成していない国が多い」**➡ ④*ll.* 9-10 many

8

countries unable to provide the most … clean water and flushing toilets より，正解。

(c)「ネパールなどで試されている新規ワクチンの有効性について適切に試験され ていない」➡ ③ *ll.* 3-4 Half of the children … received a placebo. に不一致。 また，試験を行っているかどうかは，腸チフス感染拡大の理由にはならない。 medi efficacy「有効性」

(d)「一般市民はチフスを十分に深刻なものと考えていない」➡不記載。

5．「バークレー博士が『ワクチンは最も良い時期に到来した』と考えている理由に ついて，60字以内で述べよ」

⑥ の最後の3行の内容を要約しよう。

解答例）

新規ワクチンは腸チフスの予防になるだけでなく，新規に現れた抗生剤耐性菌との 闘いの手助けになるため。

生活習慣病の因子 (Risk Factors for Lifestyle Related Diseases)

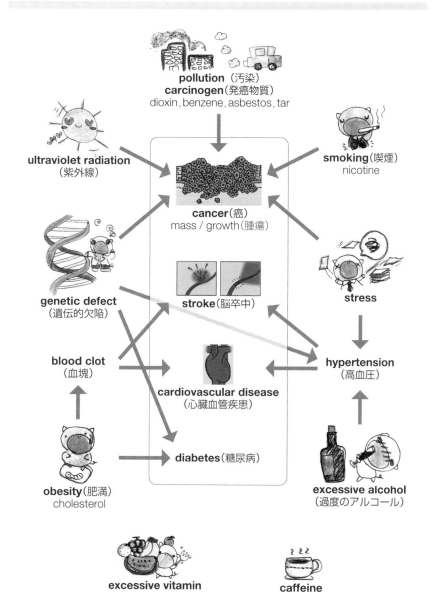

pollution (汚染)
carcinogen(発癌物質)
dioxin, benzene, asbestos, tar

ultraviolet radiation
(紫外線)

smoking(喫煙)
nicotine

cancer(癌)
mass / growth(腫瘍)

genetic defect
(遺伝的欠陥)

stroke(脳卒中)

stress

blood clot
(血塊)

cardiovascular disease
(心臓血管疾患)

hypertension
(高血圧)

8

diabetes(糖尿病)

obesity(肥満)
cholesterol

excessive alcohol
(過度のアルコール)

excessive vitamin
(過剰なビタミン)

caffeine

Chapter 9 ≫ その他

知っておきたい医系用語

● **新薬の臨床試験**

☐ **drug** ／ **medication**「薬剤」

> 新薬が許可されるまで
> 新薬の **safety**（安全性）と **validity**（有効性）の確認のため，**animal testing**（動物実験）と **clinical test**（臨床試験）が行われる。

☐ **randomized-control trial**「無作為対照試験」被験薬を投与する介入群と，従来の薬剤や偽薬を投与する対照群とに無作為に分け，両者を比較対照することで薬剤の有効性を評価するやり方。

☐ **double blinded study**「二重盲検試験」偽薬と被験薬を用いて薬効を対照する際，思いこみによるプラセボ効果を排除するため，どちらが被験薬であるか，被験者も医師も知らない状態で行う試験のやり方。

☐ **placebo effect**「プラセボ〔偽薬〕効果」薬効のない偽薬でも，「薬を飲んだから治る」と思いこむことで改善効果が生まれること。

☐ **drug's side effects**「薬剤の副作用」　☐ **interaction**「相互作用」

☐ **concomitant use of drugs** ／ **combination of drugs**「薬剤の併用」

● **院内感染**

☐ **nosocomial infection**「院内感染」MRSA「メチシリン耐性黄色ブドウ球菌」やVRE「バンコマイシン耐性腸球菌」などの抗生物質耐性菌によるものが特に問題。

☐ **contaminated blood products**「汚染血液製剤」

☐ **hepatitis**「肝炎」

● **麻　薬**

☐ **non-legal drugs**「非合法ドラッグ」　☐ **drug trafficking**「薬物売買」

☐ **mental [physical] dependence**「精神的［身体的］依存性」

☐ **addiction**「常用性」　☐ **toxication**「中毒」

☐ **withdrawal symptoms**「禁断症状」　☐ **drug abuse**「薬物乱用」

● **代替医療**

☐ **alternative medicine**「代替医療」西洋医学などの通常医療以外の医療。

☐ **Chinese medicine**「漢方医学」

代替医療（Alternative Medicine）

16 天然痘とワクチン

東京慈恵会医科大学（医学部医学科） 564 語

1 **Smallpox** was one of the most (1)dreaded diseases in human history. Caused by **the variola virus**, it was **a leading cause of death** in Europe from the 11th to the 20th centuries. When European explorers arrived in the Americas, they brought smallpox with them, and the (2)ensuing epidemic wiped out up to 90% of the native population. By the 20th century, smallpox had killed hundreds of millions of people worldwide. And yet, this horrible disease became the first disease in human history to become completely eliminated. How this happened is an interesting story in medical history.

2 Smallpox is **an extremely contagious disease** spread by **human to human contact**. It is not **carried or spread** by animals. The most common method of transmission was **inhalation of respiratory droplets**, although it was also possible to **contract it through contact** with objects that had been handled by infected people. After infection, the virus would (A)incubate for about two weeks, during which time **the patient was asymptomatic**, but the virus was quietly **multiplying** inside the body. Once this period was over, the infected person would first experience symptoms similar to the flu: **fever, chills, muscle aches, and general malaise**. Shortly after the first general symptoms, the more specific sign of **a red rash** would appear on the hands, feet, and face. The rash would then spread over the body in the form of **small raised blisters or pocks**, which is where the name smallpox comes from. The virus would infect the bones and **organs**, causing fatal (B)complications. **The mortality rate for smallpox** was 30% or higher, and those who survived were left with characteristic **pock scars** on their faces and bodies.

3 It became common knowledge that **those who were infected with smallpox** would not **contract the disease again**. Thus, in the early 18th century, the (C)practice of variolation became popular in Europe in which people would rub themselves with a small amount of pus or scabs taken from the **sores of an infected individual**. The idea was that this would give them a **mild form of smallpox** that would make them immune. About 2 % of people who became infected with smallpox this way died, but that was a much better **survival rate** than catching the disease normally, so it became very popular.

4 Then, in 1796, a physician named Edward Jenner decided to try a new

1　天然痘は人類史上最も恐ろしい病気の1つだ。それは**天然痘ウイルス**によって引き起こされ，11世紀から20世紀のヨーロッパで，主要な死因であった（※cause of death「死因」）。ヨーロッパの探検家がアメリカ大陸に到達した時，一緒に天然痘も持ち込み，その結果起きた大流行で先住民の90%が死亡した。20世紀までに，天然痘により世界で何億もの人が死亡した。それでも，この恐ろしい病気は，人類史上において完全に撲滅された初めての病気になった（※eliminate「～を撲滅する」）。いかにして撲滅したかは，医学史上，興味深い話である。

2　天然痘は，ヒトの接触感染によって拡大する極めて伝染力が強い病気である。それは動物によって媒介〔運び屋に〕されたり，拡大されたりしない。感染者が触れた物体に接触することで伝播する可能性もあるものの，最も多い伝播経路は呼吸飛沫の吸入であった（※transmission「伝播」 inhalation「吸気」 respiratory「呼吸の」）。感染後，ウイルスは約2週間潜伏し，その期間は，患者は無症状だが，ウイルスは静かに体内で急速に増殖している。いったんこの（潜伏）期間が終わると，感染者には，最初に，熱，悪寒，筋肉痛，全身倦怠感といった，インフルエンザに似た症状がでる。そのような最初の全身症状の直後に，天然痘特有の赤い発疹が手，足，顔に出現するだろう（※general symptoms「全身症状」）。それから，発疹が小さくて盛り上がった水疱，膿疱の形で，全身に広がるだろう。すなわち，これが天然痘という名前の由来である。ウイルスは骨や臓器にも感染し，致命的な合併症を引き起こす。天然痘の死亡率は30%以上で，生存者は，顔やからだに特有の痘痕〔あばた〕が残る（※mortality「死亡率」）。

3　天然痘に感染した人は再度罹患することはないというのは常識となった。したがって，18世紀初め，ヨーロッパでは種痘の実施が一般的となった。それでは〔種痘の実施では〕，感染者個体の皮膚のただれた部分から採取された少量の膿疱や痂皮〔かさぶた〕を体にすり込んだ（※variolation「種痘」 rub「すり込む」 pus or scabs「膿疱や痂皮〔かさぶた〕」 sores「ただれ」）。これは，軽度の天然痘を人々に感染させ，彼らに免疫を作らせるという考えであった（※mild「軽度の」 immune「免疫」）。この方法で天然痘に感染した人のおよそ2%が死亡したが，それは通常感染した場合よりもずっと高い生存率であったため，この治療法が広まった。

4　そして1796年にエドワード゠ジェンナーという名の医師が新しい治療法を試みる

technique. It was already known that dairymaids, women whose job was to milk cows, were safe from smallpox if they had already contracted a similar but harmless cow disease called **cowpox**. Jenner (3)extracted pus from an infected blister on the hand of a dairymaid and rubbed it into **a small cut** on an eight-year-old boy's arm. The boy became briefly ill, then got better. A month later, Jenner rubbed pus from **a smallpox lesion** into a cut on the boy's arm, but the boy did not become sick. Jenner called his new treatment vaccination, from vacca, the Latin word for cow.

5 Almost 200 years after Edward Jenner **administered his first vaccination**, smallpox was finally eliminated by (D)a rigorous global campaign of quarantine and vaccination conducted by the WHO from 1967 to 1977. In 1980, the WHO officially declared that smallpox no longer existed outside of the laboratory. No cure for the disease was ever found, but thanks to Dr. Jenner, we have been free of the (4)menace of smallpox for almost 40 years.

>>> 解 説

☑速読攻略
設問 1 (1)・(2)の選択肢を先に読み，解答を探しながら 1 を読み進めよう。

1.
(1) the most dreaded diseases「最も恐ろしい病気」
　　1. contagious「感染性の」
　　2. deadly「死に至る」
　　3. feared「恐ろしい」⇒正解。
　　4. dangerous「危険な」
(2) the ensuing epidemic「その後に続く大流行」
　　1. preceding「先行する」
　　2. unexpected「思いがけない」
　　3. widespread「広がった」
　　4. following「続く」⇒正解。

☑速読攻略
設問 1 の(3)・(4)を解く前に，設問 2 の(A)・(B)の選択肢を頭に入れ，解答を探しながら 2 を読み進めよう。同時に設問 3 と 4 に目を通し，ともに 2 の内容なので，正解を探しながら読もう。

決心をした。牛の搾乳に従事していた女性は，天然痘に似ているが害はない牛痘と呼ばれる病気に一度罹患した経験があれば，天然痘にかかる心配はないということが当時もうすでに知られていた。ジェンナーは酪農婦の手の感染した水疱から膿疱を抽出し，8歳の少年の腕の小さな切り傷にすり込んだ。少年は少しの間気分が悪くなったが，その後回復した。1カ月後，ジェンナーは天然痘の病変から採取した膿疱をその少年の腕の切り傷にすり込んだが，少年は病気にならなかった。ジェンナーはこの新しい治療法を，ラテン語で牛という言葉，ワッカにちなみ，ワクチンと命名した（※ call A ～「A を～と呼ぶ」）。

5　エドワード゠ジェンナーが最初のワクチン接種を実施してからおよそ200年後，1967年から1977年にかけて世界保健機関（WHO）によって行われた徹底的な世界規模の検疫とワクチン接種のキャンペーンによって，天然痘はついに根絶された（※ administer vaccination「ワクチン接種を実施する」）。1980年に，世界保健機関は，研究室以外には天然痘がもはや存在しないと公式に宣言した（※根絶宣言が出された）。天然痘の治療薬は発見されていなかったが，ジェンナー医師のおかげで，およそ40年の間，我々は天然痘の脅威から免れている（※医療内容が急速に変わる例：アメリカ FDA（食品医薬品局）が，2021年6月に天然痘の治療薬ブリンシドフォビルを承認した）。

(3) extracted「抽出した」

　1. **obtained**「手に入れた」➡正解。

　2. isolated「単離した，分離した」

　3. blended「混ぜ合わせた」

　4. produced「生産した」

　medi pus「膿」リンパ球，大食細胞や組織成分の分解産物を含む。

9

イラスト 茨木保

You might isolate the virus from the pus, but not the pus from the blister.
「膿からウイルスを分離するだろうが，水疱から膿を分離しないだろう」

174

⑷ free of the menace of smallpox「天然痘の脅威を免れている」

  1. epidemic「大流行」

  2. mortality「死亡数，モータリティ」

  3. threat「脅威」➡正解。

  4. horror「恐怖」

2.

(A)

  1. incubate「潜伏する」➡正解。

   medi incubation period「潜伏期間」 latent period「潜伏感染期」

  2. conceal「～を隠す」

  3. migrate「移住する」

  4. modify「～を修正する」

(B)

  1. injury「ケガ」

  2. complications「合併症」➡正解。

   medi cause complications「合併症を引き起こす」

  3. toxicity「毒性」

  4. disorders「障害，疾患」

☑速読攻略

設問 2 (C)を読み，解答を考えながら，③を読もう。設問 5 も確認し，同時に解きながら読み進めよう。

(C) the（　　）of variolation（「人痘接種〔種痘〕」）became popular
接種＝治療方法なので 2「実施」が正解となる。

  1. exercise「行使」

  2. practice「実施」➡正解。

  3. problem「問題」

  4. treatment「治療」

(D)「天然痘はついに（　　）キャンペーンによって撲滅された」

  1. an intentional「意図的な」

  2. a challenging「困難な」

  3. an ambiguous「あいまいな」

  4. a rigorous「徹底的な，厳格な」➡正解。

3．「天然痘は通常どのように感染したか」➡通常の感染経路については②を参照。

1.「動物との接触感染」

2.「飛沫感染」➡正解。

　②*ll.* 2-3 The most common method of transmission was inhalation …と一致。

3.「物の表面を触ること」

4.「不衛生な洗濯されていない物」

4．「天然痘の感染の特徴的な指標（症状）は何か」➡主な症状については②を参照。

1.「全身に水疱」➡正解。

　②*ll.* 10-11 The rash would then spread over …と一致。

2.「初期症状はインフルエンザに似た症状」

3.「最初の2週間は無症状」

4.「骨や臓器にも広がり，死に至る」

5．「なぜ故意に天然痘に感染しようとしたのか」➡③を参照。

1.「感染者の膿疱から天然痘に感染すると危険がないと信じられていた」➡不記載。

2.「感染した痂皮から弱い天然痘に感染した場合は，膿疱の傷跡は残らない」➡不記載。

3.「種痘の症状は天然痘の症状より軽い」➡不記載。

4.「通常よりも弱い天然痘を発現し，生存すれば天然痘から守られた」➡正解。

　③*ll.* 5-6 this would give them a mild form… と一致。

6．「ジェンナー医師はどのように天然痘のワクチンを作ったのか」➡④を参照。

1.「牛痘に感染している牛から材料を取り出した」➡不記載。

2.「天然痘に感染している少年の腕の切り傷から膿疱を抽出した」➡少年ではなく，牛痘に感染した酪農婦の手の水疱から膿疱を取り出したので，不一致。

3.「免疫のある安全な疾患の感染者の傷口から液体を取り出した」➡正解。

　④*ll.* 4-5 Jenner extracted pus from …「（牛痘に感染している）酪農婦の水疱から，膿を抽出した」と一致。

4.「天然痘の水疱から取った膿疱と，牛痘の水疱から取った膿疱を合わせて，少年の腕にすり込んだ」➡不記載。

7．「ジェンナー医師のワクチンの試験方法は倫理的だと思うか，それとも非倫理的だと思うか。自分の意見を支持する理由を少なくとも1つ挙げよ」

8歳の子供を被験者として選んだことに対して倫理的かどうかを考える。

9

倫理的であるとする解答例）

These days, before a medicine is used, clinical trials are carried out and the medicine is used after its efficacy has been demonstrated. However, if we consider the social conditions at the time, the sacrifice of one person was unavoidable.

「現在では，実用化する前に臨床試験が行われ，その有効性が実証されてから実用化されるが，当時の社会的背景を考えると，一個人の犠牲は仕方がない」

非倫理的であるとする解答例）

An eight-year-old child is thought to have a long future and a weak immune system, so we ought to choose adults who are able to consent to the experiment as subjects.

「8歳の子供は将来も長く，免疫も弱いと考えられるため，被験者としては，成人で，試験に同意を得られた人を選ぶべきである」

知って得する医学用語の成り立ち

　医学用語は，接頭語，接尾語がくっついたり，語が組み合わされたりしてできています。たとえば，

　　　　cavity は「**腔**」という，「**身体の空間の部分**」を表す語で，

　　　　oral は「**口の**」，

　　　　nasal は「**鼻の**」を表します。

　これらを組み合わせると，

　　　　oral cavity「**口腔**」，nasal cavity「**鼻腔**」となります。

　この **cavity** のような語を覚えておくと，医系英文を読む際に役立ちます。

類推例

たとえば，pleural cavity という用語が出てきたとき，**cavity** が「身体の空間の部分」を表すことを知っていれば，**pleural** の意味を知らなくても，「どこかの部位の空洞になったところ」とイメージすることができます。ちなみに，pleural cavity は「**胸膜腔**」です。

覚えておこう！

□ **cavity**「**腔**」　◆ nasal cavity「鼻腔」

□ **duct**「**管**」　◆ bile duct「胆管」

□ **tube**「**管**」　◆ fallopian tube「卵管」［fəlóupiən t(j)úːb］

□ **cord**「神経や腱などの**索状**（よられたひも状の）**組織**」

　　　　　　　◆ belly cord「へその緒」

□ **vessel**「**管**」　◆ blood vessel「血管」　◆ lymphatic vessel「リンパ管」

接尾語

□ **-itis**「**炎症**」　◆ gastritis「胃炎」［ɡæstráitis］（gastro-「胃の」）

接頭語

□ **hemo-**「**血液の**」（hemoglobin「ヘモグロビン」から簡単に覚えられますね）

　　　　　　◆ hemorrhage「大出血」［héməridʒ］

9

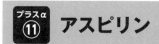

1　In many countries, **analgesic painkillers** are available in many retail outlets, from the downtown pharmacy to the neighborhood corner store, and even in some supermarkets. **Over-the-counter** (OTC) **painkillers** are those drugs that **can be self-administered** for short periods of time without the direction of a doctor. Accessible, inexpensive and easy to take, OTCs have their advantages, but there are drawbacks as well.

2　The most widely used analgesic medication in the world today is the OTC painkiller, **aspirin**. **The active ingredient** in aspirin is **acetylsalicylic acid, an estimated 40,000 tons of which is consumed** each year, ranking it second only to alcohol as the most consumed drug in the world.

3　Aspirin is used to **relieve minor aches and pains**, to **reduce fever**, and as a medication to **decrease swelling**. As it serves as a type of blood thinner, aspirin **is** also **used long-term, at low doses,** to help prevent **heart attacks** in people at high risk.

4　This drug **was** first **isolated** by Felix Hoffmann, a chemist with the German company, Bayer, in 1899. The name "aspirin" was created by Bayer, and derived from *Spiraea ulmaria*, the botanical name for **the herbal plant** known as meadowsweet in English. Hoffmann discovered that this plant was a good source of acetylsalicylic acid.

5　Plant extracts had been used to treat **headaches, pains,** and **fevers** since antiquity. For example, the father of modern medicine, Hippocrates, who lived between 460 BC and 377 BC, left historical records describing the use of **powders** made from the bark and leaves of the willow tree to **treat these symptoms**.

6　Hoffmann's drug rapidly proved popular in the first half of the 20th century, but its profitability soon led to fierce competition, and its market share declined after the introduction of its main rivals, paracetamol in 1956, and ibuprofen in 1969. Aspirin sales **revived considerably** in the last decades of the 20th century, and remain strong in the 21st century, largely because of its widespread use as **a preventive treatment for heart attacks**. It has also been suggested that taking aspirin before air travel may **decrease the risk** of deep-vein thrombosis (DVT). This condition **is caused by** the long period of sitting

1　多くの国では，鎮痛剤はダウンタウンの薬局から，近隣の街角の店や一部のスーパーマーケットに至るまで，多くの小売店で入手可能である。**市販薬の鎮痛剤は医師の指示がなくても，短期間自身で服用できる**（※ administered「投与される」という受動態を能動態で訳すと自然）薬剤である。簡単に入手でき，安価で，服用が容易であるので，市販薬は利点があるが，欠点も同様にある。

2　今日，もっとも広く服用される鎮痛薬は，市販の鎮痛剤の**アスピリン**である。アスピリンの活性成分は，アセチルサリチル酸で，アスピリンの毎年の**推定消費量は，年間4万トン**で，世界でもっとも消費される薬剤として，アルコールに次いで第2位にランクされている。

3　アスピリンは軽度の疼痛を緩和し，解熱，および腫れ〔腫脹〕の軽減に用いられる。アスピリンはまた，血液を薄めるので，心臓発作のリスクが高い人に予防の手助けの目的で，長期低用量で服用される。

4　1899年，ドイツのバイエル薬品（株式会社）の化学者であったフェリックス＝ホフマンが初めてこの薬を**分離した**（※受動態を能動態で訳すと自然）。その名称「アスピリン」は，バイエル薬品によって名付けられた。英語の meadowsweet（※「シモツケソウ」）として知られる薬草の学術名 *Spiraea ulmaria* に由来する。ホフマンは，この薬草がアセチルサリチル酸のよい抽出源であることを発見した。

5　植物からの抽出物は，古代から，頭痛，疼痛，熱の治療に用いられてきた。たとえば，紀元前460年から紀元前377年に生存した，「近代医学の父」であるヒポクラテスは，これらの症状の治療に，柳の樹皮と葉から作った粉末の使用を記述した歴史的な記録を残している。

6　ホフマンの薬は，20世紀前半に急速に広まったことが明らかとなっているが，その収益性は直ちに，市場の厳しい競争に巻き込まれ，その主要なライバルである，1956年のパラセタモールおよび1969年のイブプロフェンの導入後〔が出回り〕，ホフマンの薬の市場占有率は減少した。アスピリンの販売は，20世紀終わりの数十年にかなり回復し，21世紀においても好調のままである。その主な理由は，心臓発作の予防薬として，広く服用されているためである。飛行機旅行の前にアスピリンを服用すると，深部静脈血栓症（DVT）のリスクを低減する可能性も示唆されている。DVTは，長時間運動せず，座ったままでいることで引き起こされ，飛行機旅行その

without exercise, not the air travel itself.

[7] Recently, fresh **evidence** suggests that **the over-the-counter pain reliever** may be a powerful tool in **cancer prevention** as well. A 2010 study by Oxford University, involving over 25,000 patients, showed that taking **a small daily dose** of aspirin for four to eight years substantially reduces mortality from a range of common cancers by at least 20% .

[8] However, despite its many apparent benefits, consumers need to be careful about **taking too much aspirin**, as they should be about any other painkiller, as it **has proven side effects. Taking overly large doses** too often can lead to stomach problems, as well as **dizziness** and **excessive sweating**.

もののせいではない。

7　最近，新しいエビデンスによると，市販の鎮痛剤は，癌予防においても強力な手段である可能性が示唆されている。25,000名を超える患者を対象に行った，オックスフォード大学の2010年の研究では，4年から8年アスピリンを毎日少量服用すると，実質上，広範な一般的な癌による死亡率が少なくとも20パーセント低減することが示唆された。

8　しかし，その数多くの明白な恩恵にもかかわらず，アスピリンには副作用が証明されているため，他の鎮痛剤についてと同様，消費者は，過度のアスピリンの服用には注意する必要がある。過度の量をあまりに頻繁に服用すると，めまいや過剰な発汗だけでなく，胃の疾患が生じる場合がある。

9

日本大学（医学部）　　　　　　　　　　　⏱目標3分　400語

① In my own speciality of **colorectal surgery**, there are only about 10 national robotic programmes. I have a niche within **colorectal surgery dealing with the pelvic floor** and probably have performed the most **robotic pelvic floor operations** in the country. In a sudden impulse of vanity, I attempted to show this fact off to my mother, who asked, with complete sincerity, if I was 'not good enough to operate without one'.

② In the last 10 years, there really has only been one type of **surgical robot** available, going by the fantastic name of da Vinci. It consists of **a surgeon console** and a slave unit with all robotic surgery performed using **keyhole techniques** (that is, involving a few **small incisions in the abdominal wall** through which a miniature video camera and surgical instruments are **inserted**).

③ I start all operations just like a normal keyhole procedure and then, when everything is ready, **the robot slave unit** is placed next to the patient. This slave unit has robotic arms. These arms are attached to **keyhole instruments** that in turn enter the patient's body through small incisions **at different sites**. I will then leave the patient and go and sit in the surgeon console, which is usually at the side of **the operating theatre** (but can be miles away). I use hand and foot controls in the surgeon console to control the slave unit arms and instruments to operate.

④ The beauty of the robot is that it allows **3D vision**, as opposed to most **normal keyhole surgery** utilising **2D**, and this improved depth perception(S) benefits(V) the surgery when space is limited. If I've drunk too much coffee the robotic system **cuts out my tremor**. Additional precision comes from the scaling down of my hand movements: that is, if I move my hands 6 cm in the surgeon console, the robotic instruments only move 1 cm. Normal keyhole instrument tips have a limited range of movement, but robotic instruments have similar dexterity to the human wrist, making tasks such as throwing a knot easy.

⑤ There are limitations to using **the robot for surgery**. In **abdominal surgery**, **normal keyhole surgeons** can move from one part of the abdomen to another **with ease**, whereas robotic platforms are cumbersome and clumsy in this regard. Research has only shown one type of surgery (**prostate cancer**

1 　私自身の専門分野である結腸直腸手術では，国産ロボットプログラム〔内視鏡手術支援ロボット〕は約10しかない。私の得意分野は骨盤底を扱う結腸直腸手術である。そして国内で最も多くロボット（支援）骨盤底手術を行っているだろう。突然衝動的に虚栄心にかられて，私はこの事実を母に自慢しようとしたが，母は本当にまじめな表情で，私が「ロボットを用いないで充分な手術ができないのか」と尋ねた（※ show off「見せびらかす」）。

2 　ここ10年間，たった1種類の手術ロボットだけが利用可能で，ダ・ヴィンチという素晴らしい名前で通っている。それはサージョンコンソールと，スレーブユニットとから構成されていて，すべてのロボット外科手術は鍵穴技術〔キーホール技術〕を用いて行われる（つまり，非常に小さいビデオカメラと外科手術器具を腹壁を通って挿入し，腹壁に2，3の小切開を伴っている（※ incision「切開」））。

3 　私は，通常の鍵穴手術の手順のように，すべての手術を始め，完全に準備が整うと，ロボットスレーブユニットを患者の横に置く（※受動態を能動態で訳す）。このスレーブユニットにはロボットアームがあり，これらのアームはキーホール器具に取り付けられている。このキーホール器具を，今度は異なる場所で，小切開部を通して患者の体内に入れる。私はそれから患者から離れ，サージョンコンソールに行って座る。それはたいてい手術室の側にある（しかし距離を離すこともできる）。私はスレーブユニットアームと手術用器具をコントロールするために，サージョンコンソールで手足のコントロールを用いる〔手足の動きを操る〕。

4 　ロボットの長所は，2D映像を用いる通常のキーホール手術とは対照的に，ロボットが3D映像を可能にすることである。この立体感の認識が改善されて〔改善された立体感の認識(S)〕空間が限られている（狭い空間では）と手術に有利になる(V)。もし私がコーヒーを飲み過ぎていた場合は，ロボットシステムが私の震えを無くす。手の動きを減らすことで，さらに精度が向上する。つまり，私がサージョンコンソールで手を6センチ動かしても，ロボットの器具は1センチしか動かない。通常のキーホール器具の先端は，動作に限界範囲がある〔作動範囲に限界がある〕が，ロボット器具は人間の手首と同じ器用さ〔正確さ〕があり，糸結びといったような作業を容易にする（※ make A easy「Aを容易にする」）。

5 　手術用ロボットを使うには限界がある。腹部手術においては，人が行う普通のキーホール手術の外科医は，一部の腹部から別の場所へと容易に（術野を）移動することができるが，ロボットのプラットホーム〔基盤〕は，この点において，面倒で使いづらいのである。研究により，一種の手術（前立腺癌の手術）だけはロボット手術が

184

surgery）to be better robotically. Other procedures seem to have no **better outcome**.

［From Meet your new surgeon: da Vinci the robot, Spectator Life on May 12, 2016 by Shahab Siddiqi］

手術用ロボット（The Robot for Surgery）

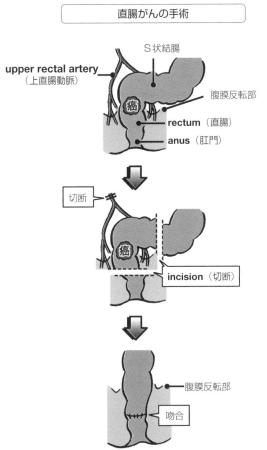

直腸がんの手術

S状結腸

upper rectal artery
（上直腸動脈）

腹膜反転部

癌

rectum（直腸）

anus（肛門）

切断

癌

incision（切断）

腹膜反転部

吻合

※吻合とは，切除し残った部分をつなぐこと。

イラスト 茨木保

より良いことが示唆された。他の処置はより良い結果は得られないようである（※
outcome「結果」）。

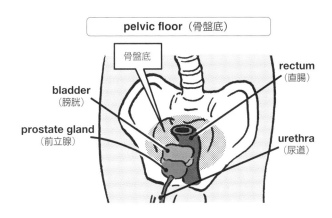

pelvic floor（骨盤底）

骨盤底

bladder
（膀胱）

prostate gland
（前立腺）

rectum
（直腸）

urethra
（尿道）

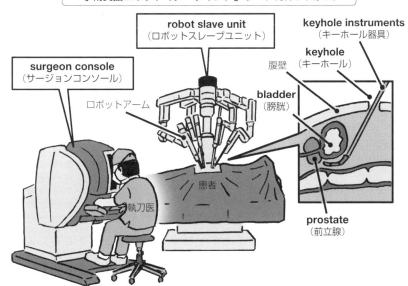

手術支援ロボット「ダ・ヴィンチ」サージカルシステム

robot slave unit
（ロボットスレーブユニット）

keyhole instruments
（キーホール器具）

keyhole
（キーホール）

腹壁

surgeon console
（サージョンコンソール）

ロボットアーム

bladder
（膀胱）

患者

執刀医

prostate
（前立腺）

9

ペニシリン

🕐 目標 4 分　336 語

① The several kinds of penicillin **synthesized** by various species of the mold *Penicillium* may be divided into two classes: **the naturally occurring penicillins** (those formed during the process of mold fermentation) and **the semisynthetic penicillins** (those in which the structure of **a chemical substance** —— **6 aminopenicillanic acid** —— found in all penicillins is altered in various ways). Because it is possible to change the characteristics of the antibiotic, different types of penicillin are produced for different therapeutic purposes.

② The naturally occurring penicillins, **penicillin G (benzylpenicillin)** and **penicillin V (phenoxymethylpenicillin)**, are still **used clinically**. Because of **its poor stability in acid**, much of penicillin G is broken down as it passes through the stomach; as a result of this characteristic, it must be given by intramuscular injection, which limits its usefulness. Penicillin V, on the other hand, typically is given orally; it is more resistant to digestive acids than penicillin G.

③ All penicillins work in the same way —— namely, by **inhibiting the bacterial enzymes** responsible for cell wall synthesis in **replicating microorganisms** and by activating other enzymes to break down the protective wall of the microorganism. As a result, they are effective only against microorganisms that are actively replicating and producing cell walls; they also therefore do not harm human cells (which fundamentally lack cell walls).

④ Some strains of previously susceptible bacteria, such as *Staphylococcus*, have developed a specific resistance to the naturally occurring penicillins; these bacteria(S) either produce(V1) **β-lactamase**, an enzyme that disrupts the internal structure of penicillin and thus destroys the antimicrobial action of the drug, or they(S) lack(V2) cell wall receptors for penicillin, greatly reducing the ability of the drug to enter bacterial cells. This has led to the production of the penicillinase-resistant penicillins (second-generation penicillins). While able to resist the activity of β-lactamase, **these agents** are not as effective against *Staphylococcus* as the natural penicillins, and they are associated with an increased risk for **liver toxicity**. Moreover, some **strains of *Staphylococcus*** have become resistant to **penicillinase-resistant penicillins**; an example is methicillin-resistant ***Staphylococcus* aureus (MRSA)**.

[From Penicillin, ENCYCLOPÆDIA BRITANNICA]

1　多種の「ペニシリン」属によって合成される数種類のペニシリンは，大きく2種類に分類されるだろう。すなわち，天然型ペニシリン（カビの発酵過程で形成されたもの）と半合成ペニシリン（すべてのペニシリンにみられる化学物質6-アミノペニシラン酸の構造をさまざまな方法で変える）である。抗生物質の特性を変更するのは可能なので，異なる種類のペニシリンを異なる治療目的で生成する（※受動態を能動態で訳す）。

2　天然型ペニシリンであるペニシリンG（ベンジルペニシリン）とペニシリンV（フェノキシメチルペニシリン）は，現在も臨床で用いられている。ペニシリンGの多くは（胃）酸で不安定であるため，胃を<u>通過する</u>間に<u>分解される</u>。この特性の結果として，筋肉注射で投与しなくてはならず，そのことが，有用性を限定的にしている。一方，ペニシリンVは，通常経口投与され，ペニシリンGより，消化管の酸性（胃酸）に対して<u>耐性がある</u>（※ be given「投与する」）。

3　すべてのペニシリンは，同様に作用する。つまり，微生物を複製する際の細胞壁合成を<u>担う</u>細菌酵素を抑制し，また，微生物の防壁を<u>分解する</u>別の酵素を活性化することによって作用する（※ inhibit「抑制する」　構文説明：in the same way by *A* and by *B*）。その結果，ペニシリンは，細胞壁を活発に複製し，生成している微生物に対してのみ有効である。つまり，ペニシリンは（基本的に細胞壁がない）ヒト細胞には害を及ぼさない。

4　「ブドウ球菌」といった，以前<u>感染しやすかった</u>細菌株は，天然型ペニシリンへの<u>特有の耐性</u>を発現しているものがある。すなわち，これらの細菌は(S)，ペニシリンの内部構造を崩壊し，それが故に薬剤の抗菌作用を破壊する〔なくす〕酵素であるβ-ラクタマーゼを生成する(V1)か，または，ペニシリンに対する細胞壁受容体を欠損し(V2)，細菌細胞に侵入する薬剤能力を大幅に低減させるかのいずれかである（※構文説明：, greatly reducing は分詞構文で，「その結果大幅に…を低減する」　β-lactamase, an enzyme that disrupts…「β-ラクタマーゼ，すなわち…を破壊する酵素」　antimicrobial action「抗菌作用」）。この結果，ペニシリナーゼ耐性ペニシリン（第2世代ペニシリン）の作成につながった。この製剤はβ-ラクタマーゼの活性への耐性になりえるが，天然ペニシリンほど，「ブドウ球菌」へ有効<u>ではなく</u>，肝臓毒性のリスク増加と<u>関連している</u>（※ the activity「活性」）。さらに，ブドウ球菌株には，ペニシリナーゼ耐性ペニシリンへの耐性になるものもある。例えば，メチシリン耐性黄色ブドウ球菌（MRSA）など。

9

巻末付録 医学論文読解のための必須単語

● 患　者
- subject「被験者，被検体」
- case「症例」
- infected person「感染者」

● 期間，時点
- incubation period「潜伏期」
- initiation「最初」 ◆ at the initiation of medication「薬剤投与開始時」
- onset「初め」 ◆ the onset of a disease「病気の始まり」

● 症　状
- symptom「主観的症状」pain, headache など患者しかわからない症状。
  A subjective feelings or sensations a patient has
- sign「客観的症状」fever, vomiting など外から見てわかる症状。
  An objective phenomenon which can be observed by another person
- manifestation「症状などの発現」

● 「妨げる」「止める」
- disturb「～を妨げる」
  ◆ sleep disturbance「睡眠障害」
- block ／ obstruct ／ hinder ／ impede ／ interrupt ／ hamper「～を阻止する，妨害する」妨害の結果悪影響を及ぼす。
  ◆ Blood clots block［obstruct ／ hinder ／ impede ／ interrupt］the blood flow.「血餅によって，血流が遮断される」
  ◆ Nicotine causes blood vessels to constrict, which hampers the flow of blood.「ニコチンは血管を収縮させ，血流を妨げる」
- halt ／ stop「～を中止する」
  ◆ halt the administration of the vaccine「ワクチン投与を中止する」
- inhibit ／ prohibit「～を禁止する，抑制する」
  ◆ inhibit the reaction（＝inhibition）「反応抑制」
- interfere with ～「～に干渉する」
  ◆ interfere with the reaction「反応に干渉する」

☐ **intervene in ～**「～に干渉する」状況をよくするために用いる。

◆ seek for medical intervention「医療介入を求める」

☐ **curb ／ regulate**「（コントロールできるように）～を抑制する，調整する」

"curb" always means "reduce", while "regulate" can include "increase."

◆ curb［regulate］blood sugar levels「血糖値を抑制する」

● 「進める」「活性化する」「誘発する」

☐ **proceed ／ promote ／ urge**「～を進める，促進する，促す」

◆ The reaction will proceed ／ S promote the reaction ／ S urge *A* to *do*「*A* が～するのを促す」

☐ **stimulate ／ activate**「～を刺激する，活性化する」

◆ stimulate ／ activate the immune system「免疫系を刺激／活性化する」

☐ **induce ／ trigger**「～を誘導する，～の引き金〔原因〕となる」

● 「致死率」「死亡率」「罹患率」「有病率」

☐ **case-fatality rate**「致死率」

$$致死率 = \frac{疾病による死亡者数／年}{疾病の罹患者数／年} \times 100$$

☐ **mortality rate ／ death rate**「モータリティ レイト」特定の期間の特定の地域での死亡率。

$$死亡率 = \frac{一定期間内死亡者数}{総人口} \times 100$$

☐ **morbidity**「罹患率」手術などによる合併症の発生率。

☐ **incidence**「インシデンス」疾患の新規発生率。

$$インシデンス = \frac{新患者発生数}{疾患にかかる危険のある人口集団}$$

☐ **prevalence rate**「有病率」

$$有病率 = \frac{一定期間疾患を有している数}{人口集団}$$

● カタカナ表記例

☐ **vector**「ベクター」

☐ **evidence**「エビデンス」

☐ **monitoring**「モニタリングする」監視する。観察し，記録する。

☐ **screening**「スクリーニングする」特定の条件下で，複数の対象の中から，条件に合致する対象を選別する。ふるいにかける。

☐ **splicing**「スプライシング」

● 「有効性」「効果」「評価」
☐ **efficacy** ／ **validity** ／ **effectiveness**「有効性，効果」
☐ **evaluation** ／ **assessment**「評価」
☐ **verification**「検証，実証」

● 系，部位
☐ **Respiratory system**「呼吸器系」
☐ **Circulatory system**「循環器系」
☐ **Nervous system**「神経系」
☐ **Reproductive system**「生殖器系」
☐ **Immune system**「免疫系」
☐ **Digestive system**「消化器系」

● 病　気
☐ **ailment** ／ **disease** ／ **malady**「病気」
　◆ fight against［ward off］a disease「病気と闘う」
☐ **ail**「苦しめる」
☐ **disorder**「疾患，障害」
　◆ mental disorder「精神障害」
☐ **disability**「障害」
　◆ physical disability「身体障碍」
☐ **deficiency** ／ **defect**「欠損」
　◆ gene defect「遺伝子欠損」　◆ genetic deficiency「遺伝病」
☐ **disturbance**「疾患，障害」
　◆ sleep disturbance［disorder］「睡眠障害」
☐ **impairment**「障害」
　◆ visual impairment「視力障害」
☐ **culprit**「敵」比喩的に「病原体，病因」に用いる。

● 感　染
☐ **epidemic**「大流行」
☐ **pandemic**「（世界的）流行病」
☐ **outbreak**「アウトブレイク」
☐ **plague**「疫病，伝染病」

□**infectious disease**「感染症，伝染病」
◆ infection「感染」 ◆ infected person「感染者」
□**contagious disease**「伝染病」

● 注 射
□**inoculate**「接種する」
◆ inoculate against typhoid ／ give an inoculation for typhoid「腸チフスの予防接種をする」
□**shot** ／ **injection**「注射」
◆ give a shot ／ give an injection「注射を打つ」
□**immunization** ／ **vaccination**「予防接種」
◆ give an immunization shot［a vaccination］「予防接種をする」
□**vaccine**「ワクチン」
◆ give a vaccine ／ get vaccinated「ワクチンを接種する」
◆ develop a new vaccine「新しいワクチンを開発する」
◆ get［vaccinated］for measles「はしかの予防接種をうける」

● 菌
□**agent**「菌，薬剤」
□**strain**「① （菌）株 ②緊張，緊張させる」
◆ drug resistant strain「薬剤耐性株」
□**virus**「ウイルス」
□**bacteria**「細菌」ウイルスとは異なるので注意。
◆ drug resistant bacteria「薬剤耐性菌」
□**pathogen** ／ **germ**「病原菌」ウイルス，細菌，真菌などの総称。
□**fungus**「真菌」
□**mold** ／ **mould**「カビ」

医学論文読解のための必須単語クイズ

Part 1

問1） 下の枠内から適切な語句を選び，記号を括弧に入れなさい。

1. (　　) nausea and vomiting　**2.** (　　) dyspnea　**3.** (　　) constipation

4. (　　) diarrhea　**5.** (　　) persistent cough

6. (　　) chest pain　**7.** (　　) slight [mild] fever

8. (　　) moderate fever　**9.** (　　) high fever

10. (　　) stabbing pain　**11.** (　　) arthritis

> (a) 中等度の熱　(b) 微熱　(c) 高熱　(d) さすような痛み　(e) 胸痛
> (f) 便秘　(g) 下痢　(h) 呼吸困難　(i) 持続性咳　(j) 吐き気と嘔吐
> (k) 関節炎 (-itis 炎症)

▶ 上記の語句を用いて，I have（名詞：症状，病名）「症状がある」のようにいう。
また，I feel（形容詞または名詞）で状態を表す。
I feel lightheaded [painful ／ feverish].「ふらつきます／痛みがあります／熱っぽいです」

問2） 下の枠内から適切な語句を選び，記号を括弧に入れなさい。

1. We report a (　　　) of diabetes mellitus in a middle-aged male.
「中年男性の糖尿病の症例を報告する」

2. 200 (　　　) took part in the randomized control study.
「200 名の被験者が 無作為化比較試験に参加した」

3. The tPA treatment is administered within 90 minutes of symptom (　　　).
「tPA 療法＝血栓溶解療法（thrombolytic therapy）を症状の発症から 90 分以内に施行する」

4. If a (　　　) with hypertension eats food high in salt, the blood sodium increases, resulting in higher blood pressure.
「高血圧の患者が塩分の高い食事をすると，血中ナトリウム値が上昇し，さらに血圧が上昇する」

> (a) patient　(b) subjects ／ research participants　(c) onset　(d) case

> **問1）**　**1**—(j)　**2**—(h)　**3**—(f)　**4**—(g)　**5**—(i)　**6**—(e)　**7**—(b)　**8**—(a)
> 　　　　**9**—(c)　**10**—(d)　**11**—(k)
> **問2）**　**1**—(d)　**2**—(b)　**3**—(c)　**4**—(a)

194

Part 2

問 1) 下の枠内から適切な語句を選び，記号を括弧に入れなさい。

1. (　　) 予防する　　　　2. (　　) 症状がでる　　　3. (　　) 診察する
4. (　　) 問診　　　　　　5. (　　) 検査をする　　　6. (　　) 除外する
7. (　　) 同定する　　　　8. (　　) 決定する　　　　9. (　　) 診断する
10. (　　) 治療する　　　11. (　　) 薬剤投与する　12. (　　) 塗り薬をつける
13. (　　) 手術を施行する　14. (　　) 経過観察をする　15. (　　) 副作用
16. (　　) 合併症

(a) prevent　　　　　(b) consult　　　　　(c) examine
(d) identify　　　　　(e) complications　　　(f) side［adverse］effects
(g) rule out　　　　　(h) determine　　　　(i) treat
(j) perform［conduct／undertake］surgery　(k) administer medicine［a drug］
(l) signs and symptoms develop［appear／occur］　(m) apply an ointment
(n) diagnose　　　　(o) history taking　　　(p) follow up

問 2) 下の枠内から適切なものを選び，記号を括弧に入れなさい。

1. (　　) 傾向　　　　2. (　　) 分類　　3. (　　) 特徴
4. (　　) 部位・領域　5. (　　) 体質

(a) classification／categorization
(b) region／area／site／location
(c) disposition／inclination／propensity
(d) constitution
(e) feature／characteristics／trait

問 1)　1—(a)　2—(l)　3—(b)　4—(o)　5—(c)　6—(g)　7—(d)　8—(h)　9—(n)
　　　　10—(i)　11—(k)　12—(m)　13—(j)　14—(p)　15—(f)　16—(e)
問 2)　1—(c)　2—(a)　3—(e)　4—(b)　5—(d)

Part 3

問 1) 下の枠内から適切な語句を選び，記号を括弧に入れなさい。

1. (　　) 重篤な合併症　**2.** (　　) 重度の感染症（重症感染症）

3. (　　) 慢性症状　**4.** (　　) 軽度の疼痛

5. (　　) 中等度の症状　**6.** (　　) 急性呼吸器感染症

(a) mild pain　　(b) serious complications　　(c) moderate symptoms
(d) acute respiratory infection　　(e) severe infection　　(f) chronic symptom

問 2) 下の枠内から適切な語句を選び，記号を括弧に入れなさい

1. The usual adult (　　　) is 60 mg of loxoprofen sodium orally three times a day.

2. The CDC recommends a third (　　　) of an mRNA COVID-19 vaccine.

3. (　　　) an eye drop 3 or 4 times a day.

4. A patient (　　　) the surgery.

5. A doctor (　　　) the surgery.

6. A doctor (　　　) a fever reducer.

(a) dose　　(b) dosage　　(c) apply　　(d) receives／undergoes
(e) administers　　(f) conducts／performs／undertakes

問 1)　**1** —(b)　　**2** —(e)　　**3** —(f)　　**4** —(a)　　**5** —(c)　　**6** —(d)
問 2)　**1** —(b)　　**2** —(a)　　**3** —(c)　　**4** —(d)　　**5** —(f)　　**6** —(e)

Part 4

問1） 左の日本語の意味の単語を下の枠内からすべて選び，記号で答えなさい。

1. 増加する　　increase, rise, enhance

2. 減少する　　decrease, drop, reduce, slide into

3. 無くす

4. 変化する　　change, alter

(a) eliminate	(b) shrink	(c) boost	(d) delete	(e) escalate
(f) diminish	(g) soar	(h) plunge	(i) eradicate	(j) decline
(k) elevate	(l) sag	(m) convert		

▶ 上記の動詞を修飾する副詞：significantly, greatly, widely, considerably, rapidly

問2） 下の枠内から，1～5のProcedureに関する語句を選び，記号で答えなさい。

1. 同定する

2. スクリーニングする（審査する，ふるい分ける）

3. モニターする

4. 追跡調査をする

5. 穿刺する

(a) puncture	(b) identify	(c) screen	(d) follow up	(e) monitor

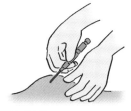

イラスト 茨木保

穿刺とは，血液や体液，細胞などの採取のために，体外から血管，体腔内，内臓に針を刺すこと。

問1）　**1**—(c)・(e)・(g)・(k)　**2**—(b)・(f)・(h)・(j)・(l)　**3**—(a)・(d)・(i)　**4**—(m)
問2）　**1**—(b)　**2**—(c)　**3**—(e)　**4**—(d)　**5**—(a)

Part 5

以下の医学英単語は一般英語と意味が異なります。

問1） 左の英語の語句の意味を右の日本語から選び，記号で答えなさい。

1.	acute	A.	組織
2.	chronic cough	B.	臓器
3.	admit	C.	慢性咳
4.	discharge	D.	急性の
5.	administer	E.	投与する
6.	tissue	F.	入院させる
7.	organ	G.	退院させる，分泌（物），分泌する
8.	membrane	H.	点眼薬をさす，軟膏を塗る
9.	apply eye drops／apply ointment	I.	膜

問2） 左の英語の語句の意味を右の日本語から選び，記号で答えなさい。

1.	solution	A.	伝導する（伝導度）
2.	resolution	B.	調剤，製剤
3.	dissolve	C.	溶かす
4.	preparation	D.	溶液
5.	concentration	E.	濃度
6.	constrict／shrink／contract	F.	拡大する，緩む
7.	relax／enlarge	G.	収縮する
8.	conduct（conductivity）	H.	解像度，解決

問1）　1―D　2―C　3―F　4―G　5―E　6―A　7―B　8―I　9―H
問2）　1―D　2―H　3―C　4―B　5―E　6―G　7―F　8―A

Part 6

以下の医学英単語は一般英語と意味が異なります。

問1） 左の英語の語句の意味を右の日本語から選び，記号で答えなさい。

1. opening		A.	反応，反応する
2. incision		B.	被験者
3. reaction／respond		C.	穴，開口部
4. reversible		D.	切開
5. positive		E.	収縮する
6. negative		F.	陰性の
7. subject		G.	陽性の
8. constrict		H.	可逆的な
9. blockage／obstruction／occlusion		I.	狭窄
10. stenosis／narrowing		J.	閉塞

以下の医学英単語は体内物質の移動によく用いられます。

問2） 左の英語の語句の意味を右の日本語から選び，記号で答えなさい。

1. permeate		A.	干渉，介入
2. penetrate／go through		B.	移動する
3. spread to／radiate		C.	分泌する
4. circulate		D.	～へ広がる
5. travel to／move to		E.	浸透する
6. secrete		F.	突き抜ける
7. seep in／seep out		G.	染み込む，染み出る
8. invade／infiltrate		H.	侵入する，湿潤する
9. intervention		I.	循環する

問1） 1－C 2－D 3－A 4－H 5－G 6－F 7－B 8－E 9－J 10－I
問2） 1－E 2－F 3－D 4－I 5－B 6－C 7－G 8－H 9－A

赤本メディカルシリーズ
Akahon Medical Series

私立医大の英語〔長文読解編〕

3訂版

別冊問題編

矢印の方向に引くと
本体から取り外せます

ゆっくり丁寧に取り外しましょう

教学社

·· CONTENTS ··

　本書では，重要な医系テーマごとに，9つの章(**Chapter**)に分類しています。それぞれの **Chapter** 内には，私大医学部の入試問題から厳選した問題を掲載しています。

　出題英文が難化する傾向にある私大医学部の入試対策として，速く読むことを意識した訓練を積んでおくことが，極めて重要です。

長文読解 に加えて，**速読訓練** として，*Science* や *Nature* など，医学論文レベルの英文も扱っています。発展学習として是非活用してください。

　★は掲載英文の難易度を示します。おおむね読みやすい英文から順に配列しています。取り組む際の参考にしてください。

★★	やや易	★★★	標準
★★★★	やや難	★★★★★	超難問

問題の英文について

一部書かれた年代が古い英文も含みますが，本書では過去の大学入試で出題された問題を素材とし，医学において普遍性のあるテーマを精選しています。

別冊　問題編

Chapter 1 » 医　療
Medicine

🎓 自治医科大学（医学部）　　　　　　　　　　　⏰ 目標 15 分

次の英文を読み，1 〜 8 の問題に最も適した答えを選べ。

　　The communication skills of health care professionals can make their *interactions with patients easier and bring about a better treatment result. Medical professionals need to be good at both verbal and nonverbal communication. Nonverbal behavior, such as facial expressions, voice tone, eye contact, hand movements and other gestures, often modifies what is spoken, expressing more about a person's thoughts and feelings. Besides controlling their own nonverbal behavior, observing and interpreting the patient's nonverbal messages are essential skills for health care providers.

　　Attentive listening can help caregivers recognize the patient's needs. This requires **empathy. Patients are often unable to identify their feelings and have difficulty talking about them. So, while listening, health care providers need to put themselves in the patient's situation.

　　Various verbal skills are also (5)critical for ***therapeutically effective communication. They include such (6)techniques as clarifying what is meant by a patient's statement and asking open-ended questions. Clarifying a patient's statement is to make a guess and restate the basic message if necessary. The following example shows how to clarify what is implied.

　　Patient : There is no point in asking for a pain pill.

　　Nurse :　Are you saying that no one gives you a pill when you have pain?
　　　　　　Or, are you saying that the pills are not helping your pain?

　　Open-ended questions and statements, such as "How did you feel in that situation?," "I'd like to hear more about that," and "Tell me about that," can invite patients to (7) and explain their feelings.

　　Just as it is important to learn ways of fostering therapeutic exchanges, it is also helpful to recognize responses that interfere with effective communication. Below are some examples of such nontherapeutic forms of expression.

　　Feelings expressed by patients such as anger or worry often make caregivers uncomfortable. Common responses to those situations are: "Don't worry about it, everything will be fine." or "Please don't cry." Such responses ****inhibit the expression of feelings. It is best to encourage the patient to voice his/her feelings and examine them objectively.

Judgmental statements that indicate how patients should feel deny a patient's true feelings and suggest that they are inappropriate. An example of such statements is: "You shouldn't complain about the pain, many others have gone through this same experience without complaint."

In addition to these communication strategies, health care providers need to be aware that a person's style of communication is often affected by factors such as his/her health condition, stress level, fatigue, education, and culture. Good therapeutic communication skills are at the heart of all the medical professions. These skills can lead to accurate assessment and improvement of a patient's health status and well-being.

*interactions　相互関係　　　　　**empathy　感情移入
***therapeutically　治療上　　　　****inhibit　抑制する

1 ～ 4 の問題については，本文の論旨に最も適したものを選べ。

1. Nonverbal communication _____.
　Ⓐ often reveals the health care provider's feelings more than verbal messages
　Ⓑ is as important as verbal communication in getting across health care providers' messages to patients
　Ⓒ is more useful than verbal communication in understanding patients' needs
　Ⓓ and verbal communication of a patient need to be controlled by caregivers

2. Health care providers need to _____ to recognize the patient's need.
　Ⓐ observe the patient's behavior carefully
　Ⓑ listen to the patient's complaint
　Ⓒ feel sympathy with the patient
　Ⓓ put themselves in the patient's shoes

3. Caregivers need to _____, so that they do not interfere with effective communication.

  Ⓐ encourage patients not to worry about their conditions

  Ⓑ be non-judgmental and encourage patients to speak up

  Ⓒ be objective and examine patients' opinions emotionally

  Ⓓ suppress their emotion and patients' complaints

4. Good communication skills can _____.

  Ⓐ help promote caregivers' status

  Ⓑ be essential for patients to be taken care of appropriately

  Ⓒ promote social welfare and health care

  Ⓓ be useful for caregivers to help patients

5. 下線語(5) critical と最も意味の近い単語を一つ選べ。

  Ⓐ good   Ⓑ helpful

  Ⓒ essential   Ⓓ useful

6. 本文中にあるⒶ～Ⓓの単語の最も強いアクセントのある母音が，下線語(6) techniques の最も強いアクセントのある母音と同じものを選べ。

  Ⓐ professional

  Ⓑ treatment

  Ⓒ caregiver

  Ⓓ interpret

7. 空所 (7) に入る最も適切な語を選べ。

  Ⓐ have

  Ⓑ hear

  Ⓒ draw

  Ⓓ discover

8. 本文の表題として最も適切なものを選べ。

  Ⓐ Importance of Nonverbal Communication for Caregivers

  Ⓑ How to Improve Communication Skills in Hospital

  Ⓒ How Communication Affects Patient-Doctor Relationship

  Ⓓ Usefulness of Communication Skills for Medical Professionals

Chapter 2 ≫ 生殖器系／遺伝子
The Reproductive System

順天堂大学（医学部）　　　　　　　　　　　　⏰ 目標 15 分

次の英文を読んで，下記の設問に答えなさい。

I've just had my genome scanned, and unfortunately the test results show that I have some common mutations that give me a slightly increased genetic risk for diabetes and heart disease. More worrisome is the news that I have three times the average risk for getting Alzheimer's disease.

On the other hand, the test also shows that I don't have lots of other dangerous mutations, like those associated with various forms of cancer. All in all, the analysis of 130 of my genetic markers suggests that my overall health expectancy is better than that of the average person. This should be comforting news. But it also makes me wonder about the future.

This kind of genetic screening may be the Next Big Thing in medicine. It offers a glimpse of how genetics will transform human life in this century. "We'd like to do away with much of the health care system," said Charles Cantor, the chief scientific officer of Sequenom, the genetic discovery company that tested my DNA. "We'd like to keep people very healthy, until they die suddenly and painlessly of old age. I think genetic screening will give doctors and patients much better disease prevention tools."

What is scary is not the technology itself. Rather, it is that we are slipping toward "our post-human future," as Francis Fukuyama put it, without public understanding or debate, and without adequate laws to prevent genetic discrimination.

The kind of broad genetic scan that I underwent may be commonly available to the general public within ten years. Such screening could give the benefits of alerting people to their medical weaknesses so that they could get early treatment for diseases, possibly saving their lives.

But genetic screening also will raise many difficult personal and ethical questions we need to wrestle with now, rather than simply allowing them to go unanswered. Among the problems — getting the results of a genetic screening can be emotionally troubling to the patient. "People need to be really sure they want to do this," emphasized Dr. Harry Osterer, the genetic specialist who advised me. For example, do people really want to know that they are at risk for Alzheimer's? Such information can change the way people see themselves.

And then, what about issues of privacy and discrimination? For example, should voters be allowed to see the genetic records of candidates for political offices? What if the genetic records of a presidential candidate showed that he or she had a high risk for some disease? Would this affect the way people voted? What if genetic records were stolen, or made up falsely by opponents?

And then, what about the effects on the medical insurance system? Would people whose gene-scans showed low risk of disease stop paying for insurance, believing it an unnecessary use of money? This could make insurance companies go bankrupt. And on the other hand, insurance companies might be tempted to engage in genetic discrimination. They might, for example, try to reject people whose gene-scans showed higher risk for dangerous diseases.

So now, while this technology is still in its infancy, is the time to debate this issue and to enact suitable laws to prevent genetic discrimination. Genetic technology is a grand technology we are quickly moving toward, but we need to shape it, rather than allow it to shape us.

© The New York Times

注：genome　ゲノム　　　　　　　　　mutation　変異
　　Alzheimer's　アルツハイマー（症）　gene　遺伝子

設問　上記の英文の内容に合うように各設問の選択肢①～⑤の中から最も適したもの
を選び，その番号を記しなさい。

1. What is the author most concerned about in this article?
① his fear of getting Alzheimer's disease
② the effects of gene-scanning on the insurance system
③ the possibilities of genetic discrimination
④ the emotional pain caused by gene-scanning
⑤ the effects of gene-scanning on the political system

2. What does Charles Cantor think about the possibilities of genetic screening?

① He worries about our post-human future.

② He worries about people dying of old age.

③ He wants to do away with the health care system.

④ He predicts that it will help prevent many diseases.

⑤ He worries about its cost.

3. After getting the results of his gene-scan test, what was the main effect on the author?

① He realized he would get Alzheimer's.

② He realized he would get cancer.

③ He found that his life expectancy was better than average.

④ He decided that gene-scanning shouldn't be used.

⑤ He worried about the cost of gene-scanning.

4. What are the main kinds of problems suggested by the phrase "our post-human future"?

① emotional problems

② ethical problems

③ economic problems

④ physical problems

⑤ historical problems

5. What are the benefits that are most likely to come from genetic screening?

① earlier diagnosis and treatment of genetic-related diseases

② cost reduction of medical treatment

③ solving problems in medical ethics

④ increasing trust between doctors and patients

⑤ encouraging greater privacy in medical treatment

6. Which of the following is NOT suggested as a possible result of gene-scanning technology?

① It could allow us to transform human life.

② It could affect the way we vote.

③ It could help save lives.

④ It could raise social and economic questions.

⑤ It could keep the technology in its infancy.

7. What do you think the author would suggest as the most important?

① banning genetic screening

② banning genetic technology

③ reforming the medical insurance system

④ passing laws to prevent genetic discrimination

⑤ training doctors in gene-scanning technology

3 　長文読解　　　　　　　　　　　　　★★★★

北里大学（医学部）　　　　　　　　　　　　　　目標 20 分

2

次の英文を読み，下記の設問に答えなさい。

　　Scientists have long known that specific genes are associated with a number of serious diseases and birth defects. Scientists have used this knowledge to develop tests to identify defective genes, which are the result of mutation: a natural process that alters genetic material. Researchers have identified a large number of genes that are responsible for life-threatening conditions, such as cystic fibrosis[*1] and Huntington's disease[*2]. (　(1)　) these genes are identified, genetic tests for many such diseases become available. These tests can indicate if a person has a specific defective gene. By 2011, researchers had developed more than 2,000 genetic tests, which allow doctors to inform patients if they have inherited these genes and if they risk passing them on to their children.

　　This testing is a significant milestone in genetic research, because these tests provide people who have genetic defects (　(2)　) important information. However, the tests also introduce complex ethical issues. If patients find out that they have a dangerous genetic defect, they may not know what to do. Their decision will depend on several factors. First, in some cases, identification of the gene only suggests the likelihood that the patient will develop the disease associated with that gene. For example, women who have inherited the harmful BRCA gene mutation[*3] have a much higher chance of developing breast cancer than other women do. (　(3)　), it is likely that women with the genetic mutation will develop cancer, but it is not certain. A second important factor in the decision is whether there is a treatment, and if so, what kind of treatment. In the case of BRCA gene mutation, a frequent treatment is major surgery before the cancer develops. Women who test positive for the mutation must decide between this treatment and the possibility of dying of cancer.

　　Unfortunately, for some genetic diseases, there is no treatment, which (6)gives rise to even more complex ethical issues. Would patients want to know that they are going to die young or become very sick if there is no treatment? Some may want to know so that they can prepare themselves. If there is a chance they could pass the disease to their future children, they may decide not to have children. For others, however, the news could ruin their lives. They might prefer not to know about their condition and enjoy their lives while they are healthy. So, they may decide not to get genetic tests at all.

Most researchers expect that the next step will be gene therapy that repairs or replaces the defective gene. This would mean, for example, that BRCA patients could receive a treatment that actually changes their genetic material. If that came true, most people would probably decide to take genetic tests.

At the end of the 20th century, researchers began to develop treatments for a variety of life-threatening genetic diseases. The early results seemed very (7)encouraging, and, consequently, people with genetic diseases became hopeful that they would soon see a cure. In 2000, for example, French doctors treated babies with a rare genetic disorder, commonly (8)referred to as "bubble boy disease*4," that affected their immune systems. They injected the babies with a healthy replacement gene. Ten months later, the children's immune systems appeared completely normal.

To these early achievements, however, considerable problems and limitations were attached. Results were ((4)); success occurred in only a small number of patients with rare conditions. Sometimes the therapy caused more problems than it solved. For example, in the French case, several of the children developed leukemia*5, one of whom died. In addition, enthusiastic researchers sometimes (9)underestimated the time it would take for discoveries in the laboratory to become practical therapies, a difficulty that persists today, often leading to disappointment and a lack of confidence in the field of gene therapy.

In spite of these ((5)), many scientists pursued their research in gene therapy. They believed this form of treatment still held great potential. However, three basic technical challenges (10)stood in the way of their progress. First, gene therapy is not like other kinds of treatments in which a patient can take a pill that sends medicine throughout the body. It must be introduced into specific genes. Second, scientists need a way to deliver the therapy directly into a cell. In many cases, they have used a virus to do this, but they have to be sure that the virus will not harm the patient. Finally, they have to be sure that the new or repaired gene will not "turn off" after it is introduced into the cell.

After years of research and trials, scientists had made considerable progress in solving these problems. In the first years of the 21st century,

2

positive results began to emerge, arousing renewed interest in the field. In a small clinical trial in 2007, patients with Parkinson's disease[*6] received genes for production of an important protein that they lacked. All 12 patients experienced an improvement in their condition with no negative effects. In 2011, researchers successfully treated patients with hemophilia[*7], a disease that impairs the body's ability to clot blood, by injecting them with the healthy form of a defective gene. These were major achievements, but they are particularly exciting because the treatments are for major diseases that affect large numbers of people.

All of these positive results have revived the public's interest in gene therapy. Many researchers and scientists have renewed their belief in the prospect of its enormous potential to treat killer diseases like cancer, diabetes, cystic fibrosis, etc. However, they are now more careful to caution patients and society that many effective genetic therapies may still be years, or decades, in the future.

[*Making Connections 3 : Skills and Strategies for Academic Reading*, 3rd Edition by Kenneth J. Pakenham, Jo McEntire and Jessica Williams, pp. 27-29 © Cambridge University Press 2013]

注：[*1]cystic fibrosis 「嚢胞性線維症」肺，膵臓，消化管，汗腺などの外分泌腺の機能が損なわれる遺伝性疾患

[*2]Huntington's disease 「ハンチントン病」常染色体優性遺伝によって発病する神経変性疾患

[*3]BRCA gene mutation 「がん抑制遺伝子変異」
BRCA gene = breast cancer (susceptibility) gene

[*4]bubble boy disease 「バブルボーイ症候群，重症複合免疫不全症」アデノシンデアミナーゼという酵素の欠損に起因する免疫不全疾患

[*5]leukemia 「白血病」血球を作る細胞（幹細胞）が，骨髄中でがん化して無制限に増殖し続ける病気

[*6]Parkinson's disease 「パーキンソン病」中脳黒質にあるドーパミン神経細胞が脱落することによる中枢神経系疾患

[*7]hemophilia 「血友病」止血に必要な凝固因子が不足するため，いったん出血すると血が止まりにくい病気

12

1. 本文中の(1)～(5)の空欄に入る最も適切なものを，それぞれ①～⑤の中から一つずつ選びなさい。

(1)　① Hence　　　② In order that　　③ Once
　　 ④ Unless　　　⑤ Whereas

(2)　① against　　 ② for　　　　　　 ③ into
　　 ④ off　　　　 ⑤ with

(3)　① Besides　　 ② Instead　　　　③ Nevertheless
　　 ④ Otherwise　⑤ Thus

(4)　① cost-effective　② mixed　　　③ punctual
　　 ④ reflective　　　⑤ reluctant

(5)　① advances　　② emissions　　③ praises
　　 ④ setbacks　　⑤ utilities

2. 本文中の下線部(6)～(10)の語（句）に最も近い意味のものを，それぞれ①～⑤の中から一つずつ選びなさい。

(6)　gives rise to
　　 ① brings about　　② cuts down　　　③ speeds up
　　 ④ takes the place of　⑤ turns away

(7)　encouraging
　　 ① absurd　　　② constant　　　③ depressing
　　 ④ promising　 ⑤ unfavorable

(8)　referred to as
　　 ① called　　　② prejudiced　　③ regulated
　　 ④ unpredictable　⑤ worsened

(9)　underestimated
　　 ① held high　　② incorrectly judged　③ put emphasis on
　　 ④ took pride in　⑤ thought twice about

(10)　stood in the way of
　　 ① turned from　② ensured　　　③ paralleled
　　 ④ relied on　　⑤ blocked

3. 下記の(11)～(15)の各問に対する答えとして最も適切なものを，それぞれ①～⑤の中から一つずつ選びなさい。

(11)　According to the reading, what is the final target of developing gene therapies?

①　Permanent repair or replacement of defective genes.

②　Identification of defective genes.

③　Development of genetic tests to identify people with defective genes.

④　Development of a delivery system in which no viruses are used.

⑤　Development of a pill that sends medicine throughout the body.

(12)　According to the reading, which is an example of how genetic tests can be helpful?

①　By enhancing people's immune systems.

②　By protecting normal genes.

③　By causing complex ethical problems.

④　By preventing people from knowing whether or not they will have genetic diseases.

⑤　By helping people make informed decisions about having children.

(13)　Which of the following (A) to (E) are described in the reading as the practical challenges that genetic researchers face in developing therapies? Choose all of the three options which apply.

(A)　They have to find a good way to introduce the therapy into the cell.

(B)　They have to make sure that the new or repaired genes remain active.

(C)　They have to make sure that the patient's blood is able to clot after injuries.

(D)　They have to be sure that the viruses to be used for the therapy are not harmful.

(E)　They have to convince more medical practitioners to take part in the therapy.

①　(A), (B), and (C)　　②　(A), (B), and (D)　　③　(A), (B), and (E)

④　(B), (C), and (D)　　⑤　(B), (D), and (E)

(14) Which of the following is in accordance with the reading?

① Women who have inherited the BRCA gene mutation are less likely to develop breast cancer than those who haven't.

② Several French children suffering from a rare genetic disease were injected with a healthy replacement gene in 2000 but none of them survived the treatment.

③ Neither side effects nor unexpected fatal accidents have happened as the results of gene therapy.

④ The time associated with developing practical gene therapies is a problem that has not yet been completely overcome.

⑤ It was proven that patients with hemophilia would not benefit from gene therapy because the disease has no relation to their genes.

(15) According to the reading, which statement best summarizes the state of gene therapy today?

① It has been so successful that any kind of gene therapy has become available anywhere on Earth.

② It is likely that only patients with rare genetic diseases will ever benefit from genetic research.

③ Recent success has allowed people to expect increased availability of genetic treatments in the years to come.

④ There have been enough failures to cause serious doubts about the overall value of gene therapy.

⑤ The age when BRCA patients were forced to decide between major surgery and the possibilities of dying of cancer has already ended.

Use the content from this passage, separated into 11 sections (*sec 1 – sec 11*), to answer the *questions*.

HUMAN-PIG 'CHIMERAS[1]' MAY PROVIDE VITAL TRANSPLANT ORGANS, BUT THEY RAISE ETHICAL DILEMMAS

sec 1　Transplantation is one of modern medicine's success stories, but it is hampered[2] by a scarcity[3] of donor organs. Figures for the UK published by the NHS Blood and Transport Service show that 429 patients died in 2014–2015 while awaiting an organ. What's more, many of the 807 removed from the waiting list will have been removed because they became too ill to receive an organ and are likely to have died as a result.

sec 2　So while there is a strong ethical imperative to increase the supply of donor organs, many of the methods tried or proposed —— presumed consent, allowing organs to be bought and sold, and using lower-grade organs such as those from donors with HIV —— are themselves controversial. And even if we accept these approaches it's unlikely they will be sufficient to meet the demand.

sec 3　Gene editing techniques such as CRISPR could provide the answer. These techniques allow us to make precise changes in the DNA of living organisms with exciting prospects for treating disease —— for example by modifying human DNA to remove genes that cause disease or insert genes associated with natural immunity to conditions such as HIV/AIDS. However, gene editing the DNA of animals could prove equally important for the medical treatment of humans.

sec 4　Scientists are now working on a technique that would allow human organs to be grown inside pigs. The DNA within a pig <u>embryo</u> that enables it to grow a pancreas is deleted, and human stem cells are injected into the embryo. These stem cells have the ability to develop into any type of cell within the body, and previous experiments using rats and mice suggest that they will automatically fill the gap created by the missing pancreas genes and form a pancreas that consists of predominantly[4] genetically human cells.

sec 5 The idea of transplanting organs from pigs into humans is not new. Transplants between different species, or **xenotransplantation**, was considered promising in the 1990s but fell from favour due to the challenges of preventing the human immune system from rejecting pig organs, and concerns about the possible transmission of infectious diseases from pigs to humans. Modern gene editing techniques may help alleviate[5] both concerns: rejection is less likely since the organ will be more closely resemble a human one, while other scientists have demonstrated that CRISPR can also be used to delete retroviruses from the pig genome.

sec 6 However, some will undoubtedly protest that the risks are still too high. Often these objections appeal to the so-called **precautionary principle**, which states that action should be taken to avert risks even if their existence and magnitude is uncertain. Attractive though this idea is, the precautionary principle is only defensible if it is evidence based, and balances the risks of innovation against the known harms of not using the technology.

PRACTICAL MEDICINE MEETS PRACTICAL ETHICS

sec 7 Others will argue that it is inherently[6] wrong to create human-animal hybrids, so-called chimeras; that it is contrary to human dignity, or constitutes "playing God[7]". It's hard to understand the rationale for such claims given that humans' biological nature is neither fixed nor categorically separated from that of other organisms. Even without technological interventions we share much of our DNA with other species, host millions of non-human cells within our bodies, and may have absorbed some of their DNA by horizontal transfer.

sec 8 Even if creating human-animal chimeras is not intrinsically[8] wrong, is there an ethical problem in harvesting[9] organs from a creature that is part-human? It has been suggested that human stem cells might become incorporated into the pig's brain, making the pig "more human". But even if stem cells enhanced the pig's brain function, it seems implausible[10] that the pig would acquire anything like the cognitive sophistication[11] that would put it morally on a par with humans.

sec 9 We might question whether the use of pigs as a source of organs for humans is permissible, even leaving aside any suggestion that their moral status is somehow enhanced by the presence of human cells. Jeremy Bentham, the father of utilitarianism[12], famously wrote: "The question is not, can they reason? Nor, can they talk? But, can they suffer?"

sec 10　<u>If this</u> is the case, pigs undoubtedly qualify for moral consideration. It is often argued that since pigs and other livestock animals are routinely sacrificed for our culinary pleasure, it would be odd to prohibit their use in life-saving medical research and treatment. But meat-eating itself is under increased ethical scrutiny today which, even while it is unlikely to be banned anytime soon, makes for a <u>weak foundation</u> on which to justify extending animal exploitation to a new arena.

sec 11　Other approaches such as laboratory-grown organs, or organs grown in "zombie" animals genetically engineered to lack sentience[13], could in the future offer the benefits of the chimera technique without the <u>animal welfare problems</u>. Until then, we shouldn't try to duck difficult judgements about weighing up human and animal welfare. If the risks can be sufficiently controlled, then it's hard to envisage[14] society choosing to forego the life-saving opportunities of this technology. But we must also recognise that the choices we face now are influenced by earlier decisions about research priorities, and that these too require careful ethical consideration.

Vocabulary

(1) **chimera**: an animal of mixed genetic tissue　*(2)* **hamper**: make difficult

(3) **scarcity**: shortage　*(4)* **predominantly**: mainly

(5) **alleviate**: make less severe　*(6)* **inherently**: basically

(7) **playing God**: behaving as if all-powerful　*(8)* **intrinsically**: completely

(9) **harvesting**: collecting　*(10)* **implausible**: unbelievable

(11) **cognitive sophistication**: complex brain development

(12) **utilitarianism**: a moral philosophy　*(13)* **sentience**: ability to feel

(14) **envisage**: imagine

1. According *sec 1*, which of the following is NOT true?

① Although transplantation is a tremendous medical innovation there are problems with organ availability.

② Many people passed away while they were waiting for an organ transplant operation.

③ Of the 809 patients removed from the waiting list, 429 of them died while awaiting an organ.

④ Some patients waiting for an organ transplant operation were removed from the waiting list because their conditions got too bad.

2. In *sec 4*, which of the following is the closest in meaning to "<u>embryo</u>"?

① pig cells

② the blood of a pig

③ unborn pig in development

④ very young pig after birth

3. Which of the following best summarizes *sec 4*?

① Human organs consist predominantly of genetically human cells.

② In the future, pigs and other animals may evolve to automatically grow human organs.

③ Scientists are developing methods to grow human organs in animals.

④ Stem cells have evolved new and exciting abilities that interest scientists.

4. According to *sec 5*, which of the following best describes the early development of "<u>xenotransplantation</u>"?

① After a positive start it ran into problems.

② Gene editing lead to the transmission of disease.

③ In the 1990's costs were impractically high.

④ It was only possible to transplant organs from humans to pigs.

5. According to *sec 6*, which of the following best reflects the meaning of the "<u>precautionary principle</u>"?

① Innovation is inherently risky.

② Risks are caused by scientific evidence.

③ Risks should be assumed and avoided.

④ Risks should be disregarded for benefits.

6. Which of the following best reflects the content of *sec 7*?
① Animals exist for the benefit of humans.
② Humans are not that different from other animals.
③ It is dangerous to create human-animal hybrids.
④ Only God is allowed to modify DNA.

2

7. According to *sec 8*, which of the following could result from injecting human stem cells into a pig embryo?
① a human with higher brain functionality
② a hybrid human with pig DNA
③ a pig capable of making ethical decisions
④ a pig with a more capable brain

8. According to *sec 9* and *sec 10*, what does "If this" refer to?
① if pigs are capable of experiencing pain and fear
② if pigs are not capable of rational thought
③ if pigs are not morally equal to humans
④ if pigs contain human cells

9. In *sec 10*, why does the author describe the meat-eating argument as having a "weak foundation"?
① because eating meat is less dangerous
② because eating meat is natural and healthy
③ because many people do not think eating meat is ethical
④ because many people think genetic modification is not ethical

10. In *sec 11*, how does the author suggest that we may overcome the "animal welfare problems"?
① by altering human DNA
② by creating animals that are incapable of suffering
③ by stopping the killing of animals for meat consumption
④ by sufficiently controlling the risks

Chapter 3 神経系／脳
The Nervous System

 久留米大学（医学部医学科）　　　　　　　　　　目標 30 分

次の英文を読んで，以下の問いに答えよ。

A new machine learning approach classifies a common type of brain tumor into low or high grades with almost 98% accuracy, researchers report in the journal IEEE Access. Scientists in India and Japan, including from Kyoto University's Institute for Integrated Cell-Material Sciences (iCeMS), (1) the method to help clinicians choose the most effective treatment strategy for individual patients.

Gliomas are a common type of brain tumor affecting glial cells, which provide support and insulation for neurons. Patient treatment varies depending on the tumor's aggressiveness, so it's important to get the (2) right for each individual. Radiologists obtain a very large amount of data from MRI scans to reconstruct a 3D image of the scanned tissue. Much of the data available in MRI scans cannot be detected by the naked eye, such as details related to the tumor shape, texture, or the image's intensity.

Artificial intelligence (AI) algorithms help extract this data. Medical oncologists have been using this approach, called radiomics, to improve patient diagnoses, but accuracy still needs to be (3). iCeMS bioengineer Ganesh Pandian Namasivayam collaborated with Indian data scientist Balasubramanian Raman from Roorkee to develop a machine learning approach that can (4) gliomas into low or high grade with 97.54% accuracy.

Low grade gliomas include grade I pilocytic astrocytoma and grade II low-grade glioma. These are the less aggressive and less malignant of the glioma tumors. High grade gliomas include grade III malignant glioma and grade IV glioblastoma multiforme, which are much more aggressive and more malignant with a (5) short post-diagnosis survival time.

The choice of patient treatment largely depends on being able to determine the glioma's grading. The team, including Rahul Kumar, Ankur Gupta and Harkirat Singh Arora, used a dataset from MRI scans belonging to 210 people with high grade gliomas and another 75 with low grade gliomas.

They developed an approach called CGHF, which stands for computational decision support system for grouping gliomas using hybrid radiomics and stationary wavelet-based features.

　　They chose specific algorithms for extracting features from some of the MRI scans and then （　6　） another predictive algorithm to process this data and categorize the gliomas. They then tested their model on the rest of the MRI scans to assess its accuracy. "Our method outperformed other state-of-the-art approaches for predicting glioma grades from brain MRI scans," says Balasubramanian. "This is quite considerable."

（Ives, J. (2020). *News Medical* より一部改変）
〔Artificial intelligence enhances brain tumour diagnosis
ⓒ Mindy Takamiya/Kyoto University iCeMS, CC BY 4.0〕

1. 本文の空所(1)〜(6)に入れるのに最も適切な語を，下記の(a)〜(d)からそれぞれ1つ選び，その記号をマークせよ。

(1)　(a)　grew　　　　　　　(b)　abandoned
　　　(c)　developed　　　　(d)　condemned

(2)　(a)　diagnosis　　　　 (b)　decree
　　　(c)　oblivion　　　　　(d)　rationality

(3)　(a)　assumed　　　　　(b)　inspired
　　　(c)　decreased　　　　(d)　enhanced

(4)　(a)　classify　　　　　 (b)　confuse
　　　(c)　refuse　　　　　　(d)　exacerbate

(5)　(a)　protractedly　　　 (b)　relatively
　　　(c)　hardly　　　　　　(d)　broadly

(6)　(a)　cured　　　　　　 (b)　coerced
　　　(c)　trained　　　　　 (d)　destroyed

2. 本文の内容と適合するものを下記の(a)～(h)から 3 つ選び，その記号をマークせよ。

(a) A glioma is a common type of cell that causes brain tumors.

(b) Radiologists acquire data from MRI scans to recreate a three-dimensional image of the tissue.

(c) Low-grade gliomas are the less threatening than high-grade type gliomas.

(d) A new type of machine is learning how to approach brain tumors with high accuracy.

(e) Artificial intelligence algorithms help the patients to research their own diagnosis.

(f) The type of glioma discussed is not related to the method of treatment of the patient.

(g) Details related to the tumor shape and texture can be easily seen by looking at MRI scans.

(h) According to an Indian scientist, their method was much better for estimating types of gliomas by using MRI scans of the brain.

次の英文を読んで，設問に答えなさい。

①[Exercise (ア)<u>may help to keep</u> the brain robust in people who (イ)<u>have an increased risk</u> of (ウ)<u>Alzheimer's disease to be developed</u>, (エ)<u>according to an inspiring new study</u>]. The findings suggest that even moderate amounts of physical activity may help to slow the progression of one of the most dreaded diseases of aging. For the new study, which was published in May in *Frontiers in Aging Neuroscience*, researchers at the Cleveland Clinic in Ohio recruited almost 100 older men and women, aged 65 to 89, many of whom had a family history of Alzheimer's disease. Alzheimer's disease, characterized by a (　②　) and then quickening loss of memory and ③<u>cognitive</u> functioning, can strike anyone. But scientists have discovered in recent years that people who harbor a specific variant of a (A)<u>gene</u>, known as the APOE epsilon4 allele or the e4 gene for short, have a substantially increased risk of developing the disease. (　④　) testing among the volunteers in the new study determined that about half of the group carried the e4 gene, although, at the start of the study, none showed signs of memory loss beyond what would be normal ⑤<u>for</u> their age.

But then some studies began to suggest that exercise might affect the disease's progression. A 2011 brain scan study, for instance, conducted by some of the same researchers from the Cleveland Clinic, found that elderly people with the e4 gene who exercised regularly had significantly more brain activity during cognitive tests than people with the e4 gene who did not exercise, suggesting that the exercisers' brains were functioning better. But that study looked at the function, not the structure of the brain. (　⑥　) the physical shape of the brain, the researchers wondered, particularly in people with the e4 gene? To find out, they asked the volunteers in their new (B)<u>experiment</u> how often and intensely they exercised. About half, as it turned out, didn't move much at all. But the other half walked, jogged or otherwise exercised moderately a few times every week.

In the end, the scientists divided their volunteers into four groups, based on their e4 status and exercise habits. One group included those people with the e4 gene who did not exercise; another consisted of those with the e4 gene who did exercise; and the other two groups were composed of those without the gene who did or did not regularly exercise. The scientists then scanned their volunteers' brains, with particular emphasis on their *hippocampi. Eighteen months later, they repeated the scans. In that brief interval, the members of the group carrying the e4 gene who did not exercise had undergone significant *atrophy of their *hippocampus. It had shrunk (⑦) about 3 percent, on average. Those volunteers who carried the e4 gene but who regularly exercised, however, showed almost no shrinkage of their hippocampus. Likewise, both groups of volunteers who did not carry the e4 gene showed little change to their hippocampus. In effect, the brains of ⑧physically active volunteers at high risk for Alzheimer's disease looked just like the brains of people at much lower risk for the disease, said Stephen M. Rao, a professor at the Schey Center for Cognitive Neuroimaging at the Cleveland Clinic, who oversaw the study. Exercise appeared to have been (⑨).

Meanwhile, the brains of sedentary people at high risk appeared to be slipping, structurally, toward dysfunction. "This occurred in a very compressed time frame," said Dr. Rao, who described the differences in brain structure as "quite significant." How exercise was guarding people's hippocampi remains unclear, he said, although the e4 gene is known to alter fat metabolism within the brain, he said, as does exercise, which could be counteracting some of the undesirable effects of the e4 gene. More research needs to be done to better understand the interplay of exercise and Alzheimer's disease risk. But even so, Dr. Rao said, "there's good reason to tell people to exercise" to protect their memories. Many of us do not carry the e4 gene, but everyone has some chance of developing Alzheimer's disease. And if exercise reduces that risk in any way, Dr. Rao said, "then why not (⑩)?"

[From Gretchen Reynolds, "Can Exercise Reduce Alzheimer's Risk?," *The New York Times*, 2 July 2014
〈http://well.blogs.nytimes.com/2014/07/02/can-exercise-reduce-alzheimers-risk〉]

注) hippocampi / hippocampus：海馬　　atrophy：萎縮

1. 次の⑦〜㋑の単語の二重下線部の中で, (A)⎡gene⎤の二重下線部 "e" と同じ発音をもつものが1つだけある。それを選び, 記号で答えなさい。

⑦ juv<u>e</u>nile   ㋑ n<u>ea</u>t   ㋒ p<u>e</u>rish   ㋓ sp<u>e</u>cialty

2. 次の⑦〜㋑の単語の二重下線部の中で, (B)⎡experiment⎤の二重下線部 "e" と同じ発音をもつものが1つだけある。それを選び, 記号で答えなさい。

⑦ exp<u>e</u>rience   ㋑ exp<u>e</u>nsive   ㋒ p<u>e</u>riod   ㋓ m<u>e</u>liorate

3. ①[Exercise ㋐<u>may help to keep</u> the brain robust in people who ㋑<u>have an increased risk</u> of ㋒<u>Alzheimer's disease to be developed</u>, ㋓<u>according to an inspiring new study</u>] の下線部㋐〜㋓のうち間違っているものを1つ選び, 記号で答えなさい。

4. 文中の空欄 (②) に入る最も適切な単語を⑦〜㋓から1つ選び, 記号で答えなさい。

⑦ gradual

㋑ contemporary

㋒ sudden

㋓ overwhelming

5. 文中の下線部③cognitive の意味として最も適切なものを⑦〜㋓から1つ選び, 記号で答えなさい。

⑦ related to the process of knowing, understanding, and learning something

㋑ worthy to be remembered

㋒ having sound judgment

㋓ possessing a highly developed intellect

6. 文中の空欄 (④) に入る最も適切な単語を⑦〜㋓から1つ選び, 記号で答えなさい。

⑦ Genial

㋑ Generic

㋒ Genetic

㋓ Generous

7．文中の下線部⑤for と同じ意味の for を使っている文章を⑦〜㋔から1つ選び，記号で答えなさい。

㋐ She came back in October and set out to rearrange her wedding for a third time.

㋑ This weather is certainly unseasonal for July, with the combination of strong winds, heavy rain and depressed temperatures making it feel more like November.

㋒ He then walked off to try to get help to exchange the coins for larger ones.

㋓ We have to do this for moral reasons, and because our security depends on it.

8．文中の空欄（　⑥　）に入る最も適切な語句を⑦〜㋔から1つ選び，記号で答えなさい。

㋐ Should exercise also have affected

㋑ Might exercise also be affected

㋒ Could exercise also be affecting

㋓ Would exercise also have been affecting

9．文中の空欄（　⑦　）に入る最も適切な単語を⑦〜㋔から1つ選び，記号で答えなさい。

㋐ of　　　　㋑ with　　　　㋒ for　　　　㋓ by

10．文中の下線部⑧physically active と反対の意味を表す形容詞を1語本文中から探し出して書きなさい。

11．文中の空欄（　⑨　）に入る最も適切な単語を⑦〜㋔から1つ選び，記号で答えなさい。

㋐ progressive

㋑ aggressive

㋒ defensive

㋓ protective

12. 文中の空欄（　⑩　）に入る最も適切な語句を⑦〜㊤から1つ選び，記号で答えなさい。

⑦　get up and move

⑦　stay at home quietly

⑦　restore your memory loss

㊤　rise and shine

13. 次の⑦〜㋑の中から本文の内容と合致する内容の文章を1つ選び，記号で答えなさい。

⑦　It has been shown that people in the modern world have a higher tendency to carry the e4 gene than those in the early-modern period, because of their increasing liability toward sedentary habits.

⑦　How much physical activity people might do, a family history of Alzheimer's disease would turn out to be a minor risk factor in developing it eventually.

⑦　The physically active people are likely to volunteer for various kind of activities, which the older people might hesitate to join because of the lack of enough physical strength.

㊤　For eighteen months, the volunteers for the experiment were encouraged to exercise too intensively. As a result, their brains slipped toward dysfunction.

㋑　To what extent exercise reduces the risk of Alzheimer's disease is still to be investigated, although it has been suggested that exercise works as preventive.

以下は，睡眠と記憶の関係についての英文である。英文を読み，問題に答えなさい。

It is widely believed that memories of events and spaces are stored briefly in the hippocampus before they are combined and strengthened in the neocortex for permanent storage (Fig. 1). (a)Experts have long suspected that part of the process of turning temporary short-term memories into lasting long-term memories occurs during sleep. Now, Professor Susumu Tonegawa and his team have shown that mice prevented from "replaying" their activities from waking hours while asleep do not remember them.

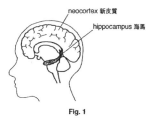

Fig. 1

At research facilities around the world, mice learn to run through complex mazes, find chocolate-flavored rewards, and after an interval, run the mazes again very efficiently, quickly collecting all the rewards. However, Professor Tonegawa and his team created mutant mice in which a change of diet blocked a specific part of the mouse hippocampus, the area of the brain responsible for learning and memory. Consequently, these mutant mice (b)could not perform these tasks.

In the experiment with these mutant mice, the researchers implanted electrodes in their brains and monitored the activities of their brain cells as the mice ran a maze and then slept (Fig. 2 & 3). Researchers examined a circuit within the hippocampus known as the synaptic pathway*. While the mice were still awake and running, they formed within their brains a pattern of neurons that was activated to recognize the maze the mice had learned to find their way through. During their post-run sleep, particularly during a deep

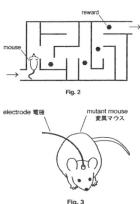

Fig. 2

Fig. 3

sleep phase called slow-wave, the specific sequence of brain cells that had been activated during the run was "replayed" in a similar sequence. However, with these mutant mice, this replay process during the slow-wave sleep was harmed. Generally, the animals were able to form long-term memories of the maze only when their synaptic pathways were functioning after the formation of the short-term memories.

Although this replay during sleep had been speculated to be important for converting the recent memory stored in the hippocampus to a more permanent memory stored in the neocortex, it had never been demonstrated. Professor Tonegawa and his team demonstrated that this pathway is essential for the transformation of a recent memory, formed within a day, into a remote memory that still exists at least six weeks later. They concluded that the synaptic pathway-mediated replay of the hippocampal memory sequence during sleep plays a crucial role in the formation of a long-term memory.

[From Sleep helps build long-term memories, MIT News on June 24, 2009 by
Deborah Halber Reprinted with permission of MIT News http://news.mit.edu/]

注：the synaptic pathway＊シナプス経路

1. 下線部(a)を日本語に訳しなさい。

2. 下線部(b)の理由を説明しなさい。

3. 変異マウスを使った実験の結果から，どのような結論を導いたのか説明しなさい。

Chapter 4 »» 呼吸器系／感染症
The Respiratory System

8 長文読解 ★★★

順天堂大学（医学部）　　　　　　　　　　　　目標 15 分

次の英文を読んで，下記の設問に答えなさい。

Asthma seems to be increasing throughout most of the developed world, yet medical experts remain unsure about its causes. Nearly every statement we might make about asthma can be challenged, including the claim that it is getting worse. One study says that asthma cases have increased by 60 percent in the past ten years and that asthma-related deaths have tripled. Yet another study claims that this supposed increase is just an illusion. According to this argument, modern people are simply more aware of asthma, more ready to go to the doctor with mild cases, and more prepared to define as asthma something that would once have been called a cold.

Still, the greater probability is that asthma problems are actually getting worse and that the cause is pollution. But what kind of pollution? Smoke has long been suspected of being a leading cause of asthma. Yet most of us today inhale far less smoke than our ancestors did, with their wood fires and poorly constructed chimneys, so it seems unlikely that smoke, alone, can have caused the recent increase. More than smoke, it seems a more common trigger for asthma is the common dust mite's droppings. These creatures thrive in modern heated indoor homes, where they live in carpets and bedding. Thus, modern homes may account for much of the increase of asthma.

But many other factors are also at work. One theory holds that people who wash too much as children or who encounter less dirt in everyday life are more likely to develop asthma; that hygiene, not lack of it, is the problem. A study of 14,000 children in Britain showed that those who washed their hands five times a day or more and bathed twice a day had a 25 percent chance of having asthma, while those who washed their hands less than three times a day and bathed every other day had only about half that risk of asthma. The theory is that dirt contains bacteria, which stimulate one part of the immune system. Our immune systems, the theory goes, are set up in such a way that they expect to be stimulated by soil bacteria early in childhood; when they are not, the result is an unbalanced system which is more likely to develop asthma. According to this theory, our bodies may need small doses of dirt to keep them healthy.

　　The other big factor in asthma, and one which still remains a mystery, is heredity. Clearly a person's genetic background plays a major role in determining his or her probabilities of developing asthma. Medical researchers are hopeful that the recent mapping of the human genetic structure will eventually lead to genetic-based cures of asthma. But such a cure still seems many years away. For now, most doctors and patients are concentrating on improving the environmental conditions which are associated with asthma. This seems to be the most cost-effective approach, and it connects with other health and social benefits as well.

4

註）　asthma　喘息　　　mite　ダニ　　　dropping　糞

設問　上記の英文の内容に合うように各設問の選択肢(a)〜(e)の中から最も適したものを選び，その記号を記しなさい。

1. Why do some experts say it is an illusion to think that asthma is increasing recently?
(a)　because pollution levels are actually less than in previous times
(b)　because people may just be more aware of asthma and reporting it more
(c)　because we can challenge every statement about asthma
(d)　because the amount of asthma cases has increased by 60% in the past 10 years
(e)　because experts remain unsure about the causes of asthma

2. What point does the article make about the connection between pollution and asthma?
(a)　Decreases in smoking have lead to decreases in asthma.
(b)　Wood fires and poorly constructed chimneys are main causes of asthma.
(c)　Pollution is not a sufficient explanation of the causes of asthma.
(d)　Smoking is the most common cause of asthma.
(e)　Smoke is the leading cause of asthma.

3. What problem of modern houses might be most related to conditions of asthma?

(a) They contain too much smoke.

(b) They produce dropping rates of asthma.

(c) They use modern accounting systems.

(d) They are too small.

(e) They provide good living places for small insects.

4. What do some experts think about the relation between hygiene and asthma?

(a) Washing hands is a cause of asthma.

(b) We should bathe more often to prevent asthma.

(c) Insufficient contact with dirt could increase the possibility of getting asthma.

(d) Contact with dirt is making us more likely to get asthma.

(e) We should stop hygiene programs in order to prevent asthma.

5. What claim is made in the third paragraph?

(a) British children are becoming more likely to get asthma.

(b) Our immune systems may need to be stimulated by exposure to some bacteria.

(c) Dirt and soil should be avoided because they contain bacteria.

(d) Our immune systems produce small amounts of bacteria.

(e) We need a balanced immune system in order to develop asthma.

6. What claim is made in the fourth paragraph?

(a) Improving environmental conditions is the most important policy for dealing with asthma today.

(b) Heredity is the most important factor in causing asthma.

(c) Environmental problems are the most important factor in causing asthma.

(d) Genetic-based cures provide the most effective means of curing asthma today.

(e) Mapping the human genetic structure has allowed us to find the cure for asthma.

Chapter 5 ≫ 免疫系
The Immune System

9 長文読解   ★★★★☆

藤田医科大学（医学部）   ⏰ 目標 20 分

次の英文を読んで，後の問いに答えなさい。

In 1893 Emil von Behring was busy investigating the properties of diphtheria toxin, the biochemical by-product of diphtheria bacteria that is [　あ　] the disease of the same name. This toxin acts as a kind of poison to normal tissues. A few years earlier von Behring and his colleague Shibasaburo Kitasato had performed an experiment that showed that immunity to diphtheria was [　い　] antitoxin elements, "antibodies," in the blood. What von Behring did not expect to find in his studies on diphtheria toxin — but to his surprise did find — was this: some animals given a *second* dose of toxin too small to injure an animal when given as a *first* dose, nevertheless had drastically exaggerated harmful responses to the tiny second dose. In some cases the response to the puny second dose was so overwhelming as to cause death. Von Behring 《A》coined the term 'hypersensitivity' (*Überempfindlichkeit*, in German) to describe this exaggerated reaction to a small second dose of diphtheria toxin. This experimental finding was so odd relative to the rest of immunological science at the time that it was essentially ignored for about ten years.

In 1898, Charles Richet and Jules Hericourt reported the same finding, this time with a toxin derived from poisonous eels. It too was noted and then ignored. Then in 1902 Paul Portier and Richet published an experimental result that caught the sustained attention of other immunologists. They reported the same exaggerated response to a second small dose of poison derived from marine invertebrates. [　う　] was their careful and detailed description of the hypersensitive response as an observable form of cardiovascular shock. Richet and Portier worked in France rather than in Germany, unlike von Behring, and a good deal of political tension and professional animosity existed between those two leading centers of immunological research. The French scientists weren't about to use a term like 'hypersensitivity' 《A》coined by a German, so they called the exaggerated response *anaphylaxis* (to highlight its harmful aspects as contrasted with *prophylaxis*, the medical term for 'protection').

During the next decade a host of prominent immunologists systematically investigated the nature of anaphylaxis, both its qualitative and its quantitative aspects. In 1903 Maurice Arthus performed the experiments that would result in the discovery of the phenomenon named [　え　] him: The Arthus reaction is a characteristic skin lesion formed by the intradermal injection of certain kinds of proteins. In 1906 Clemens von Pirquet and Bela Schick studied 《B》serum sickness, the unfortunate phenomenon whereby a small percentage of persons given standardized diphtheria or tetanus shots, which do not harm a majority of recipients, nevertheless become extremely sick from the shots. They argued that the observational evidence pointed to an immunological cause of serum sickness. To have a convenient way of referring to any medical condition in which otherwise harmless or beneficial substances paradoxically produce illness in certain persons who come into contact with them, von Pirquet and Schick 《A》coined the term *allergy* (from the Greek *allos ergos*, altered working). In the same year, Alfred Wolff-Eisner published a textbook on hay fever in which he presented the evidential case for hay fever being a form of hypersensitivity traceable to the immune system. In 1910 Samuel Meltzer made the same kind of case for asthma as a form of immunological hypersensitivity somehow localized in the lung tissues.

Notice in this account of the early days of modern immunology how a surprising observational mystery is first [　お　], then perhaps [　か　], and eventually [　き　]. Not all observational mysteries are happily resolved in such a way (some are ignored permanently); but in a large number of cases the course a given area of science takes does seem *evidence driven* in a way many other forms of knowledge gathering are not driven by observational evidence. 《C》Scientific claims deliberately run a risk: the risk of being shown to be false. Some philosophers of science have seen in this at-risk status an important contrast with other forms of human belief such as political ideology, theological doctrines, and so on.

[Robert Klee, *Introduction to the Philosophy of Science: Cutting Nature at Its Seams*, Oxford University Press, 1997 (一部改変)]

注　diphtheria toxin：ジフテリア毒素　　　antibody：抗体
　　puny：微量の　　　　　　　　　　　　　hypersensitivity：過敏症
　　eel：ウナギ　　　　　　　　　　　　　　invertebrate：無脊椎動物

cardiovascular：心臓血管系の	animosity：敵意
lesion：病変	intradermal injection：皮内注射
tetanus：破傷風	allergy：アレルギー
hay fever：枯草熱，花粉症	asthma：ぜんそく
theological：神学的	

1. 空所〔　あ　〕，〔　い　〕に入る表現として最も適当なものをそれぞれ1つ選び，その番号を答えなさい（同じものを2度使ってはいけない）。

(1)　destroyed by 　　　　(2)　due to

(3)　prevented from 　　　(4)　responsible for

2. von Behring はジフテリア毒素を同じ動物に2度にわたって投与する実験をおこなった。初回の投与でその動物に害を与えるのに必要な毒素の量を基準量として，2度目の投与において【　ア　】毒素を与えてみると，そのときの反応は【　イ　】。

(a)　基準量より多い　　(b)　基準量と同じ量の　　(c)　基準量より少ない

(d)　予想通りであった　(e)　予想より強かった　　(f)　予想より弱かった

上の空所【　ア　】と【　イ　】には，それぞれ(a)〜(f)のいずれかが入る。最も適当な組み合わせを次の(1)〜(9)から1つ選び，その番号を答えなさい。

(1)：ア-(a)　イ-(d)　　(2)：ア-(a)　イ-(e)　　(3)：ア-(a)　イ-(f)

(4)：ア-(b)　イ-(d)　　(5)：ア-(b)　イ-(e)　　(6)：ア-(b)　イ-(f)

(7)：ア-(c)　イ-(d)　　(8)：ア-(c)　イ-(e)　　(9)：ア-(c)　イ-(f)

3. 下線部《A》(3カ所ある)の 'coined' に最も近い意味の語を1つ選び，その番号を答えなさい。

(1)　criticized　　(2)　discarded　　(3)　invented　　(4)　used

4. 空所〔　う　〕には次の(1)〜(5)の語句をある順序に並べた表現が入る。2番目と4番目に入る語句の番号を答えなさい（文頭にくる文字も小文字にしてある）。

(1)　distinguished　　　　　　(2)　first described nine years earlier

(3)　their report of the same phenomenon

(4)　von Behring　　　　　　(5)　what

5. 空所〔　え　〕に入る表現として最も適当なものを1つ選び，その番号を答えなさい。

(1)　after　　(2)　in　　(3)　to　　(4)　with

6. 下線部《B》の serum sickness（血清病）の説明として最も適当なものを1つ選び，その番号を答えなさい。

⑴　1度目の接種では害のない血清が2度目の接種では害をおよぼすという，一部の人にみられる現象

⑵　ほとんどの人にとっては適量である血清接種量が，一部の人にとっては不足であり，効果を発揮せずに病気が起こってしまう現象

⑶　ほとんどの人にとっては適量である血清接種量が，一部の人にとっては過剰であり，有害な影響をおよぼす現象

⑷　ほとんどの人にはなんら害のない血清が，免疫上の理由によって一部の人に対して有害な影響をおよぼす現象

7. 空所　［　お　］，［　か　］，［　き　］にはそれぞれ次の⒜，⒝，⒞のいずれかが入る。各空所に入るものの組み合わせとして最も適当なものを1つ選び，その番号を答えなさい。

　　⒜　ignored for a bit　　　　　　⒝　noted

　　⒞　set upon with experimental frenzy　　　　　（注　frenzy：熱狂）

⑴：お－⒜　か－⒝　き－⒞　　　　⑵：お－⒜　か－⒞　き－⒝

⑶：お－⒝　か－⒜　き－⒞　　　　⑷：お－⒝　か－⒞　き－⒜

⑸：お－⒞　か－⒜　き－⒝　　　　⑹：お－⒞　か－⒝　き－⒜

8. 下線部《C》を日本語にしなさい。

9. 本文の内容と一致するものを2つ選び，その番号を答えなさい。

⑴　von Behring は過敏症という現象を発見したが，それがその後，北里柴三郎と共同での抗体の研究へとつながっていった。

⑵　von Behring が発見した過敏症という現象はしばらくのあいだ無視されたが，後に広く関心をもたれて，組織的な免疫学研究へと発展していった。

⑶　同じ現象を指すのに 'hypersensitivity' と 'anaphylaxis' という2つの語が存在した背景には，ドイツとフランスという免疫学研究の2つの中心地の間の敵対関係があった。

⑷　枯草熱やぜんそくは過敏症の一種ではあるが，免疫系の働きに関係する過敏症とは異なったタイプのものである。

⑸　一部の科学哲学者の考えでは，科学と政治イデオロギーの相違は，自然界を対象とするか人間社会を対象とするかという扱う対象の違いに根ざしている。

Use the content from this passage, separated into 16 sections *(sec 1 - sec 16)*, to answer the *questions*.

sec 1　A generation ago, peanut allergies seemed to be a rare occurrence. Today, they're getting much more attention in the news —— with stories popping up all the time of children with severe and life-threatening reactions to peanuts. So what's going on here?

sec 2　Peanut allergies are still relatively rare —— affecting about 1 to 2 percent of children in the United States. But some studies have indeed found evidence that the number of reported nut allergies is increasing over time.

sec 3　That said, it's tough to disentangle[1] this from broader trends. Allergies on the whole have been increasing, says Wesley Burks, an allergy expert and chair of pediatrics[2] at UNC School of Medicine. Peanut allergies seem, for the most part, to be part of **this broader mysterious trend**.

sec 4　Meanwhile, scientists have recently done a surprising flip[3] on what they think causes peanut allergies. Up until recently, many medical experts thought that exposure to peanuts in the womb or in early life was the trigger[4]. Now, they're not so sure and have some evidence that a lack of exposure to peanuts might cause allergies. Here's a guide to what researchers know so far on the topic.

sec 5　Until recently, most experts recommended that pregnant and nursing mothers should avoid eating peanuts altogether. They assumed that exposure to peanuts early in life was what was causing peanut allergies.

sec 6　Parents followed the advice —— but peanut allergies continued to rise in the United States anyway. So, in 2008 the American Academy of Pediatrics released a report stating that there wasn't any evidence to support restricting mothers' and babies' diets.

sec 7　Since then, there's been more research on the topic. In 2014, a study came out in the Journal of the American Medical Association that observed a **correlation** between mothers eating more nuts being less likely to have children with peanut and tree-nut allergies. The study was quite large, involving 8,205 children, 140 of whom had nut allergies.

5

38

sec 8   But this was just a correlational observation, not a controlled experiment[5]. A newer, ongoing study led by Gideon Lack of King's College London should provide better answers. The experiment enrolled 640 children at high risk of developing peanut allergies and randomly assigned[6] some of them to eat peanuts three times a week and some of them to never eat peanuts at all for their first three years of life. The researchers will then look at which kids develop peanut allergies by age five.

sec 9   Lack is also leading a separate study of 1,303 families to test out what happens when babies are exposed to several foods while they're still being breastfed[7].

sec 10   It could turn out that peanut allergies develop in utero, through breast milk, or by eating peanuts. These studies should help find out.

sec 11   Another possible **culprit**? Peanut dust. Peanuts are such a fundamental part of many Americans' diets that peanut dust is found in our homes, and there's evidence that some children with a specific genetic profile are susceptible[8] to developing peanut allergies through skin exposure.

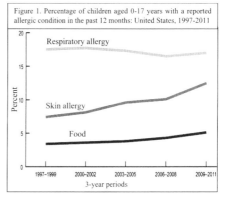

Figure 1. Percentage of children aged 0-17 years with a reported allergic condition in the past 12 months: United States, 1997-2011

sec 12   If researchers can figure out what causes peanut allergies, then they may be able to give parents better advice to prevent more children from developing them in the first place.

sec 13   But what about those who are already allergic? Are they doomed to **peanut-butter-free-existence** for the rest of their lives?

sec 14   Maybe not. Right now, the best advice for those with peanut allergies is to avoid foods with peanuts and to be trained how to use an adrenaline pen in the rare case of an anaphylactic shock[9].

sec 15   But scientists are also developing treatments that might reduce how allergic children are. In the past decade or so, researchers started compiling good evidence that by very carefully exposing children to tiny bits of peanut, they could very slowly work up children's tolerance[10].

sec 16   Patients eat tiny doses of peanut or use a peanut patch worn on the skin, and medical professionals stand ready to jump in with an adrenaline shot in case of a severe reaction. Over time, as the dose increases, the body learns that the peanut is not the enemy.

Vocabulary

(1) **disentangle**: separate ideas that have become confused　*(2)* **pediatrics**: medical specialty dealing with children　*(3)* **surprising flip**: an unexpected reversal　*(4)* **trigger**: something that causes a reaction　*(5)* **controlled experiment**: a trial where everything is held constant except for one variable　*(6)* **randomly assign**: give out without regular pattern　*(7)* **breastfed**: fed with mother's milk　*(8)* **susceptible**: likely to be affected by　*(9)* **anaphylactic shock**: a life-threatening allergic reaction　*(10)* **tolerance**: ability to take something without being harmed

Article by Susannah Locke (2014) https://www.vox.com/2014/11/6/7163713/peanut-allergy-symptoms
Figure 1 by CDC/NCHS, Health Data Interactive, National Health Interview Survey (slightly modified to fit one page)

5

1. In *sec 3*, what does "<u>this broader mysterious trend</u>" refer to?
① a decrease in peanut allergies
② all allergy rates are decreasing
③ all allergy rates are increasing
④ an increase in peanut allergies

2. According to *sec 4* to *sec 7*, what is the current medical stance regarding peanut consumption among pregnant women?
① They can eat peanuts if they want to.
② They can eat tree-nuts.
③ They cannot eat peanuts.
④ They must not eat too many peanuts.

3. In *sec 7*, which of the following is closest in meaning to "<u>correlation</u>"?
① dichotomy
② identicalness
③ inequality
④ relationship

4. In *sec 7* and *sec 8*, what is a limitation of the 2014 study by the Journal of the American Medical Association?

① It enrolled 640 children at high risk of developing peanut allergies.

② It involved 8,205 children.

③ It observed a correlation between mothers who eat more nuts having fewer children with nut allergies.

④ It was not a controlled experiment.

5. In *Figure 1*, which of the following phrases best describes the increase in food allergy rates from 1997 to 2011?

① a dramatic increase

② a hidden increase

③ a slight increase

④ an inverse increase

6. In *sec 11*, which of the following is closest in meaning to "**culprit**"?

① allergy

② cause

③ criminal

④ thing

7. In *sec 11*, which of the following is NOT true about peanut dust?

① It is common due to Americans eating large amounts of peanuts.

② It is rarely found in American homes.

③ It may affect children with a particular set of genes.

④ It may lead to allergies through skin contact.

8. In *sec 13*, what does the phrase "**peanut-butter-free-existence**" mean?

① Peanut butter can be freely eaten.

② Peanut butter causes no allergic reaction.

③ Peanut butter costs no money.

④ Peanut butter is never eaten.

9．Which of the following best reflects the content of *sec 15*?

① In past decades, scientists and patients work hand in hand to prevent anaphylactic shock which is caused by ingesting tiny bits of peanuts through the use of adrenaline pens.

② In the past few years, scientists are unsure why children with allergies would want to eat small amounts of peanuts despite their allergies.

③ Recently, researchers have been working on new approaches to treating allergies, such as exposing patients to small amounts of peanut fragments.

④ Scientists are conducting new studies on children with allergies in which the children work out a tiny bit to understand the true nature of their peanut allergy.

10．Which of the following would be the best title for this article?

① A Rise in Peanut Harvests

② Hypo-Allergenic Peanut Recipes

③ What are the Symptoms of Peanut Allergy?

④ Why are Peanut Allergies on the Rise?

5

Chapter 6 » 癌
Oncology

 日本大学（医学部）　　　　　　　　　　　　🕐 目標 15 分

This is an article about "Cures for Cancer." Read it and answer the questions. Write your answers **in Japanese** in the answer sheet.

There will probably never be a cure for all cancers but a considerable amount of progress has been made recently. In the early 1970s, United States President Richard Nixon declared war on cancer. The U.S. has since then given nearly 70 billion dollars to its National Cancer Institute. This does not include money spent by drug companies and charities in researching ways of combating the disease. Yet despite the vast sums spent, the mortality rate of cancer has increased from 163 per 100,000 people in 1971 to 194 per 100,000 in 2001. By contrast, deaths from other major diseases such as heart attacks and strokes have fallen in that period.

Fortunately, behind these numbers lies some good news. Researchers are finding new ways of treating cancers so that while there may not be any "magic bullet" discovered for cancer within the next 10 or 20 years, over the long term, cancer may be more treatable so that it becomes more like a 1) chronic condition than a fatal diagnosis.

Cancer is connected with the fact that our bodies are constantly reproducing cells. Cancer is basically the unregulated growth of unhealthy cells, many of which grow into 2) tumors. Current cancer therapies simply attack all cells which are reproducing. This means that both healthy and unhealthy cells are killed. This causes side effects such as dizziness and fatigue. However, recently developed anticancer drugs target only 3) cancerous cells. They work at the molecular level and don't kill healthy cells which are 4) dividing. This approach looks very promising and may produce treatments which are effective and have fewer side effects. However, all patients are different and there are many different kinds of cancer so a doctor needs to 5) match the appropriate drug to the patient.

Many anticancer drugs are very poisonous to the body so researchers have developed vehicles to deliver these to the cancerous areas using 6) variants of bacteria and viruses. For example, injecting a modified cold virus into the body could kill cancer cells or even carry $_{7)}$ radioactive materials to the cancerous area. Most important, however, is early detection. Even a small tumor can contain a billion cancerous cells so scanning a patient's body with MRI or other techniques is an essential part of diagnosis. Such scanning techniques can reveal even a small number of cancer cells developing so this may mean that more people will be diagnosed with cancer but will result in a better chance of treating it.

1) chronic :   (of disease) lasting for a long time
2) tumor :   a mass of cells that grow in a way that is not normal
3) cancerous : of cancer
4) dividing :   splitting
5) match :   provide
6) variant :   something that is slightly different from the usual form of something
7) radioactive : containing radiation (＝a form of energy that can harm living things)

6

1. How does the number of people dying of cancer compare with those dying from other diseases mentioned in this article?

2. How do the newly developed cancer treatments differ from the previous cancer treatments?

3. Why do doctors have to be careful when prescribing treatments for cancer sufferers?

4. Why are greater numbers of people likely to be diagnosed with cancer in the future?

44

Read the following passage and write the answers to the questions on the answer sheet.

　　The worst cancer cells don't sit still. Instead they metastasize —— migrate from their original sites and establish new tumors in other parts of the body. Once a cancer spreads, it is harder to (A). A study by developmental biologists offers a fresh clue to how cancer cells (1)acquire the ability to invade other tissues —— a prerequisite for metastasis. It reveals that invasion requires cells to stop dividing. Therefore, the two (B) —— invasion and proliferation —— are mutually exclusive. The finding could inform cancer therapies, which typically target rapidly proliferating cancer cells.

　　David Matus of Stony Brook University and David Sherwood of Duke University turned (C) a transparent worm to elucidate this invading process. During the worm's normal development, a cell known as the anchor cell breaks through a structure called the basement membrane, which initially separates the uterus from the vulva. The process is similar to how human cancer cells invade basement membranes to enter the bloodstream, which carries them to distant sites. So biologists have adopted *Caenorhabditis elegans* as a metastasis model organism, which they can easily image and genetically manipulate.

　　After turning on and off hundreds of genes in *C. elegans*, Matus's team found a gene that regulated anchor cell invasion. When it was turned off, the anchor cell failed to invade the basement membrane. But the anchor cell also did something unexpected: it began to divide. Conversely, when the researchers inhibited cell proliferation, the anchor cell stopped dividing and began to invade again. Further experiments showed that halting cell division was both necessary and sufficient for invasion. Although (2)anecdotal observations by pathologists have suggested this either/or situation might be the case, the new study is the first to uncover the genetic mechanism that explains why these two processes must be mutually exclusive. The results were published in October in the journal *Developmental Cell*.

　　The study also explains the long-standing but mysterious observation by cancer biologists that the invading front of many tumors does not contain dividing cells; instead the invasive cells lead the dividing cells behind them and push forward into healthy tissue as the tumor grows in size. "This research changes how we think about cancer at some level," Matus says. "We think of cancer as a disease of uncontrolled cell division, and in fact, many cancer drugs are designed to target these dividing cells. But our study suggests that we need to figure out how to target these nondividing cells, too, as these are the ones that are invasive."

Before the (3)insight makes its way into cancer treatments, however, it will need further testing. "Now we can take that simple model and go to more complex systems —— like breast cancer tumors," says Andrew Ewald, a cancer cell biologist at Johns Hopkins University. Metastatic breast cancer alone (D) about 40,000 deaths every year in the U.S., but the five-year survival rate is nearly 100 percent if caught before the cancer spreads.

[Adapted from Callier, Viviane. "Divide or Conquer." *Scientific American*, January 2016, p. 17]

6

1. Choose the correct word from the list to fill in blanks (A) ~ (D).

(A) 1. exclude　　　2. reject　　　3. discard　　　4. eliminate

(B) 1. processes　　2. discoveries　3. methods　　4. dilemmas

(C) 1. on　　　　　2. out　　　　3. away　　　　4. to

(D) 1. accounts for　2. takes up　　3. gives up　　4. comes from

2. Choose the best meaning for the underlined word.

(1) acquire:　1. attain　　　2. experience　3. reach　　　4. proceed

(2) anecdotal:　1. scientific　2. mysterious　3. statistical　4. subjective

(3) insight:　1. conclusion　2. discovery　3. awareness　4. research

3. What was the purpose of this study?

1. To find out how to prevent cancer cells from metastasizing.

2. To clarify how cancer moves to a new part of the body.

3. To reveal the mechanism by which cancer cells divide.

4. To discover how to stop cancer cells from multiplying.

4. How did the scientists conduct their research?
 1. They modified anchor cells from a worm to mimic the metastasis process of cancer cells.
 2. They injected cancer cells into the basement membrane of a transparent worm so they could observe how the cells spread.
 3. They observed how certain cells in a growing worm could be induced into moving from one part of the body to another.
 4. They noticed that anchor cells of a certain worm invade the worm's basement membrane similarly to human cancer cells.

5. What did the scientists discover?
 1. Anchor cells cannot migrate through the body while they are dividing.
 2. Cancer cells can be prevented from metastasizing if a certain gene is turned off.
 3. Each cancer cell is specialized to either invade or divide but cannot do both.
 4. Anchor cells and cancer cells do not behave in the same way in the body.

6. How ought future cancer treatments be changed to be more effective?
Answer in English using your own sentence(s).

Chapter 7 》》 循環器系・心臓血管系／生活習慣病
The Circulatory / Cardiovascular System / Life-Style Disease

13 速読訓練 ★★★★

🎓 久留米大学（医学部医学科）　　　　　⏰ 目標 25 分

次の英文を読んで，以下の問いに答えよ。

Columbia University scientists have demystified a metabolic enzyme that could be the next major molecular target in cancer treatment. The team has successfully determined the 3D structure of human ATP-citrate lyase (ACLY) —— which plays a key role in cancer cell （ 1 ） and other cellular processes —— for the first time.

The findings represent a first step in better understanding the enzyme in order to create effective molecular targeted （ 2 ） for patients. While previous experiments have succeeded with fragments of the enzyme, the current work reveals the full structure of human ACLY at high resolution.

ACLY is a metabolic enzyme that controls many processes in the cell, including fatty acid synthesis in cancer cells. By inhibiting this enzyme, the researchers hope to control cancer growth. In addition, the enzyme has other roles, including cholesterol biosynthesis, so inhibitors against this enzyme could also be useful toward （ 3 ） cholesterol levels.

Targeted therapy is an active area of cancer research that involves identifying specific molecules in cancer cells that help them grow, divide and spread. By targeting these changes or blocking their effects with therapeutic drugs, this type of treatment interferes with the （ 4 ） of cancer cells.

Earlier this year, another group of researchers presented results of a phase 3 clinical trial for bempedoic acid, an oral therapy for the treatment of patients with high cholesterol. The drug, a first-generation ACLY inhibitor, was shown to reduce low-density lipoprotein (LDL) cholesterol by 30% when taken alone and an additional 20% in combination with statins.

ACLY has been found to be over-expressed in several types of cancers, and experiments have found that "turning off" ACLY leads cancer cells to stop growing and dividing. Knowledge of the complex molecular architecture of ACLY will point to the best areas to focus on for inhibition, paving the way for targeted drug development.

7

The scientists performed an imaging technique known as cryogenic electron microscopy (cryo-EM) to resolve the complex structure of ACLY. Cryo-EM allows for high-resolution imaging of frozen biological (5) with an electron microscope. A series of 2-dimensional images are then computationally reconstructed into accurate, detailed 3D models of intricate biological structures like proteins, viruses, and cells.

A critical part of the drug discovery process is to understand how the compounds work at the molecular level. This means determining the structure of the compound bound to the target, which in this case is ACLY.

The cryo-EM results revealed an unexpected mechanism for effective inhibition of ACLY. The team found that a significant change in the enzyme's structure is needed for the inhibitor to bind. This structural change then indirectly blocks a substrate from binding to ACLY, averting enzyme activity from occurring as it should. This (6) mechanism of ACLY inhibition could provide a better approach for developing drugs to treat cancer and metabolic disorders.

(Wei, J. et al. (2019). *Nature* より一部改変)

[From Scientists Map 3D Structure of Promising Molecular Target for Cancer Treatment, Columbia University Fundamental Science News on April 3, 2019 by Meeri Kim]

1． 本文の空所(1)～(6)に入れるのに最も適切な語を，下記の(a)～(d)からそれぞれ1つ選び，その記号をマークせよ。

(1) (a) proclamation (b) shortages
   (c) proliferation (d) scarcity

(2) (a) bases (b) marrow
   (c) satellites (d) therapies

(3) (a) making (b) controlling
   (c) inspiring (d) switching

(4) (a) progression (b) deterioration
   (c) embodiment (d) classification

(5) (a) germs (b) duties
   (c) illnesses (d) specimens

(6) (a) menial (b) novel
   (c) rustic (d) outdated

2. 本文の内容と適合するものを下記の(a)〜(h)から 3 つ選び，その記号をマークせよ。

(a) ACLY plays a very important function in cancer cell production.

(b) The primary goal of this research was to test a new drug for cancer treatments.

(c) One type of ACLY inhibitor can reduce LDL by between 30% and 50%.

(d) An enzyme's structure cannot be extensively altered.

(e) The research did not enable us to see ACLY at high resolution.

(f) Trying to solve the structure of ACLY was not an option for the researchers.

(g) It is difficult to identify which kinds of cancer cells grow and spread.

(h) Discovering new drugs requires scientists to look at compounds at an extremely minute level.

7

Chapter 8 》 消化器系／生活習慣病
The Digestive System / Life-Style Disease

14 長文読解 ★★★

🎓 北里大学（薬学部） ⏲ 目標 25 分

次の英文を読み，下記の設問に答えなさい。

Doctors and medical researchers are often hesitant to abandon a long-established idea. So it was with the discovery that gastric ulcers[*1] can result from bacterial infection. Until the mid-1990s, doctors blamed the acid build-up that supposedly caused gastric ulcers on stress and eating spicy foods, calling the causes "hurry, worry, and curry." The finding in the 1970s that drugs which block acid production ⬜(1)⬜ ulcers seemed to confirm the hypothesis that excess acid caused them. For decades, the standard treatment for ulcers in the stomach or small intestine used to be a mild-tasting diet, stress reduction, acid blocking drugs, or surgery. The idea that an ulcer was ⬜(2)⬜ due to a bacterial infection that could be easily, quickly, cheaply, and permanently cured seemed ridiculous.

Helicobacter pylori —— the key to a cure for gastric ulcer patients —— was identified in the laboratory of J. Robin Warren at Royal Perth Hospital in western Australia. Warren, a pathologist[*2] who examined gastric biopsies[*3], realized that spiral-shaped bacteria were always present in tissue that showed signs of inflammation[*4]. Convinced that his observation was significant, he inspired the interest of Barry Marshall, then a medical resident, and together they ⬜(3)⬜ to isolate the source of the infection. They tried, without success, to grow the bacteria from stomach biopsies for months —— until the cultures[*5] were accidentally left in the incubator[*6] over the Easter holidays. Easter weekend in 1982 was a long, 4-day break and, as a result, the culture plates on which they had been trying to grow the mysterious cells taken from a stomach were left 4 days longer than the usual 2 days. With the longer incubation time, they discovered ⬜(4)⬜ a large growth of bacteria with helix-shaped cells. They called the new bug *Helicobacter pylori*.

Isolating *Helicobacter pylori* was significant, but it still did not establish whether the bacteria were the cause of the inflammation or whether they occurred as a result of it. Barry Marshall proposed a way to help determine the choice between these two hypotheses. He knew he had a healthy stomach and had never had gastritis[*7] or an ulcer. If the bacteria caused the inflammation, they ____(5)____ in him. So on a hot July day in 1984, Marshall decided to swallow a solution[*8] containing the bug. Marshall got sick. He had headaches, vomiting[*9], abdominal[*10] discomfort, and irritability. Endoscopic[*11] examination proved he had acute gastritis, which cleared up without treatment by the fifteenth day. A second volunteer who also took the suspect bacteria was ill for several months. A 2-month treatment using an antibacterial agent and bismuth[*12] was required to eradicate the organism. Other researchers, using laboratory animals, soon confirmed the ____(6)____ link between *Helicobacter pylori* and gastritis and then a link to ulcers, too. Studies also showed an increased incidence of ulcers in persons infected with the bacteria.

Most patients with gastric ulcers have the bacteria in their stomach, as do many other people without ulcers, ____(7)____ that additional factors such as stress are also needed for ulcer formation. In about 80% of the infected people, the infection seems not to produce any ill effects. Nevertheless, the bacteria produce a toxin —— a poison which damages the cells of the stomach wall. In susceptible people, the amount of this toxin reaches a level which overcomes (ア) the natural defenses of the cells and initiates the formation of an ulcer.

It took the best part of a decade to convince doctors that these bacteria were really living in the stomach and could cause ulcers. (イ) Skepticism was fuelled by the fact that all bacteria would normally be killed by the large amount of acid in the stomach. Yet it was eventually found that the *Helicobacter* bacteria ____(8)____ partly because they live within the layer of mucus[*13] which the stomach secretes[*14] to protect itself against the acid, and partly because they produce the enzyme[*15], urease[*16]. This enzyme converts urea, a chemical made by stomach cells, to ammonia which neutralizes the acidity in the mucus immediately surrounding the bacteria, creating a non-acidic microzone that protects the bacteria.

We now know that many ulcers result from bacterial infection. The realization that antibiotics can effectively cure stomach ulcers may be one of the most significant medical ____(9)____ in the 20th century. The *Helicobacter* story shows that, in a time of "big science" and "mega research projects", there is still opportunity for individual investigators to challenge accepted theories and change them, ____(10)____ .

8

註 *¹gastric ulcer「胃潰瘍」 *²pathologist「病理学者」
　 *³biopsy「生検」 *⁴inflammation「炎症」
　 *⁵culture「培養菌」 *⁶incubator「培養器」
　 *⁷gastritis「胃炎」 *⁸solution「溶液」
　 *⁹vomiting「嘔吐」 *¹⁰abdominal「腹部の」
　 *¹¹endoscopic「内視鏡の」
　 *¹²bismuth「医薬用ビスマス（蒼鉛）化合物」
　 *¹³mucus「粘液」 *¹⁴secrete「分泌する」
　 *¹⁵enzyme「酵素」
　 *¹⁶urease「ウレアーゼ」（尿素の加水分解を促す酵素）

1. 　(1)　〜　(10)　の各空欄に入るものとして最も適切なものを，それぞれ①〜⑤の
中から一つずつ選びなさい。

(1) ① reform ② reject ③ resolve
　　④ relieve ⑤ retain

(2) ① therefore ② instead ③ steadily
　　④ barely ⑤ comparatively

(3) ① stood out ② turned out ③ worked out
　　④ made out ⑤ set out

(4) ① on their return ② on second thought
　　③ on the quiet ④ on duty
　　⑤ on purpose

(5) ① did so ② would do so
　　③ will not do so ④ would not do so
　　⑤ do so

(6) ① legitimate ② causative ③ humble
　　④ exclusive ⑤ ambiguous

(7) ① implying ② implied
　　③ having implied ④ imply
　　⑤ implies

(8) ① are similar to the acid
　　② are increased by the acid
　　③ are protected from the acid
　　④ are destroyed by the acid
　　⑤ are derived from the acid

8

(9)　① statistics　　　　② confrontations
　　　③ regulations　　　④ speculations
　　　⑤ breakthroughs

(10)　① with huge burdens to patients and their families
　　　② with minor effects on the public
　　　③ with small disadvantages to challengers
　　　④ with great benefits to society and science
　　　⑤ with major advantages to researchers and doctors

2．下線部(ア), (イ)の意味内容として最も適切なものを，それぞれ①〜⑤の中から一つ
ずつ選びなさい。

(ア) the natural defenses of the cells
　　① substances able to reduce immune responses
　　② treatment of disease with medical substances that stimulate immune responses
　　③ medicinal products that inhibit the growth of or destroy microorganisms
　　④ strict hygiene that limits the risk of infection
　　⑤ immune system's ability to resist a particular infection or toxin

(イ) Skepticism was fuelled
　　① Recognition of the value of Warren and Marshall's discovery was enhanced.
　　② Many medical researchers reserved judgment on the relevance of Warren and Marshall's findings.
　　③ Doubt about the significance of Warren and Marshall's research was strengthened.
　　④ Doctors acknowledged the importance of Warren and Marshall's study.
　　⑤ Warren and Marshall's experimental results naturally aroused suspicion in other researchers.

3．(1), (2)の各英文のうち，本文の内容と一致しないものを，それぞれ①〜⑤の中から一つずつ選びなさい。

(1)
　　① When Warren and Marshall succeeded in isolating *Helicobacter pylori*, they were not sure whether the bacteria were attracted to inflamed tissue or caused the stomach inflammation.

② *Helicobacter pylori* exists in some people who do not suffer from gastric ulcers as well as those with the disease.

③ Warren and Marshall's discovery of *Helicobacter pylori* represents a triumph of scientific detective work over conservative skepticism.

④ Warren and Marshall first successfully cultured *Helicobacter pylori* by intentionally leaving the culture plates in the incubator longer than usual.

⑤ Animal experiments helped medical scientists prove the role of *Helicobacter pylori* in stomach diseases.

(2)

① *Helicobacter pylori* survives in the acid environment of the stomach by hiding in the mucus and counteracting stomach acid in its local environment.

② The story of the discovery of *Helicobacter pylori* demonstrates that scientific advances can be gained through creative insights and perseverance of independent investigators.

③ Barry Marshall's self-administration of *Helicobacter pylori* confirmed, contrary to his expectation, the connection between the *Helicobacter pylori* bacteria and gastric ulcers.

④ The idea that stomach ulcers could be caused by bacteria used to be treated with intense scorn.

⑤ Warren and Marshall discovered that *Helicobacter pylori* grew more slowly than the other bacteria that were usually cultured in laboratories.

15　速読訓練　　　　　　　★★★

慶應義塾大学（医学部）　　　　　　　目標25分

Read the passage below and answer the questions that follow it.

A new typhoid* vaccine works "fantastically well" and is being used to help stop an almost untreatable strain of the infection, doctors say. Cases of the bacterial disease fell by more than 80% in a trial reported in the *New England Journal of Medicine*. Experts said the vaccine was a game-changer and would reduce the "terrible toll wrought* by typhoid".

Typhoid fever is caused by highly contagious *Salmonella Typhi* bacteria and is spread through contaminated food and water. (1) Symptoms include prolonged fever, headache, nausea, loss of appetite, and constipation. It causes fatal complications, such as internal bleeding, in one in 100 people. Precise numbers on typhoid are hard to collect, but it affects between 11 million and 21 million people around the world each year and kills 128,000 to 161,000.

More than 20,000 children aged from nine months to 16 years took part in the trial in Kathmandu Valley, Nepal, where typhoid is a major public-health problem. Half of the children were given the vaccine, and the other half received a placebo. At the end of the first year of the study, the rate of infections was 81% lower in the group that had received the vaccine. "It works fantastically well in preventing a disease that affects some of the world's most vulnerable children," Prof. Andrew Pollard, from the University of Oxford, who has been involved in the trials, told BBC News. "The burden of typhoid is so huge that we're seeing families taking children into hospital to be treated and being plunged into poverty paying for the costs of investigation and treatment with antibiotics. The arrival of this vaccine to control the disease (2)."

The children in Nepal, as well as those taking part in other trials in Malawi and Bangladesh, will now be followed up to see how long protection lasts. Typhoid Vaccine Acceleration Consortium director Dr Kathleen Neuzil said the vaccine could "reduce disease and save lives in populations that lack clean water and improved sanitation". A vaccine is particularly needed, because typhoid has, according to a World Health Organization report, acquired a "crazy amount" of antibiotic resistance, and the world is "reaching the limit" of current treatments. Rapid urbanisation in the developing world has left many countries unable to provide the most effective preventative measure —— clean water and flushing toilets. And while there are two typhoid vaccines already available, neither is licensed for children under the age of two, so the most vulnerable people are unprotected.

Pakistan has an outbreak of what is called extensively drug-resistant (XDR) typhoid fever. "Right now in Pakistan, a strain of typhoid has developed resistance to all but one of the antibiotics we use to treat the disease, threatening to take us back to the days when typhoid killed as many as one-fifth of the people that contracted it," Dr Seth Berkley, chief executive of Gavi, the Vaccine Alliance, told BBC News. It started in Hyderbad, in Sindh province, in November 2016 and more than 10,000 people have been infected. Gavi is paying for nine million children to be vaccinated, and Sindh province will now become the first region in the world to add the vaccine to routine childhood vaccinations.

[A] Dr Berkley describes the new vaccine as a game-changer in the battle against typhoid, adding that it couldn't have arrived at a better time: "This vaccine should play a key role in bringing this dangerous disease under control and, once introduced into more countries' routine vaccination programmes, reducing the terrible toll wrought by typhoid worldwide." Prof. Pollard added, "It is really exciting to have a new intervention, in a very rapid space of time, that can not only prevent the disease but also help in the fight against antibiotic resistance."

[From Typhoid vaccine 'works fantastically well', BBC News on December 4, 2019 by James Gallagher]

注：typhoid 　　チフス
　　 wreak 　　to do great damage or harm to something

Questions

1. According to the passage, are the following statements true or false? On the answer sheet, indicate those you consider to be true with an A, and those you think are false with a B. If you think it is impossible to tell from the passage whether a particular statement is true or false, indicate this with a C.

(ア)　Two typhoid vaccines are currently in use in addition to the new one undergoing trials.

(イ)　There is more than one strain of typhoid.

(ウ)　The cost of treating typhoid fever is unaffordable for some families in Nepal.

(エ)　Health insurance does not cover typhoid fever treatment in most countries.

(オ)　Pakistan has no effective antibiotics to treat typhoid fever.

(カ)　There was a time when typhoid fever was responsible for about 20% of deaths in Pakistan.

(キ)　Typhoid fever is less likely to be fatal in infants than in any other age group.

2. Which of the following sentences would best fill the blank space marked (1)? (On the answer sheet, the space for the answer to Q2 is on the same line as the space for Q1.)

(A)　It is a disease for which no treatment is yet available.

(B)　It is a disease for which there is currently no vaccine on the market.

(C)　It is a disease of poverty, most common in countries with poor sanitation and a lack of clean water.

(D)　It is a disease that is easily spread by hygienic practices like washing vegetables in clean water.

3. Which of the following would best fill the blank space marked (2)? (On the answer sheet, the space for the answer to Q3 is on the same line as the space for Q1 and Q2.)

(A)　is a danger to us all

(B)　is a pretty exciting moment

(C)　is something we are greatly looking forward to

(D)　is something we had not planned

4. In each of the questions below, (1)–(3), select the option that best completes the sentence.

(1) Typhoid fever is
  (a) a condition which can in some cases lead to death.
  (b) a condition which causes headache and nausea without constipation.
  (c) a disease which is passed from parents to their children.
  (d) a viral disease which spreads rapidly via dirty sewage water.

(2) The new typhoid vaccine described in the article has been shown to be effective for at least
  (a) one month.
  (b) three months.
  (c) one year.
  (d) three years.

(3) A major reason given in the passage for the continued spread of typhoid fever is that
  (a) the bacteria that cause it can be transmitted through too many different routes.
  (b) many countries have not yet achieved high levels of hygiene and sanitation.
  (c) the efficacy of the new vaccine being trialled in Nepal and elsewhere has not been properly tested.
  (d) the general public are not taking the disease seriously enough.

5. Referring to the first sentence of the final paragraph (underlined and marked [A]), explain why Dr Berkley thinks the new vaccine "couldn't have arrived at a better time". Answer in Japanese, using no more than 60 characters.

Chapter 9 ≫ その他

16 速読訓練 ★★★

東京慈恵会医科大学（医学部医学科）　　　⏱ 目標 18 ～ 20 分

Read the following passage and write the answers to the questions on the answer sheet.

Smallpox was one of the most (1)dreaded diseases in human history. Caused by the variola virus, it was a leading cause of death in Europe from the 11th to the 20th centuries. When European explorers arrived in the Americas, they brought smallpox with them, and the (2)ensuing epidemic wiped out up to 90% of the native population. By the 20th century, smallpox had killed hundreds of millions of people worldwide. And yet, this horrible disease became the first disease in human history to become completely eliminated. How this happened is an interesting story in medical history.

Smallpox is an extremely contagious disease spread by human to human contact. It is not carried or spread by animals. The most common method of transmission was inhalation of respiratory droplets, although it was also possible to contract it through contact with objects that had been handled by infected people. After infection, the virus would (　A　) for about two weeks, during which time the patient was asymptomatic, but the virus was quietly multiplying inside the body. Once this period was over, the infected person would first experience symptoms similar to the flu: fever, chills, muscle aches, and general malaise. Shortly after the first general symptoms, the more specific sign of a red rash would appear on the hands, feet, and face. The rash would then spread over the body in the form of small raised blisters or pocks, which is where the name smallpox comes from. The virus would infect the bones and organs, causing fatal (　B　). The mortality rate for smallpox was 30% or higher, and those who survived were left with characteristic pock scars on their faces and bodies.

It became common knowledge that those who were infected with smallpox would not contract the disease again. Thus, in the early 18th century, the (　C　) of variolation became popular in Europe in which people would rub themselves with a small amount of pus or scabs taken from the sores of an infected individual. The idea was that this would give them a mild form of smallpox that would make them immune. About 2% of people who became infected with smallpox this way died, but that was a much better survival rate than catching the disease normally, so it became very popular.

Then, in 1796, a physician named Edward Jenner decided to try a new technique. It was already known that dairymaids, women whose job was to milk cows, were safe from smallpox if they had already contracted a similar but harmless cow disease called cowpox. Jenner (3)extracted pus from an infected blister on the hand of a dairymaid and rubbed it into a small cut on an eight-year-old boy's arm. The boy became briefly ill, then got better. A month later, Jenner rubbed pus from a smallpox lesion into a cut on the boy's arm, but the boy did not become sick. Jenner called his new treatment vaccination, from vacca, the Latin word for cow.

Almost 200 years after Edward Jenner administered his first vaccination, smallpox was finally eliminated by (D) global campaign of quarantine and vaccination conducted by the WHO from 1967 to 1977. In 1980, the WHO officially declared that smallpox no longer existed outside of the laboratory. No cure for the disease was ever found, but thanks to Dr. Jenner, we have been free of the (4)menace of smallpox for almost 40 years.

1. Choose the best meaning for underlined words (1)~(4).

(1) dreaded: 1. contagious 2. deadly   3. feared   4. dangerous

(2) ensuing: 1. preceding 2. unexpected 3. widespread 4. following

(3) extracted: 1. obtained 2. isolated   3. blended   4. produced

(4) menace: 1. epidemic   2. mortality   3. threat   4. horror

2. Choose the correct word from the list to fill in blanks (A) ~ (D).

(A) 1. incubate   2. conceal   3. migrate   4. modify

(B) 1. injury   2. complications 3. toxicity   4. disorders

(C) 1. exercise   2. practice   3. problem   4. treatment

(D) 1. an intentional 2. a challenging 3. an ambiguous   4. a rigorous

3. How was smallpox usually transmitted?
1. Through contact with animals that were sick with the variola virus
2. By breathing in water vapor exhaled by an infected person
3. By touching articles or surfaces of things that had the virus on them
4. From not adequately washing objects contaminated with the virus

4. What were the distinguishing indicators of a smallpox infection?
1. The patient developed blisters all over the body.
2. The initial symptoms were similar to the flu.
3. The patient was asymptomatic for the first two weeks of infection.
4. The virus caused death by invading the bones and organs.

5. Why did people purposely try to contract smallpox?
1. Contracting smallpox from the pus of an infected person was believed to be without risk.
2. If they contracted mild smallpox from an infected scab, they would not be scarred by pocks.
3. The symptoms of variolation were milder than symptoms of full-blown smallpox.
4. They would be protected from smallpox if they developed a weaker form and lived.

6. How did Dr. Jenner make his smallpox vaccine?
1. He took material from a cow that had the cowpox disease.
2. He extracted pus from a cut on the arm of a boy who had already had smallpox.
3. He removed fluid from a sore on a person infected with a safer disease that granted immunity.
4. He combined pus from a smallpox blister with pus from a cowpox blister and rubbed them on a boy's arm.

7. Do you think Dr. Jenner's method of testing his vaccine was ethical or unethical? Give at least one reason to support your opinion.

Kyogakusha